Qualitative Research and Case Study Applications in Education

Qualitative Research and Case Study Applications in Education

Revised and Expanded from *Case Study Research in Education*

Sharan B. Merriam

Jossey-Bass Publishers • San Francisco

Substantial discounts on bulk quantities of Jossey-Bass books are available to corporations, professional associations, and other organizations. For details and discount information, contact the special sales department at Jossey-Bass Inc., Publishers (415) 433–1740; Fax (800) 605–2665.

Jossey-Bass Web address: http://www.josseybass.com

List in Chapter Eight from Bogdan, R. C., and Biklen, S. K., *Qualitative Research for Education,* Second Edition. Copyright © 1992 by Allyn & Bacon. Reprinted by permission.

TCF Manufactured in the United States of America on Lyons Falls Turin Book. This paper is acid-free and 100 percent totally chlorine-free.

Library of Congress Cataloging-in-Publication Data

Merriam, Sharan B.
    Qualitative research and case study applications in education /
Sharan B. Merriam.—Rev. and expanded.
        p.   cm.—(A joint publication of the Jossey-Bass education
series and the Jossey-Bass higher and adult education series)
    Rev. ed. of: Case study research in education. 1st ed. 1988.
    Includes bibliographical references and index.
    ISBN 0-7879-1009-0
    1. Education—Research—Methodology. 2. Education—Research—Case
studies. 3. Case method. I. Merriam, Sharan B. Case study
research in education. II. Title. III. Series: Jossey-Bass
education series. IV. Series: Jossey-Bass higher and adult
education series.
LB1028.M396   1998
370′7′2—dc21   97-7167

SECOND EDITION
PB Printing   10 9 8 7 6 5 4

A joint publication in
The Jossey-Bass Education Series
and
The Jossey-Bass Higher Education Series

Contents

Preface   xi

The Author   xvii

Part One: The Design of Qualitative Research   1

1. What Is Qualitative Research?   3
2. Case Studies as Qualitative Research   26
3. Designing the Study and Selecting a Sample   44

Part Two: Collecting Qualitative Data   69

4. Conducting Effective Interviews   71
5. Being a Careful Observer   94
6. Mining Data from Documents   112
7. Collecting Data in Case Studies   134

Part Three: Analyzing and Reporting Qualitative Data   151

8. Analytic Techniques and Data Management   155
9. Levels of Analysis   178
10. Dealing with Validity, Reliability, and Ethics   198
11. Writing Reports and Case Studies   220

References   247

Name Index   267

Subject Index   273

Preface

Qualitative Research and Case Study Applications in Education is the second edition of *Case Study Research in Education*. As evidenced by the titles, the primary focus of this second edition is on qualitative research in general, with applications to case study as a secondary emphasis. This change is appropriate because the first edition was widely used as a basic introductory text by qualitative researchers in education. Indeed, much of the content of the first edition—data collection techniques, data analysis and the reporting of findings, and concerns about validity, reliability, and ethics—was presented as germane to all forms of qualitative research. This material has been revised, updated, and retained in the second edition. Also corresponding with the shift in focus are expanded discussions on the nature of qualitative research, on the different types of qualitative research (including case study) commonly found in education, and on how to design a qualitative study, including problem formation and sample selection.

The first edition of this book also proved useful to qualitative researchers interested in conducting case studies. In fact, at the time of its publication in 1988, the book was one of the very few detailed resources available on qualitative case study research. Several publications on case study have appeared within the last ten years, but resource material is still less available for case study than for other types of research. Moreover, there is still some confusion as to what a case study is and how it can be differentiated from other types of qualitative research. These considerations contributed to the decision to make case study a secondary focus in this edition.

The combination of a primary emphasis on qualitative research with applications to case study makes this book unique among the burgeoning literature of qualitative research. The book can be used by those who are interested only in qualitative research in general, or it can be consulted for assistance in conducting a case study in particular. To that end, Chapters Two and Seven cover case study research; sections at the ends of other chapters apply the chapter content to case studies. In addition, general points and issues throughout the book are often illustrated, when appropriate, with reference to specific case studies.

Another defining characteristic of this book is its how-to, practical focus, wherein the mechanics of conducting a qualitative study are presented in a simple, straightforward manner. Designing a qualitative study, collecting and analyzing data, and writing the research report are topics logically presented and liberally illustrated to assist the researcher desiring some guidance in the process. The revisions related to this aspect of the book have greatly benefited from ten years of additional resources, my own research, and my supervision of dozens of qualitative dissertations. The intended audiences for this book, then, are teachers, researchers, and graduate students in education who are interested in understanding qualitative research and perhaps in conducting a qualitative case study.

Overview of the Contents

The organization of this text reflects the process of conducting a qualitative research investigation. Part One contains three chapters. The first is on the nature of qualitative research, the second covers the case study as one common type of qualitative research, and the third explains the procedure for setting up a qualitative study, including selecting a sample. Part Two consists of four chapters that detail data collection techniques. The four chapters in Part Three deal with analyzing the data collected, handling concerns about reliability, validity, and ethics, and writing the final report.

Chapter One introduces qualitative research as it contrasts with positivist (or quantitative) and critical research traditions. The essential characteristics of qualitative research are presented, as are brief overviews of several types of qualitative research commonly found in education. In particular, the basic or generic qualitative study, ethnography, phenomenology, grounded theory, and qualitative case study are reviewed. Chapter One also includes a discussion of the investigator characteristics and skills needed to conduct a qualitative study.

Case study is a term used by many people in many different ways to mean many different things. The purpose of Chapter Two is to define and further differentiate case study from other qualitative approaches to a research problem. A qualitative case study is an intensive, holistic description and analysis of a bounded phenomenon such as a program, an institution, a person, a process, or a social unit. Most case studies in education draw from other disciplines for both theory and method. Chapter Two explains how concepts, theories, and techniques from anthropology, history, sociology, and psychology in particular have influenced case studies in education. Irrespective of disciplinary orientation, case studies can also be described in terms of their overall intent, whether it be to describe, to interpret, or to evaluate some phenomenon or to build theory. This chapter also reviews the strengths and limitations of qualitative case studies.

def.

Knowledge of previous research and theory can help a researcher focus on the problem of interest and select the unit of analysis most relevant to the problem. Chapter Three explains what a theoretical framework is and shows how reviewing relevant literature can contribute not only to identifying the study's theoretical framework but also to shaping the problem statement. The problem statement lays out the logic and purpose of the study and is critical to making informed decisions regarding sample selection (also covered in this chapter), data collection, and data analysis. A separate section at the end of Chapter Three discusses sample selection in case study research.

Data collection techniques are covered in the four chapters in Part Two. Chapters Four, Five, and Six examine the three primary means of collecting data in qualitative research. Interviews, discussed in Chapter Four, can range in structure from a list of predetermined questions to a totally free-ranging interview in which nothing is set ahead of time. The success of an interview depends on the nature of the interaction between the interviewer and the respondent and on the interviewer's skill in asking good questions. How to record and evaluate interview data is also covered in Chapter Four. Observations differ from interviews in that the researcher obtains a firsthand account of the phenomenon of interest rather than relying on someone else's interpretation. Chapter Five discusses what to observe, the interdependent relationship between observer and observed, and how to record observations in the form of field notes. Chapter Six presents the third primary source of case study data: documents. The term *document* is broadly defined to cover an assortment of written records, physical traces, and artifacts. Although some documents might be developed at the investigator's request, most are produced independently of the research study and thus offer a valuable resource for confirming insights gained through interviews and observations. Chapter Six covers various types of documents, their use in qualitative research, and their strengths and limitations as sources of data. The application of all three data collection strategies to case studies is the focus of Chapter Seven. Here, three case studies demonstrate the interactive nature of data collection using all three techniques.

Many texts on qualitative research devote more space to theoretical discussions of methodology and data collection than to the management and analysis of data once they have been collected. This book redresses that imbalance with two full chapters on data analysis. First reviewed in Chapter Eight are six strategies for analyzing qualitative data. Next, the importance of analyzing data *while* they are being collected is underscored; some suggestions for analysis early in the study during data collection are included. Management of the voluminous data typical of a qualitative study is another topic addressed in this chapter. Finally, a major section addresses the increasing role of computers in both management and analysis of qualitative data. Chapter Nine, which also focuses on data analysis, explains the several levels of analysis possible—ranging from developing a descriptive account of the findings to developing categories, themes, or other concepts, to interpreting the meaning of the data in even more abstract terms in the form of models or theories. The last section of Chapter Nine speaks to within-case and cross-case analysis common to case studies.

All researchers are concerned with producing valid and reliable findings. Chapter Ten explores the issues of validity and reliability in qualitative case study research. In particular, internal validity, reliability, and external validity are discussed, and strategies are offered for dealing with each of these issues. Also of concern to researchers is how to conduct an investigation in an ethical manner. Chapter Ten closes with a section on ethics, paying particular attention to ethical dilemmas likely to arise in qualitative research.

Many an educator has been able to conceptualize a study, collect relevant data, and even analyze the data, but then has failed to carry through in the important last step—writing up the results. Without this step, the research has little chance of advancing the knowledge base of education or having an impact on practice. Chapter Eleven is designed to help qualitative researchers complete the research process by writing a report of their investigation. The first half of the chapter offers suggestions for organizing the writing process—determining the audience for the report, settling on the main message, and outlining the overall report. The rest of Chapter Eleven focuses on the *content* of the report—its components and where to place them, how to achieve a good balance between description and analysis, and how to disseminate the study's findings. At the end of the chapter is a discussion of special considerations in writing a case study report.

Acknowledgments

I want to acknowledge those who have contributed in various ways to this second edition. First, there are those who challenged me *and* assisted me in thinking through the reorganization of this edition. Carolyn Clark, a friend and colleague at Texas A&M University; my husband and case study researcher, Bob Rowden; Gale Erlandson, my editor at Jossey-Bass; and two anonymous reviewers of the original text all provided me with invaluable suggestions through written comments, brainstorming sessions, and e-mail discussions. The book is immeasurably better thanks to their help. For a very specific contribution I want to thank Linda Gilbert, a Ph.D. student in instructional technology, who compiled information for me on the use of computers in qualitative research. Thanks also go to Denise Collins for designing most of the visual displays and to Lilian Hill and Lynda Hanscome, doctoral candidates here in the Department of Education, for their assistance with a wide range of technical and organizational tasks related to getting the manuscript ready for publication.

Athens, Georgia   Sharan B. Merriam
July 1997

The Author

Sharan B. Merriam is professor of adult and continuing education at the University of Georgia in Athens, where her responsibilities include teaching graduate courses in adult education and qualitative research methods and supervising graduate student research. She received her B.A. degree (1965) in English literature from Drew University, her M.Ed. degree (1971) in English education from Ohio University, and her Ed.D. degree (1978) in adult education from Rutgers University. Before coming to the University of Georgia, she served on the faculties of Northern Illinois University and Virginia Polytechnic Institute and State University.

Merriam's main research and writing activities have focused on adult education, adult development and learning, and qualitative research methods. She has served on steering committees for the annual North American Adult Education Research Conference, the Qualitative Research in Education Conference held annually at the University of Georgia, and the Commission of Professors of Adult Education; she is an active member of the American Association for Adult and Continuing Education and the Postsecondary Division of the American Educational Research Association. For five years she was coeditor of *Adult Education Quarterly*, the major research and theory journal in the field of adult education. She is also coeditor of the 1989 *Handbook of Adult and Continuing Education*.

Merriam's other books include *Philosophical Foundations of Adult Education* (with J. Elias, 1994), *Coping with Male Mid-life: A Systematic Analysis Using Literature as a Data Source* (1980), *Adult Education: Foundations of Practice* (with G. Darkenwald, 1982)—winner of the 1985 Cyril O. Houle World Award for Literature in Adult Education—*Themes of Adulthood Through Literature* (1983), *A Guide to Research for Educators and Trainers of Adults* (with E. L. Simpson, 1995, second edition)—first published in 1984 and winner of the 1984 Phillip E.

Frandson Memorial Award for Literature in Continuing Education—*Selected Writings on Philosophy and Adult Education* (editor, 1995, second edition), *Lifelines: Patterns of Work, Love, and Learning in Adulthood* (with M. C. Clark, 1991), *Learning in Adulthood* (with R. Caffarella, 1991), and most recently, *The Profession and Practice of Adult Education: An Introduction* (with R. Brockett, 1997).

Qualitative Research and Case Study Applications in Education

Part One

The Design of Qualitative Research

Few areas of practice offer as many opportunities for research as does the field of education. To begin with, education is a familiar arena. Potential researchers have had personal experience with formal schooling, usually through college, and everyone has learned in informal ways throughout their lives. Having an interest in knowing more about the field and in improving the practice of education leads to asking researchable questions, some of which are best approached through a qualitative research design. In fact I believe that research focused on discovery, insight, and understanding from the perspectives of those being studied offers the greatest promise of making significant contributions to the knowledge base and practice of education.

Choosing a study design requires understanding the philosophical foundations underlying the type of research, taking stock of whether there is a good match between the type of research and your personality, attributes, and skills, and becoming informed as to the design choices available to you within the paradigm. Part One of this book provides the conceptual foundation for doing this type of research and lays out some of the choices and decisions you will need to make in conducting a qualitative study.

The qualitative, interpretive, or naturalistic research paradigm defines the methods and techniques most suitable for collecting and analyzing data. Qualitative inquiry, which focuses on meaning in context, requires a data collection instrument that is sensitive to underlying meaning when gathering and interpreting data. Humans are best suited for this task, especially because interviewing, observing, and analyzing are activities central to qualitative research.

While all of qualitative research holds a number of assumptions and characteristics in common, there are variations in the disciplinary base that a qualitative study might draw from, in how a qualitative study might be designed, and in what the intent of the study might be. Thus a qualitative ethnographic study that focuses on culture could be differentiated from a life history study or from a study that is designed to build a substantive theory. Some major types of qualitative studies commonly found in educational research are differentiated in the first chapter.

Because of its prevalence in educational research and some general confusion surrounding its nature and use, one design in particular—the qualitative case study—has been selected for an extended discussion in Chapter Two. Definitions, types, and uses of case studies are discussed, as are the design's strengths and limitations.

Other considerations have to do with identifying the theoretical framework that forms the scaffolding or underlying structure of your study. Reviewing previous thinking and research found in the literature can help illuminate your framework as well as shape the actual problem statement and purpose of the study. Further, how you select your sample is directly linked to the questions you ask and to how you have constructed the problem of your study.

The three chapters that make up Part One of this book are thus designed to orient you to the nature of qualitative research and to qualitative case studies in particular, as well as how to frame your question or interest, state your research problem, and select a sample. Part One paves the way for subsequent chapters that focus on data collection and data analysis.

Chapter One

What Is
Qualitative Research?

Planning a research project can be compared to planning for a vacation trip. Before starting out, you consider what sort of trip most appeals to you, what you like to do, what it might cost, where you want to go, how best to get there, how long to stay, and so on. So too, there are things to think about before you begin a research project. A fundamental consideration is your philosophical orientation. What do you believe about the nature of reality, about knowledge, and about the production of knowledge? Research is, after all, producing knowledge about the world—in our case, the world of educational practice. Along with locating yourself philosophically, you might consider some of your personal attributes: How much structure are you comfortable with? Do you prefer to work with people or things? Does writing come easily for you? Or is it a struggle?

This chapter will help you plan your research journey by first briefly introducing three research paradigms, then presenting in more detail the defining characteristics of qualitative research. A third section will help you distinguish among a number of major types of qualitative research commonly found in education. The last part of the chapter reviews several personal attributes considered desirable for those engaging in qualitative research.

Three Orientations to Research

Linking research and philosophical traditions or schools of thought helps to illuminate the special characteristics of different research orientations or paradigms. Many writers, for example, trace the philosophical roots of qualitative research to phenomenology and symbolic interaction, while quantitative research is most commonly linked to positivism. Others draw upon constructivism, postpositivism, and critical social science to delineate the worldview of qualitative research. The most helpful typology for me has been the distinction that Carr and Kemmis (1986) make among three basic forms of educational research—positivist, interpretive, and critical.

Briefly, the three orientations are distinguished as follows. In *positivist* forms of research, education or schooling is considered the object, phenomenon, or delivery system to be studied. Knowledge gained through scientific and experimental research is objective and quantifiable. "Reality" in this perspective is stable, observable, and measurable. In *interpretive* research, education is considered to be a process and school is a lived experience. Understanding the meaning of the process or experience constitutes the knowledge to be gained from an inductive, hypothesis- or theory-generating (rather than a deductive or testing) mode of inquiry. Multiple realities are constructed socially by individuals. In the third orientation—*critical research*—education is considered to be a social institution designed for social and cultural reproduction and transformation. Drawing from Marxist philosophy, critical theory, and feminist theory, knowledge generated through this mode of research is an ideological critique of power, privilege, and oppression in areas of educational practice. Some forms of critical research have a strong participatory, action component (Merriam and Simpson, 1995).

Differences among these three philosophical orientations as they would play out in a research study can be illustrated by showing how investigators from different perspectives might go about conducting research on the topic *dropping out of high school,* or, as it is now commonly referred to, *noncompletion.* From a positivist perspective you might begin by hypothesizing that students drop out of high school because of low self-esteem. You could then design an intervention program to raise the self-esteem of students at risk. You set up an experiment controlling for as many variables as possible, and then measure the results.

The same topic from an interpretive or qualitative perspective would not test theory, set up an experiment, or measure anything. Rather, you might be interested in understanding the experience of dropping out from the perspective of the noncompleters themselves, or you might be interested in discovering which factors differentiate noncompleters from those who may have been at risk but who nevertheless completed high school. You will need to interview students, perhaps observe them in or out of school, and review documents such as counselors' reports and personal diaries.

Finally, from a critical research perspective, you would be interested in how the social institution of school is structured such that the interests of some members and classes of society are preserved and perpetuated at the expense of others. You would investigate the way in which schools are structured, the mechanisms (for example, attendance, tests, grade levels) that reproduce certain patterns of response, and so on. You might also design and carry out the study in collaboration with high school noncompleters. This collective investigation and analysis of the underlying socioeconomic, political, and cultural causes of the problem is designed to result in collective action to address the problem (if, indeed, noncompletion is identified as the problem by students themselves).

Thus getting started on a research project begins with examining your own orientation to basic tenets about the nature of reality, the purpose of doing research, and the type of knowledge to be produced through your efforts. Which orientation is the best fit with your views? Which is the best fit for answering the question you have in mind? The rest of this book is devoted to explaining how to conduct an interpretive or qualitative research investigation in education.

Characteristics of Qualitative Research

Qualitative research is an umbrella concept covering several forms of inquiry that help us understand and explain the meaning of social phenomena with as little disruption of the natural setting as possible. Other terms often used interchangeably are *naturalistic inquiry, interpretive research, field study, participant observation, inductive research, case study,* and *ethnography.* Some writers refer to these and other terms as types of qualitative research. Tesch (1990), for example lists over forty types. Lancy (1993) compares the "mighty oak" forest of quantitative research to the "mixed forest" of qualitative research in which there are "distinct trees representing different species or, at least subspecies. In many cases their growth has not been spectacular and some trees appear to be almost moribund. That is, whole traditions seem to spring up ('critical ethnography,' Anderson 1989) while others slowly die out ('ecological psychology,' Barker and Gump 1964)" (Lancy, 1993, p. 3). Later in this chapter I will delineate among several major types of qualitative research most often found in educational research. First, however, some essential characteristics cut across all forms of qualitative research.

The key philosophical assumption, as I noted earlier, upon which all types of qualitative research are based is the view that reality is constructed by individuals interacting with their social worlds. Qualitative researchers *are interested in understanding the meaning people have constructed,* that is, how they make sense of their world and the experiences they have in the world. Qualitative research "implies a direct concern with experience as it is 'lived' or 'felt' or 'undergone'" (Sherman and Webb, 1988, p. 7).

In contrast to quantitative research, which takes apart a phenomenon to examine component parts (which become the variables of the study), qualitative research can reveal how all the parts work together to form a whole. It is assumed that meaning is embedded in people's experiences and that this meaning is mediated through the investigator's own perceptions. Patton (1985) explains:

> [Qualitative research] is an effort to understand situations in their uniqueness as part of a particular context and the interactions there. This understanding is an end in itself, so that it is not attempting to predict what may happen in the future necessarily, but to understand the nature of that setting—what it means for participants to be in that setting, what their lives are like, what's going on for them, what their meanings are, what the world looks like in that particular setting—and in the analysis to be able to communicate that faithfully to others who are interested in that setting. . . . The analysis strives for depth of understanding [p. 1].

The key concern is understanding the phenomenon of interest from the participants' perspectives, not the researcher's. This is sometimes referred to as the *emic,* or insider's perspective, versus the *etic,* or outsider's view. An entertaining example of the difference in the two perspectives can be found in Bohannan's classic, *Shakespeare in the Bush* (1992). As she tells the story of *Hamlet* to elders in a West African village, they instruct her on the "true meaning" of the drama, based on their beliefs and cultural values.

A second characteristic of all forms of qualitative research is that *the researcher is the primary instrument for data collection and analysis.* Data are mediated through this human instrument, the researcher, rather than through some inanimate inventory, questionnaire, or computer. Certain characteristics differentiate the human researcher from other data collection instruments: the researcher is responsive to the context; he or she can adapt techniques to the circumstances; the total context can be considered; what is known about the situation can be expanded through sensitivity to nonverbal aspects; the researcher can process data immediately, can clarify and summarize as the study evolves, and can explore anomalous responses (Guba and Lincoln, 1981).

A third characteristic of qualitative research is that *it usually involves fieldwork.* The researcher must physically go to the people, setting, site, institution (the field) in order to observe behavior in its natural setting. This is customarily done by anthropologists whose interest is to learn about other cultures. Most investigations that describe and interpret a social unit or process necessitate becoming intimately familiar with the phenomenon being studied. An occasional qualitative study has been undertaken using documents alone (such as written materials or photographs), but these are the exceptions.

Fourth, qualitative research *primarily employs an inductive research strategy.* That is, this type of research builds abstractions, concepts, hypotheses, or theories rather than tests existing theory. Often qualitative studies are undertaken because there is a lack of theory, or existing theory fails to adequately explain a phenomenon. There are thus no hypotheses to be deduced from theory to guide the investigation. Qualitative researchers build toward theory from observations and intuitive understandings gained in the field. In contrast to deductive researchers who "hope to find data to match a theory, inductive researchers hope to find a theory that explains their data" (Goetz and LeCompte, 1984, p. 4). Typically, qualitative research findings are in the form of themes, categories, typologies, concepts, tentative hypotheses, even theory, which have been inductively derived from the data.

Finally, since qualitative research focuses on process, meaning, and understanding, *the product of a qualitative study is richly descriptive*. Words and pictures rather than numbers are used to convey what the researcher has learned about a phenomenon. There are likely to be researcher descriptions of the context, the players involved, and the activities of interest. In addition, data in the form of participants' own words, direct citations from documents, excerpts of videotapes, and so on, are likely to be included to support the findings of the study.

In addition to the characteristics common to all types of qualitative research, several others are more or less common to most forms of qualitative research. Ideally, for example, the design of a qualitative study is emergent and flexible, responsive to changing conditions of the study in progress. This is not always the case, however, as thesis and dissertation committees, funding agencies, and human subjects review boards often require the design of the study to be specified ahead of time. Sample selection in qualitative research is usually (but not always) nonrandom, purposeful, and small, as opposed to the larger, more random sampling of quantitative research. Finally, the investigator in qualitative research spends a substantial amount of time in the natural setting of the study, often in intense contact with participants.

By way of a summary, Table 1.1 displays a comparison of these characteristics of qualitative research with the more familiar positivist-quantitative approach. Such a comparison helps to illuminate some of the basic differences between the two types of research. However, as many experienced researchers can attest, this table sets up a somewhat artificial dichotomy between the two types; it should be viewed as an aid to understanding differences, not as a set of hard-and-fast rules governing each type of research. In the actual conduct of research, differences on several points of comparison are far less rigid than the table suggests. Finally, there is an ongoing debate in the literature about the extent to which the methods of data collection and analysis characteristic of one paradigm can be utilized in the other (Smith and Heshusius, 1986; Kidder and Fine, 1987; Firestone, 1987; Gage, 1989; Reichardt and Rallis, 1994).

Table 1.1. Characteristics of Qualitative and Quantitative Research.

Point of Comparison	Qualitative Research	Quantitative Research
Focus of research	Quality (nature, essence)	Quantity (how much, how many)
Philosophical roots	Phenomenology, symbolic interactionism	Positivism, logical empiricism
Associated phrases	Fieldwork, ethnographic, naturalistic, grounded, constructivist	Experimental, empirical, statistical
Goal of investigation	Understanding, description, discovery, meaning, hypothesis generating	Prediction, control, description, confirmation, hypothesis testing
Design characteristics	Flexible, evolving, emergent	Predetermined, structured
Sample	Small, nonrandom, purposeful, theoretical	Large, random, representative
Data collection	Researcher as primary instrument, interviews, observations, documents	Inanimate instruments (scales, tests, surveys, questionnaires, computers)
Mode of analysis	Inductive (by researcher)	Deductive (by statistical methods)
Findings	Comprehensive, holistic, expansive, richly descriptive	Precise, numerical

Major Types of Qualitative Research

As noted earlier, qualitative research is an umbrella term that has numerous variations. Depending on the writer, such variations may be called *orientations* (Tesch, 1990), *theoretical traditions* (Patton, 1990), *strategies of inquiry* (Denzin and Lincoln, 1994), *genres* (Wolcott, 1992), or *major traditions* (Jacob, 1987, 1988; Lancy, 1993). A short review of several of these typologies serves to underscore the vast variety of qualitative research, as well as the lack of consensus as to major types.

Tesch's (1990, p. 58) list of forty-five approaches to qualitative research is a mix of designs (action research, case study), data analysis techniques (content analysis, discourse analysis), and disciplinary orientations (ethnography, oral history). She later collapses these into three basic orientations—language-oriented, descriptive-interpretive, and theory-building (Tesch, 1990). She acknowledges that these distinctions are far from rigid; indeed, overlap often occurs.

Taking a different approach, Patton (1990) anchors different types of qualitative research in "the kinds of questions a particular researcher will ask" (p. 66). Different disciplines or scholarly traditions lead to different questions. He identifies ten perspectives, their disciplinary roots, and what the focus of a research study in each would be. The ten traditions he lists are ethnography, phenomenology, heuristics, ethnomethodology, symbolic interactionism, ecological psychology, systems theory, chaos theory, hermeneutics, and orientational inquiry (by which Patton means a particular ideological or political perspective).

Taking yet another tack, Denzin and Lincoln (1994) include the following chapters under "strategies of inquiry": case studies; ethnography and participant observation; phenomenology, ethnomethodology, and interpretive practice; grounded theory; biographical method; historical social science; and clinical research. Finally, Lancy (1993) explores what he calls the major traditions of qualitative research in education. These include anthropological, sociological, and biological perspectives, the case study, personal accounts, cognitive studies, and historical inquiry.

While examples of qualitative studies in education can be found framed from any one of these perspectives or disciplinary orientations, certain types of qualitative studies are much more prevalent in education than others. Following are five types of qualitative research commonly found in education—the *basic* or *generic qualitative study, ethnography, phenomenology, grounded theory,* and *case study.* While these types can be distinguished from each other, they all share the essential characteristics of qualitative research—*the goal of eliciting understanding and meaning, the researcher as primary instrument of data collection and analysis, the use of fieldwork, an inductive orientation to analysis,* and *findings that are richly descriptive.* Table 1.2 summarizes the five types of qualitative research to be discussed in more detail in this chapter.

Basic or Generic Qualitative Study

For lack of a better label, the term *basic* or *generic qualitative study* refers to studies that exemplify the characteristics of qualitative research discussed earlier. Many qualitative studies in education do not focus on culture or build a grounded theory; nor are they intensive case studies of a single unit or bounded system. Rather, researchers who conduct these studies, which are probably the most common form of qualitative research in education, simply seek to discover and understand a phenomenon, a process, or the perspectives and worldviews of the people involved.

The basic qualitative study in education typically draws from concepts, models, and theories in educational psychology, developmental psychology, cognitive psychology, and sociology. Data are collected through interviews, observations, or document analysis. Findings are a mix of description and analysis—an analysis that uses concepts from the theoretical framework of the study (see Chapter Three). The analysis usually results in the identification of recurring patterns (in the form of categories, factors, variables, themes) that cut through the data or in the delineation of a process. In these studies the analysis does not extend to building a substantive theory as it does in grounded theory studies. Neither are these case studies; there is no bounded system or functioning unit that circumscribes the investigation.

Three examples of basic qualitative studies are Blankenship's (1991) study of male nursing students, Herzog's (1995) study of censorship and public school teachers, and Levinson and Levinson's

Table 1.2. Common Types of Qualitative Research in Education.

Type	Characteristics	Example
Basic or Generic	• Includes description, interpretation, and understanding • Identifies recurrent patterns in the form of themes or categories • May delineate a process	• Meaning-making in transformational learning (Courtenay, Merriam, and Reeves, forthcoming)
Ethnography	• Focuses on society and culture • Uncovers and describes beliefs, values, and attitudes that structure behavior of a group	• A study of twenty successful Hispanic high school students (Cordeiro and Carspecken, 1993)
Phenomenology	• Is concerned with essence or basic structure of a phenomenon • Uses data that are the participant's and the investigator's firsthand experience of the phenomenon	• The role of intuition in reflective practice (Mott, 1994) • Practices inhibiting school effectiveness (Aviram, 1993)
Grounded Theory	• Is designed to inductively build a substantive theory regarding some aspect of practice • Is "grounded" in the real world	• A framework for describing developmental change among older adults (Fisher, 1993)
Case Study	• Is intensive, holistic description and analysis of a single unit or bounded system • Can be combined with any of the above types	• A comparative case study of power relationships in two graduate classrooms (Tisdell, 1993)

(1996) study of women's development. Blankenship wanted to uncover the factors that differentiate male nursing students who complete their studies from those who do not. The literature on participation and motivation framed her study. She discovered from interviewing eight graduates and six nongraduates that both groups had family support and saw nursing as a means of upward mobility. Separating the two groups were participants' image of nursing and of themselves as nurses; time participants needed to finish the degree (graduates had more realistic expectations with regard to image and time); and commitment to the student role versus other adult roles (for graduates, the student role was not negotiable).

Herzog (1995) was interested in the impact of censorship experiences on the educational philosophy and curriculum practices of public school teachers. Thirteen teachers in southern Appalachian communities were interviewed; they identified fifty-five censorship events, most of which were between teacher and parent. Herzog discusses her results in terms of the conflicts between traditional values and modern pressures. In the third example, Levinson and Levinson (1996) studied women's development based on in-depth interviews with fifteen homemakers, fifteen corporate business women, and fifteen academics. This was a follow-up study to his 1978 qualitative study of male development in which he interviewed forty men in midlife. In studying women, Levinson and Levinson found that women experience the same alternating pattern of tumultuous, structure-building periods followed by stable periods of development.

An Ethnographic Study

Ethnography is a form of qualitative research employed by anthropologists to study human society and culture. While *culture* has been variously defined, it essentially refers to the beliefs, values, and attitudes that structure the behavior patterns of a specific group of people. D'Andrade (1992,) outlines the criteria used to determine what is called *cultural.*

> To say something is cultural is—at a minimum—to say that it is shared by a significant number of members of a social group; shared in the sense of being behaviorally enacted, physically

possessed, or internally thought. Further, this something must be recognized in some special way and at least some others are expected to know about it; that is, it must be intersubjectively shared. Finally for something to be cultural it must have the potential of being passed on to new group members, to exist with some permanency through time and across space [p. 230].

An educational ethnography typically deals with the culture of a school community, such as Peshkin's (1986) study of a fundamentalist Christian school, or the culture of a specific group within an educational community, such as Cordeiro and Carspecken's (1993) study of Hispanic high school achievers.

Confusion results when the term *ethnography* is used interchangeably with *fieldwork, case study, participant observation,* or *qualitative research.* For anthropologists, the term has two distinct meanings. *Ethnography* is, first, a set of methods used to collect data, and second, the written record that is the product of using ethnographic techniques. *Ethnographic techniques* are the strategies researchers use to collect data about the social order, setting, or situation being investigated. Common techniques of data gathering are interviewing, conducting documentary analysis, examining life histories, creating investigator diaries, and observing participants. Just using these techniques, however, does not necessarily produce an ethnography in the second sense of the word. An *ethnography is a sociocultural interpretation of the data.* As interpretive descriptions or reconstructions of participants' symbolic meanings and patterns of social interaction, "ethnographies re-create for the reader the shared beliefs, practices, artifacts, folk knowledge, and behaviors of some group of people" (LeCompte and Preissle, 1993, pp. 2–3).

An ethnography then, presents a sociocultural analysis of the unit of study. Concern with the cultural context is what sets this type of study apart from other types of qualitative research. Wolcott (1980) distinguishes sharply between the techniques of ethnography and the ethnographic account itself. "Specific ethnographic techniques are freely available to any researcher who wants to approach a problem or setting descriptively. It is the essential anthropological concern for cultural context that distinguishes ethnographic method from fieldwork techniques and makes genuine ethnography distinct from other 'on-site-observer' approaches. And when cultural interpretation is the goal, the ethnographer must be thinking like an anthropologist, not just looking like one" (p. 59).

In tracing the history of educational ethnography from its roots in the first decades of this century to the present, LeCompte and Preissle (1993) note that culture "remains a unifying construct of this tradition" (p. 13). Whatever the unit of study—students, schools, learning, curriculum, informal education—an ethnographic study is characterized by its sociocultural interpretation. An ethnographic study of a junior high school, for example, would take into account the community at large and its cultural context. The history of the neighborhood, socioeconomic factors, the community's racial and ethnic makeup, the attitudes of parents, residents, and school officials toward education—all would be important considerations in this ethnographic study.

Phenomenology

Phenomenology is a school of philosophical thought that underpins all of qualitative research—and herein lies much of the confusion surrounding the writing in this area. Qualitative research draws from the philosophy of phenomenology in its emphasis on experience and interpretation, but a researcher could also do a phenomenological study using the particular "tools" of phenomenology.

In the conduct of a phenomenological study, the focus would be on the essence or structure of an experience (phenomenon). According to Patton (1990), this type of research is based on

the assumption that *there is an essence or essences to shared experience.* These essences are the core meanings mutually understood through a phenomenon commonly experienced. The experiences of different people are bracketed, analyzed, and compared to identify the essences of the phenomenon, for example, the essences of loneliness, the essence of being a mother, or the essence of being a participant in a particular program. *The assumption of essence, like the ethnographer's assumption that culture exists and is important, becomes the defining characteristic of a purely phenomenological study* [p. 70, emphasis in original].

The task of the phenomenologist, then, is to depict the essence or basic structure of experience. Prior beliefs about a phenomenon of interest are temporarily put aside, or bracketed, so as not to interfere with seeing or intuiting the elements or structure of the phenomenon. When belief is temporarily suspended, consciousness itself becomes heightened and can be examined in the same way that an object of consciousness can be examined.

Spiegelberg (1965), one of the main architects of the phenomenological method of research, has outlined the process of conducting a study. First, a researcher must have an "intuitive grasp" (p. 659) of the phenomenon, and then follow up by investigating several instances or examples of the phenomenon to gain a sense of its general essence. The next steps are to apprehend relationships among several essences and then to systematically explore "the phenomena not only in the sense of *what* appears, whether particulars or general essences, but also of the way in which things appear" (p. 684, emphasis in original). Next to be determined is how the phenomena have come into consciousness; next, beliefs about the phenomena are bracketed, and finally, the meaning of the phenomena can be interpreted.

In an example described by Merriam and Simpson (1995), if we were "to phenomenologically analyze our own learning, we would first describe what is 'subjectively experienced,' such as the setting, the feelings, and reactions to the content involved. In attending to its 'modes of appearing,' we might see that learning involves a sensory experience, a mental activity, and/or an emotional dimension. Finally, the ways in which learning 'constitutes itself in consciousness' involve tracing the sequence of steps through which learning establishes itself or takes shape in our consciousness" (p. 92). We might then bring the experience of our learning into consciousness, analyze it, and attempt to grasp its meaning.

A phenomenological study by Mott (1994) investigated how adult education practitioners use intuition in their practice. Using the steps in the research process proposed by Spiegelberg (1965), she found that intuition aids in the presentation and synthesis of perception, guides practice, and enhances professional competence. In another study by Howard (1994), a phenomenological approach was employed to study the computer experience of eight adult, first-time users. The author notes that this kind of study involves interpretation of the "text" of the experience. "This, then, is a phenomenological investigation of the experiences of those persons who have sat down to the keyboard and can articulate the experience of being introduced to a computer. Another interpretation of the 'text' may help us 'see' computer technology as if for the first time" (p. 34). Four major themes capture the meaning of the experience in Howard's study. These are "(a) The Encounter, (b) The Learning Experience, (c) Becoming Computer Literate, and (d) Alterity: The Computer as Other" (p. 35).

While phenomenology is not easily summarized, Moustakas (1994, p. 27) captures many of its principal tenets in the following statement: "The challenge facing the human science researcher is to describe things in themselves, to permit what is before one to enter consciousness and be understood in its meanings and essences in the light of intuition and self-reflection. The process involves a blending of what is really present with what is imagined as present from the vantage point of possible meanings; thus a unity of the real and the ideal."

Grounded Theory

Grounded theory is a specific research methodology introduced in 1967 by sociologists Glaser and Strauss in their book, *The Discovery of Grounded Theory*. As is true in other forms of qualitative research, the investigator as the primary instrument of data collection and analysis assumes an inductive stance and strives to derive meaning from the data. The end result of this type of qualitative research is a theory that emerges from, or is "grounded" in, the data—hence, grounded theory. Rich description is also important but is not the primary focus of this type of study. As Strauss and Corbin (1994) note, "The major difference between this methodology and other approaches to qualitative research is its emphasis upon theory development" (p. 274).

The type of theory developed is usually "substantive" rather than formal or "grand" theory. Substantive theory has as its referent specific, everyday-world situations such as an innovative middle school science program, the coping mechanisms of returning adult students, or stages of late-life development. A substantive theory has a specificity and hence usefulness to practice often lacking in theories that cover more global concerns.

A substantive theory consists of categories, properties, and hypotheses. Categories, and the properties that define or illuminate the categories, are conceptual elements of the theory. Hypotheses are the relationships drawn among categories and properties. These hypotheses are tentative and are derived from the study. They are not set out at the beginning of the study to be tested, as is true in quantitative research.

As with ethnography and phenomenology, grounded theory has its own jargon and procedures for conducting a study. Very familiar to all qualitative researchers is the set of procedures for analyzing data. The constant comparative method of data analysis is widely used in all kinds of qualitative studies, whether or not the researcher is building a grounded theory. This perhaps explains the indiscriminate use of the term *grounded theory* to describe other types of qualitative research. Basically, the constant comparative method involves comparing one segment of data with another to determine similarities and differences (for example, one quote about returning to school as an adult with another quote by the same or another participant). Data are grouped together on a similar dimension. This dimension is tentatively given a name; it then becomes a category. The overall object of this analysis is to seek patterns in the data. These patterns are arranged in relationship to each other in the building of a grounded theory. (See Chapter Nine for more discussion on the constant comparative method.) Examples of grounded theory studies can be found in a reader compiled by Glaser (1993), as well as in journals from various fields. Fisher (1993), for example, in a grounded theory study of the experiences of older adults ranging in age from sixty to ninety-four, found that developmental change in this stage of life could be described in five age-independent periods. As Strauss and Corbin (1994, p. 277) note, "The diffusion of this methodology seems recently to be increasing exponentially in numbers of studies, types of phenomena studied, geographical spread, and disciplines (education, nursing, psychology, and sociology, for example)."

Case Study

Those with little or no preparation in qualitative research often designate the case study as a sort of catch-all category for research that is not a survey or an experiment and is not statistical in nature. While case studies can be very quantitative and can test theory, in education they are more likely to be qualitative. A case study design is employed to gain an in-depth understanding of the situation and meaning for those involved. The interest is in process rather than outcomes, in context rather than a specific variable, in discovery rather than confirmation. Insights gleaned from case studies can directly influence policy, practice, and future research.

Case studies are differentiated from other types of qualitative research in that they are intensive descriptions and analyses of a *single unit* or *bounded system* (Smith, 1978) such as an individual, program, event, group, intervention, or community. "From Volunteer to Advocate: The Empowerment of an Urban Parent," for example, is a case study of one low-income, single mother who participated in a decision-making process at her daughter's school (Etheridge, Hall, and Etheridge, 1995). Case studies can and do accommodate a variety of disciplinary perspectives. Qualitative case studies in education are often framed with the concepts, models, and theories from anthropology, history, sociology, psychology, and educational psychology. For example, an analysis of the culture of a group such as Gibson's (1988) study of Punjab (from Northern India) immigrants in an American high school could be labeled an ethnographic case study. Likewise, a description and analysis of a school, program, intervention, or practice as it has evolved over time would be a historical case study. A case study of a single student learning math concepts would most likely draw from concepts and theories of learning found in educational psychology. These would all be educational case studies as well, since the focus is on some aspect of educational practice.

While case study has been included in this typology as a form of qualitative research, I also single it out for special attention because case studies are so prevalent in education, and yet the number of available resources for case study researchers is so scant. The literature on case study methodology has expanded in the last few years, but it still lags behind other types. In fact, there is still much confusion as to what constitutes a case study, how it differs from other forms of qualitative research, and when it is most appropriate to use. In Chapter Two, I will address these and other issues related to qualitative case study research.

In summary, the five types of qualitative research presented here are commonly found in educational research. They share the common characteristics of qualitative research, while at the same time each can be distinguished from the others in terms of disciplinary orientation (ethnography, phenomenology), function (grounded theory), or form (case study, basic or generic qualitative study). The five can, and often do, work in conjunction with one another. Thus you could conduct an ethnographic case study or a basic or generic qualitative study using the framework and investigative tools of phenomenology. A case study might also build a substantive theory. For example, three of these forms were combined in Aviram's (1993) study of practices inhibiting school effectiveness in an Israeli boarding school. The methodology of this study was guided by phenomenology; at the same time, it is a case study (one school was studied) and an ethnography (culture was an important construct).

The Researcher

In a qualitative study the investigator is the primary instrument for gathering and analyzing data and, as such, can respond to the situation by maximizing opportunities for collecting and producing meaningful information. Conversely, the investigator as human instrument is limited by being human—that is, mistakes are made, opportunities are missed, personal biases interfere. Human instruments are as fallible as any other research instrument. The extent to which a researcher has certain personality characteristics and skills necessary for this type of research needs to be assessed, just as a rating scale or survey form would be assessed in other types of research.

To begin with, the qualitative researcher must have an enormous *tolerance for ambiguity*. Throughout the research process—from designing the study, to data collection, to data analysis—there are no set procedures or protocols that can be followed step by step. The guidelines and the experiences of others can help, but the researcher must be able to recognize that the best way to proceed will not always be obvious. The very lack of structure is what makes this type of research appealing to many, for it allows the researcher to adapt to unforeseen events and change direction in pursuit of meaning. The investigator's role in qualitative research can be compared to that of a detective. At first everything is important; everyone is suspect. It takes time and patience to search for clues, to follow up leads, to find the missing pieces, to put the puzzle together. For those who work best in a structured situation and have no patience with ambiguity, a more traditional research design is recommended.

Even designing the study can be stressful to the person who prefers an established format. Decisions have to be made as to sample selection (which can be ongoing), how data will be collected, who and how many participants will be interviewed or observed, what documents will be read, and so on. These procedures are far from routine. Once design decisions are made, gaining access to a site and actually meeting the players in the field can be an unsettling experience. Where does the researcher start? What questions should be asked of whom? What should be observed in the field? How should data be dealt with as they are being collected? And how does that process affect what additional data are needed? At every step of the way, the investigator must exercise discretion. The certainty of predetermined data analysis procedures is not to be found in this type of research. Qualitative research thus places the investigator in a largely uncharted ocean. For some it becomes an adventure full of promise for discovery; for others, it can be a disorienting and unproductive experience.

Sensitivity, or being highly intuitive, is a second trait needed in this type of research. The researcher must be sensitive to the context and all the variables within it, including the physical setting, the people, the overt and covert agendas, and the nonverbal behavior. The researcher must be sensitive to the information being gathered. What does it reveal? How can it lead to the next piece of data? How well does it reflect what is happening? Finally, the researcher must be aware of any personal biases and how they may influence the investigation.

This notion of sensitivity pervades the literature on doing qualitative research of any sort. Speaking of evaluators using naturalistic inquiry, Guba and Lincoln (1981) make the point that qualitative evaluators do not measure. Rather, "they do what anthropologists, social scientists, connoisseurs, critics, oral historians, novelists, essayists, and poets throughout the years have done.

They emphasize, describe, judge, compare, portray, evoke images, and create, for the reader or listener, the sense of having been there" (p. 149).

Being sensitive in the data-gathering phase of the study involves a keen sense of timing—of knowing when enough has been observed. In interviewing it means knowing when to allow for silence, when to probe more deeply, when to change the direction of the interview. Every sense of the investigator must be alert to cues and nuances provided by the context.

Sensitivity to the data during collection is also important. Most first-time qualitative researchers have trouble "reading" their data. While a number of resources present techniques for analyzing data, it is still a highly idiosyncratic, intuitive, and lonely process, the success of which depends on the investigator's sensitivity and analytical powers. In speaking of developing theory from data, Glaser (1978) writes that throughout the process

> of generating theory is reliance on the social psychology of the analyst; that is, . . . skill, fatigue, maturity, cycling of motivation, life cycle interest, insights into and ideation from the data. Generating theory is done by a human being who is at times intimately involved with and other times quite distant from the data—and who is surely plagued by other conditions in . . . life. . . . Within the analyst, as the research continues, is a long term biographical and conceptual build up that makes [the researcher] quite "wise" about the data— how to detail its main problems and processes and how to interpret and explain them theoretically [p. 2].

In producing a qualitative study, the researcher must also be sensitive to the biases inherent in this type of research. As LeCompte and Preissle (1993) observe, qualitative research "is distinguished partly by its admission of the subjective perception and biases of both participants and researcher into the research frame" (p. 92). Because the primary instrument in qualitative research is human, all observations and analyses are filtered through that human being's worldview, values, and perspective. It might be recalled that one of the philosophical assumptions underlying this type of research is that reality is not an objective entity; rather, there are multiple interpretations of reality. The researcher thus brings a construction of reality to the research situation, which interacts with other people's constructions or interpretations of the phenomenon being studied. The final product of this type of study is yet another interpretation by the researcher of others' views filtered through his or her own. Many people are uncomfortable negotiating these layers of meaning and worry about the subjectivity involved. Sensitivity thus extends to understanding how biases or subjectivity shape the investigation and its findings. Peshkin (1988) discusses the issue with regard to his "subjectivities" in being a Jewish scholar studying a fundamentalist Christian school. He concludes that subjectivity "can be seen as virtuous, for it is the basis of researchers making a distinctive contribution, one that results from the unique configuration of their personal qualities joined to the data they have collected" (p. 55).

Apart from being able to tolerate ambiguity and being a sensitive observer and analyst, the qualitative research investigator must also be *a good communicator.* A good communicator empathizes with respondents, establishes rapport, asks good questions, and listens intently. Guba and Lincoln (1981) write that one of the "hallmarks of outstanding anthropological and sociological studies to date has been the empathy with which they have presented major actors, performers, and informants" (p. 140). Further, they say, "the extent to which inquirers are able to communicate warmth and empathy often marks them as good or not-so-good data collectors" (p. 140).

Empathy is the foundation of rapport. A researcher is better able to have a conversation with a purpose—an interview, in other words—in an atmosphere of trust. "The purpose of interviewing," writes Patton (1990), "is to find out what is in and on someone else's mind" (p. 278). Since what is in and on someone's mind cannot be directly observed or measured, the interviewer has to ask questions in such a way as to obtain meaningful information. Fortunately, interviewing is a skill that can be developed with practice.

Another vital communication skill is listening. The good qualitative researcher "looks and listens everywhere." It is only by listening "to many individuals and to many points of view that value-resonant social contexts can be fully, equitably, and honorably represented" (Guba and Lincoln, 1981, p. 142). "Hearing" what is not explicitly stated but only implied, as well as noting the silences, whether in interviews, observations, or documents, is an important component of being a good listener.

Being a good communicator involves more than oral skills. You also need to be able to write, for there is an enormous amount of writing in qualitative research. Besides writing field notes during observations, you write memos to yourself about methodological aspects of the study, about emerging findings, about your own reactions and reflections. The final report is usually a lengthy, written narrative. As Lancy (1993) observes, "Every aspect of one's work as a qualitative researcher demands more writing than would be the case for a quantitative scholar. Writing is to qualitative research what mathematics is to quantitative research" (p. 234).

There are many lists of the ideal investigator's characteristics in the literature of qualitative research. Commenting on these lists of desirable attributes, Guba and Lincoln (1981) wryly observe that a person who possessed all of the suggested qualities "not only could be a good inquirer but undoubtedly would make a good president, a fine doctor, another Margaret Mead, or could lead the United Nations to a peaceful resolution of world conflict. . . . They are above all human beings who attend carefully to the social and behavioral signals of others and who find others intrinsically interesting" (pp. 144–145). The three chosen for discussion here—tolerance for ambiguity, sensitivity, and communication skills—capture what most writers consider to be essential for those who conduct this type of research. The question of whether a person can acquire these characteristics, however, has not been answered. If the personality characteristics are present to some degree, skills can probably be cultivated; certainly communication skills can be developed to a higher level in almost everyone. And of course the more experience a person has in doing this type of research, the more likely it is that the needed skills can be developed. Also recommended for prospective researchers are training sessions or workshops, apprenticeships, or small-scale pilot studies. A researcher can determine whether conducting this type of inquiry would be a comfortable process and, at the same time, refine the skills needed for doing so.

Summary

In this chapter I reviewed some important foundational information related to qualitative research, beginning with the positivist-quantitative, interpretive-qualitative, and critical-philosophical orientations toward research. Next, I discussed the essential characteristics of qualitative research: the focus is on interpretation and meaning; the researcher is the primary instrument in data collection and analysis; research activities include fieldwork; the process is primarily inductive; and rich description characterizes the end product. The third section of the chapter focused on five types of qualitative research commonly found in education—the basic or generic qualitative study, ethnography, phenomenology, grounded theory, and case study. Finally, I discussed the important attributes that researchers doing qualitative research should have: a tolerance for ambiguity, sensitivity to context and data, and good communication skills.

Chapter Two

Case Studies as Qualitative Research

Most teachers, graduate students, and researchers in education and other applied social sciences have encountered case studies in their training or work. But while many have heard of case study research, there is little consensus on what constitutes a case study or how this type of research is done. Some of the confusion stems from the fact that, as I pointed out in Chapter One, case study is often equated with fieldwork, ethnography, participant observation, qualitative research, naturalistic inquiry, grounded theory, or exploratory research. The use of the terms *case history, case record,* and *case method,* sometimes in conjunction with *case study,* further confuses the issue.

Case studies, especially qualitative case studies, are prevalent throughout the field of education. From Wolcott's (1973) classic case study, *The Man in the Principal's Office,* to case studies of students, programs, schools, innovations, teachers, and policies, this type of research has illuminated educational practice for nearly thirty years.

The prevalence of qualitative case study research and the lingering uncertainty about its nature and appropriate usage suggest that a chapter like this one is needed—a chapter devoted to presenting case study research as one type of qualitative research. The first section of the chapter defines the case study and describes when it is appropriate as a research design. A second section reviews the various types of case studies, including multisite and comparative designs. In the final section, the strengths and weaknesses of this type of qualitative research are evaluated.

Case Study Defined

Part of the confusion surrounding case studies is that the *process* of conducting a case study is conflated with both the unit of study (the case) and the product of this type of investigation. Yin (1994), for example, defines case study in terms of the research process. "A case study is an empirical inquiry that investigates a contemporary phenomenon within its real-life context, especially when the boundaries between phenomenon and context are not clearly evident" (p. 13). Stake (1994, 1995), however, focuses on trying to pinpoint the *unit of study*—the case. In the first edition of this book, I defined case study in terms of its *end product:* "A qualitative case study is an intensive, holistic description and analysis of a single instance, phenomenon, or social unit" (Merriam, 1988, p. 21). Wolcott (1992) also sees it as "an end-product of field-oriented research" (p. 36) rather than a strategy or method.

Of course each of these approaches reveals something about case studies and contributes to a general understanding of the nature of this kind of research. However, in the ten years since the first edition of this book, I have concluded that the single most defining characteristic of case study research lies in delimiting the object of study, the case. Smith's (1978) notion of the case as a *bounded system* comes closest to my understanding of what defines this type of research. Stake (1995) adds that "the case is an integrated system" (p. 2). Both definitions allow me to see the case as a thing, a single entity, a unit around which there are boundaries. I can "fence in" what I am going to study. The case then, could be a person such as a student, a teacher, a principal; a program; a group such as a class, a school, a community; a specific policy; and so on. Miles and Huberman (1994) think of the case as "a phenomenon of some sort occurring in a bounded context" (p. 25). They graphically present it as a circle with a heart in the center. The heart is the focus of the study, while the circle "defines the edge of the case: what will not be studied" (p. 25).

If the phenomenon you are interested in studying is not intrinsically bounded, it is not a case. One technique for assessing the boundedness of the topic is to ask how finite the data collection would be, that is, whether there is a limit to the number of people involved who could be interviewed or a finite amount of time for observations. If there is no end, actually or theoretically, to the number of people who could be interviewed or to observations that could be conducted, then the phenomenon is not bounded enough to qualify as a case. Stake (1995) clarifies this distinction as follows. "The case could be a child. It could be a classroom of children or a particular mobilization of professionals to study a childhood condition. The case is one among others. . . . An innovative program may be a case. All the schools in Sweden can be a case. But a relationship among schools, the reasons for innovative teaching, or the policies of school reform are less commonly considered a case. These topics are generalities rather than specifics. The case is a specific, a complex, functioning thing" (p. 2).

The bounded system, or case, might be selected because it is an instance of some concern, issue, or hypothesis. It would be, in Adelman, Jenkins, and Kemmis's (1983) words, "*an instance drawn from a class*" (p. 3, emphasis in the original). If the researcher is interested in the process of mainstreaming children into regular classes, for example, he or she could select a particular instance of mainstreaming to study in depth. An instance could be an individual child, a specific program, or a school. A case might also be selected because it is intrinsically interesting; a researcher could study it to achieve as full an understanding of the phenomenon as possible. Choosing to study a college counseling program for returning adult students is an example of selecting a case for its intrinsic interest. In both situations—the mainstreaming process and the counseling program—the case is identified as a bounded system. "The most straightforward examples of 'bounded systems' are those in which the boundaries have a common sense obviousness, e.g. an individual teacher, a single school, or perhaps an innovatory programme" (Adelman, Jenkins, and Kemmis, 1983, p. 3).

Unlike experimental, survey, or historical research, case study does not claim any particular methods for data collection or data analysis. Any and all methods of gathering data, from testing to interviewing, can be used in a case study, although certain techniques are used more than others. Since this book focuses on qualitative research, data-gathering and analysis techniques characteristic of qualitative research are emphasized. The decision to focus on qualitative case studies stems from the fact that this design is chosen precisely because researchers are interested in insight, discovery, and interpretation rather than hypothesis testing. Case study has in fact been differentiated from other research designs by what Cronbach (1975) calls "interpretation in context" (p. 123). By concentrating on a single phenomenon or entity (the case), the researcher aims to uncover the interaction of significant factors characteristic of the phenomenon. The case study focuses on holistic description and explanation. As Yin (1994) observes, case study is a design particularly suited to situations in which it is impossible to separate the phenomenon's variables from their context.

Several writers have advanced definitions of the case study that are congruent with this discussion. Wilson (1979), for example, conceptualizes the case study as a process "which tries to describe and analyze some entity in qualitative, complex and comprehensive terms not infrequently as it unfolds over a period of time" (p. 448). MacDonald and Walker's (1977) definition of a case study as "the examination of an instance in action" (p. 181) is congruent with Guba and Lincoln's (1981) statement that the purpose is "to reveal the properties of the class to which the instance being studied belongs" (p. 371). Becker (1968) defines the purposes of a case study as twofold, that is, "to arrive at a comprehensive understanding of the groups under study" and "to develop general theoretical statements about regularities in social structure and process" (p. 233).

The case study can be further defined by its special features. Qualitative case studies can be characterized as being particularistic, descriptive, and heuristic.

Particularistic means that case studies focus on a particular situation, event, program, or phenomenon. The case itself is important for what it reveals about the phenomenon and for what it might represent. This specificity of focus makes it an especially good design for practical problems—for questions, situations, or puzzling occurrences arising from everyday practice. Case studies "concentrate attention on the way particular groups of people confront specific problems, taking a holistic view of the situation. They are problem centered, small scale, entrepreneurial endeavors" (Shaw, 1978, p. 2).

Descriptive means that the end product of a case study is a rich, "thick" description of the phenomenon under study. *Thick description* is a term from anthropology and means the complete, literal description of the incident or entity being investigated. Case studies include as many variables as possible and portray their interaction, often over a period of time. Case studies can thus be longitudinal (see Huber and Van de Ven, 1995). They have also been labeled *holistic, lifelike, grounded,* and *exploratory.* The description is usually qualitative—that is, instead of reporting findings in numerical data, "case studies use prose and literary techniques to describe, elicit images, and analyze situations. . . . They present documentation of events, quotes, samples and artifacts" (Wilson, 1979, p. 448).

Heuristic means that case studies illuminate the reader's understanding of the phenomenon under study. They can bring about the discovery of new meaning, extend the reader's experience, or confirm what is known. "Previously unknown relationships and variables can be expected to emerge from case studies leading to a rethinking of the phenomenon being studied. Insights into how things get to be the way they are can be expected to result from case studies" (Stake, 1981, p. 47).

Olson (in Hoaglin and others, 1982, pp. 138–139) has developed a list of case study characteristics that may illuminate the nature of this research design. These "aspects," as she refers to them, can be loosely grouped under three of the major characteristics just discussed. Three statements reflect the case study's *particularistic* nature:

- It can suggest to the reader what to do or what not to do in a similar situation.
- It can examine a specific instance but illuminate a general problem.
- It may or may not be influenced by the author's bias.

Several aspects of a case study listed by Olson address its *descriptive* nature. A case study can

- Illustrate the complexities of a situation—the fact that not one but many factors contributed to it.
- Have the advantage of hindsight yet can be relevant in the present.
- Show the influence of personalities on the issue.

- Show the influence of the passage of time on the issue—deadlines, change of legislators, cessation of funding, and so on.
- Include vivid material—quotations, interviews, newspaper articles, and so on.
- Obtain information from a wide variety of sources.
- Cover many years and describe how the preceding decades led to a situation.
- Spell out differences of opinion on the issue and suggest how these differences have influenced the result.
- Present information in a wide variety of ways . . . and from the viewpoints of different groups.

The *heuristic* quality of a case study is suggested by these aspects. A case study can

- Explain the reasons for a problem, the background of a situation, what happened, and why.
- Explain why an innovation worked or failed to work.
- Discuss and evaluate alternatives not chosen.
- Evaluate, summarize, and conclude, thus increasing its potential applicability.

Attempts to define case study often center on delineating what is unique about the research design. As I mentioned earlier, the uniqueness of a case study lies not so much in the methods employed (although these are important) as in the questions asked and their relationship to the end product. Stake (1981) takes this notion one step further and claims that knowledge learned from case study is different from other research knowledge in four important ways. Case study knowledge is

- More concrete—case study knowledge resonates with our own experience because it is more vivid, concrete, and sensory than abstract.
- More contextual—our experiences are rooted in context, as is knowledge in case studies. This knowledge is distinguishable from the abstract, formal knowledge derived from other research designs.

- More developed by reader interpretation—readers bring to a case study their own experience and understanding, which lead to generalizations when new data for the case are added to old data. (Stake considers these generalizations to be "part of the knowledge produced by case studies" [p. 36].)
- Based more on reference populations determined by the reader—in generalizing as described above, readers have some population in mind. Thus, unlike traditional research, the reader participates in extending generalization to reference populations (Stake, 1981, pp. 35–36).

In defining a phenomenon such as a case study, it is often helpful to point out what it is *not.* Case study research is not the same as casework, case method, case history, or case record. *Casework* denotes "the developmental, adjustment, remedial, or corrective procedures that appropriately follow diagnosis of the causes of maladjustment" (Good and Scates, 1954, p. 729). *Case method* is an instructional technique whereby the major ingredients of a case study are presented to students for illustrative purposes or problem-solving experiences. Case studies as teaching devices have become very popular in law, medicine, and business. "For teaching purposes, a case study need not contain a complete or accurate rendition of actual events; rather, its purpose is to establish a framework for discussion and debate among students" (Yin, 1994, p. 2). *Case history*—the tracing of a person, group, or institution's past—is sometimes part of a case study. In medicine and social work, case histories (also called *case records*) are used in much the same sense as casework—to facilitate service to the client.

Determining when to use a case study as opposed to some other research design depends upon what the researcher wants to know. Yin (1994, p. 9) suggests that for "how" and "why" questions the case study has a distinct advantage. Also, the less control an investigator has over "a contemporary set of events," and/or if the variables are so embedded in the situation as to be impossible to identify ahead of time, case study is likely to be the best choice. Bromley (1986) writes that case studies, by definition, "get as close to the subject of interest as they possibly can, partly by means of direct observation in natural settings, partly by their access to subjective factors (thoughts, feelings, and desires), whereas experiments and surveys often use convenient derivative data, e.g. test results, official records. Also, case studies tend to spread the net for evidence widely, whereas experiments and surveys usually have a narrow focus" (p. 23).

Case study is a particularly suitable design if you are interested in process. Process as a focus for case study research can be viewed in two ways. "The first meaning of process is monitoring: describing the context and population of the study, discovering the extent to which the treatment or program has been implemented, providing immediate feedback of a formative type, and the like. The second meaning of process is causal explanation: discovering or confirming the process by which the treatment had the effect that it did" (Reichardt and Cook, 1979, p. 21). Collins and Noblit's (1978) case study of a desegregated high school in Memphis, Tennessee, illustrates the two meanings of process. They discuss the city, the setting, and the extent to which desegregation had been implemented. They also describe how each of the school system's three subsystems (administrative, academic, student) affected the process of interracial schooling. Of particular interest were the differing experiences of the school under two different principals, the climate in the classrooms before and after desegregation, and the students' extracurricular activities. In summarizing the importance of a process rather than an outcome as justification for selecting a case study, Sanders (1981) writes, "Case studies help us to understand processes of events, projects, and programs and to discover context characteristics that will shed light on an issue or object" (p. 44).

Finally, a case study might be selected for its very uniqueness, for what it can reveal about a phenomenon, knowledge we would not otherwise have access to. Abramson (1992) underscores the value of unique or atypical cases. "First, since such data are rare, they can help elucidate the upper and lower boundaries of experience. Second, such data can facilitate . . . prediction by documenting infrequent, non-obvious, or counterintuitive occurrences that may be missed by standard statistical (or empirical) approaches. And finally, atypical cases . . . are essential for understanding the range or variety of human experience, which is essential for understanding and appreciating the human condition" (p. 190). Kline's (1981) case study of a back-to-industry program for vocational instructors at a junior college is an example of a somewhat atypical case. At the end of her study, only three such programs could be located in the United States.

In summary, then, the qualitative case study can be defined in terms of the process of actually carrying out the investigation, the unit of analysis (the bounded system, the case), or the end product. As the product of an investigation, a case study is an intensive, holistic description and analysis of a single entity, phenomenon, or social unit. Case studies are particularistic, descriptive, and heuristic and not to be confused with casework, case method, case history, or case record. As in all research, the choice of a case study design depends upon what the researcher wants to know.

Types of Qualitative Case Studies

Qualitative case studies in education can be further defined by arranging them into categories or types based on disciplinary orientation or by function, that is, whether the overall intent is to describe, interpret, or evaluate some phenomenon or to build theory. Also addressed in this section are multisite or comparative case designs.

Disciplinary Orientation

Certain fields of study use case study research for specific purposes. Law, medicine, psychology, and social work, for example, often employ case studies on behalf of individual clients. Political science, business, journalism, economics, and government have found case studies helpful in formulating policy. Case studies in education can focus on individual students—to diagnose learning problems, for example. More commonly, though, case study research in education is conducted so that specific issues and problems of practice can be identified and explained; researchers in education often draw upon other disciplines such as anthropology, history, sociology, and psychology both for theoretical orientation and for techniques of data collection and analysis.

As I discussed in the first chapter, anthropology has influenced qualitative research generally and education specifically. A case study focusing on, for example, the culture of a school, a group of students, or classroom behavior would be an *ethnographic* case study.

In explaining ethnography, Bogdan and Biklen write, "Researchers in this tradition say that an ethnography succeeds if it teaches readers how to behave appropriately in the cultural setting, whether it is among families in an African American community (Stack, 1974), in the school principal's office (Wolcott, 1973), or in the kindergarten class (Florio, 1978)" (Bogdan and Biklen, 1992, p. 38).

A second type of case study found in education is the *historical* case study. Just as ethnographic case studies distinguish between technique and account, so do historical case studies. This type of research employs techniques common to historiography—in particular, the use of primary source material. The handling of historical material is systematic and involves distinguishing between primary and secondary sources. The nature of the account also distinguishes this form of case study. In applied fields such as education, historical case studies have tended to be descriptions of institutions, programs, and practices as they have evolved in time. Historical case studies may involve more than a chronological history of an event, however. To understand an event and apply that knowledge to present practice means knowing the context of the event, the assumptions behind it, and perhaps the event's impact on the institution or participants.

Bogdan and Biklen (1992), in their discussion of types of case study, list historical organizational case studies as one form common in educational research. These studies focus on a specific organization and trace its development. "You might do a study, for example, of a 'free school,' tracing how it came into being, what its first year was like, what changes occurred over time, what it is like now (if it is still operating), or how it came to close (if it did)" (p. 62). The key to historical case studies, organizational or otherwise, is the notion of investigating the phenomenon over a period of time. The researcher still presents a holistic description and analysis of a specific phenomenon (the case) but presents it from a historical perspective.

Historical research is essentially descriptive, and elements of historical research and case study often merge. Yin (1994) discusses the two approaches:

> Histories are the preferred strategy when there is virtually no access or control. Thus, the distinctive contribution of the historical

method is in dealing with the "dead" past—that is, when no relevant persons are alive to report, even retrospectively, what occurred, and when an investigator must rely on primary documents, secondary documents, and cultural and physical artifacts as the main sources of evidence. Histories can, of course, be done about contemporary events; in this situation, the strategy begins to overlap with that of the case study.

The case study is preferred in examining contemporary events, but when the relevant behaviors cannot be manipulated. Thus, the case study relies on many of the same techniques as a history, but it adds two sources of evidence not usually included in the historian's repertoire: direct observation and systematic interviewing. Again, although case studies and histories can overlap, the case study's unique strength is its ability to deal with a full variety of evidence—documents, artifacts, interviews, and observations—beyond what might be available in the conventional historical study [p. 8].

An example of how historical research can be differentiated from a case study that is historical in nature might be as follows. A study of urban public schools in the late 1800s would rely primarily on public school records for data. A case study of an urban school in the 1960s would use public documents as well, but it might also make use of television or videotaped reports and interviews of persons who had been directly associated with the case.

A third type of qualitative case study employs concepts, theories, and measurement techniques from psychology in investigating educational problems. The focus of a *psychological* case study is on the individual. The most famous precedent for case study in psychology was set by Freud in the early 1900s. His intensive self-analysis, combined with case studies of a few individuals, led to uncovering the unconscious life that is repressed but that nevertheless governs behavior.

Psychologists investigating learning have had the most direct relevance to education. Again there are famous precedents for using case study to gain insight into learning processes. Ebbinghaus in the late nineteenth century, for example, self-administered thousands of tasks in the study of memory (Dukes, 1965). His findings provided the basis for memory research for the next half century. Piaget in studying his own children developed a theory about the stages of cognitive structure that has had an enormous impact on curriculum and instruction. Indeed, his theory is still being tested and refined in educational research investigations. Finally, many studies in child and adult development have employed a qualitative case study as the mode of inquiry, such as Vaillant's (1977) findings about mental health derived from longitudinal case studies of ninety-five Harvard men.

The focus on the individual as a way to investigate some aspect of human behavior characterizes the psychological case study. In education a case study of an individual, program, event, or process might well be informed by a psychological concept. A case study of an elderly learner might draw upon Piaget's theory of cognitive development, for example, or research on behavior change might inform a case study of a patient education program.

Case studies in education might also draw upon theory and technique from sociology. Rather than focusing on an individual, the past, or on culture, *sociological* case studies attend to the constructs of society and socialization in studying educational phenomena. Sociologists are interested in demographics; social life and the roles people play in it; the community; social institutions such as the family, church, and government; classes of people including minority and economic groups; and social problems such as crime, racial prejudice, divorce, and mental illness. Hamel (1993), who traces the history of case studies in both anthropology and sociology, writes that "as a sociological approach, the case study strives to highlight the features or attributes of social life. This is true whether the latter is perceived as a set of interactions, as common behavior patterns, or as structures" (p. 2). Educational case studies drawing upon sociology have explored such topics as student-peer interaction as a function of high school social structure, the effect of role sets on teachers' interactions with students, the actual versus the hidden school curriculum, the relationship of schooling to equalities and inequalities in society at large, and so on (LeCompte and Preissle, 1993).

Thus sociology, like history, anthropology, and psychology, has influenced the theory and methods of case studies in education. What makes these case studies in *education* is their focus on questions, issues, and concerns broadly related to teaching and learning. The setting, delivery system, curriculum, student body, and theoretical orientation may vary widely, but the general arena of education remains central to these studies.

Overall Intent

Irrespective of disciplinary orientation, case studies can also be described by the overall intent of the study. Is it intended to be largely descriptive? Interpretive? To build theory? To present judgments about the worth of a program?

A *descriptive* case study in education is one that presents a detailed account of the phenomenon under study—a historical case study that chronicles a sequence of events, for example. Lijphart (1971) calls descriptive case studies "atheoretical." They are "entirely descriptive and move in a theoretical vacuum; they are neither guided by established or hypothesized generalizations nor motivated by a desire to formulate general hypotheses" (p. 691). They are useful, though, in presenting basic information about areas of education where little research has been conducted. Innovative programs and practices are often the focus of descriptive case studies in education. Such studies often form a database for future comparison and theory building. Moore (1986), for example, conducted case studies of high school interns to find out how newcomers in organizations learn. He developed case studies of interns in such diverse settings as a furniture-making shop, an animal protection league, a hospital speech clinic, a food cooperative, a museum, and a labor union. With these descriptive studies he later devised a conceptual framework about learning in nonschool settings. Whatever the area of inquiry, basic description of the subject being studied comes before hypothesizing or theory testing.

Interpretive case studies, too, contain rich, thick description. These descriptive data, however, are used to develop conceptual categories or to illustrate, support, or challenge theoretical assumptions held prior to the data gathering. If there is a lack of theory, or if existing theory does not adequately explain the phenomenon, hypotheses cannot be developed to structure a research investigation. A case study researcher gathers as much information about the problem as possible with the intent of analyzing, interpreting, or theorizing about the phenomenon. A researcher might study how students come to an understanding of mathematical concepts, for example. Rather than just describing what was observed or what students reported in interviews, the investigator might take all the data and develop a typology, a continuum, or categories that conceptualize different approaches to the task. In another example, Medina (1987) studied the literacy-related activities of a rural farm family and interpreted the data in terms of the meaning of functional literacy in a rural context. The *level* of abstraction and conceptualization in interpretive case studies may range from suggesting relationships among variables to constructing theory. The model of analysis is inductive. Because of the greater amount of analysis in interpretive case studies, some sources label these case studies *analytical*. Analytical case studies are differentiated from straightforward descriptive studies by their complexity, depth, and theoretical orientation (Shaw, 1978).

Evaluative case studies involve description, explanation, and judgment. Much has been written about naturalistic evaluation, responsive evaluation, and qualitative evaluation (Guba and Lincoln, 1981; Patton, 1987, 1990, 1996; Stake, 1981; Greene, 1994; LeCompte and Preissle, 1993). Guba and Lincoln (1981) conclude that case study is the best reporting form for evaluations. For them, case study is best because it provides thick description, is grounded, is holistic and lifelike, simplifies data to be considered by the reader, illuminates meanings, and can communicate tacit knowledge. Above all else, though, this type of case study weighs "information to produce judgment. Judging is the final and ultimate act of evaluation" (p. 375).

Kenny and Grotelueschen (1980) offer several reasons for choosing a case study design when doing an evaluation. "Case study can be an important approach when the future of a program is contingent upon an evaluation being performed and there are no reasonable indicators of programmatic success which can be formulated in terms of behavioral objectives or individual differences" (p. 5). Case study is appropriate when the objective of an evaluation is "to develop a better understanding of the dynamics of a program. When it is important to be responsive, to convey a holistic and dynamically rich account of an educational program, case study is a tailormade approach" (p. 5). They also argue that a case study design can be justified on the basis that sometimes it is important to leave an account. "This goal of case study is essentially descriptive and of historical significance" (p. 5). Finally, "case study can be supported as the common language approach to evaluation" (p. 5). Using common language, as opposed to scientific or educational jargon, allows the results of a study to be communicated more easily to nonresearchers.

Other writers have identified other types of case studies, such as oral or life history case studies (Lawrenson, 1994), clinical case studies (Borg and Gall, 1989), action research case studies (Stenhouse, 1988), and journalistic case studies (Yin, 1994).

Multiple Case Studies

A number of terms can be used when researchers conduct a study using more than one case. These are commonly referred to as *collective case studies, cross-case, multicase* or *multisite studies,* or *comparative case studies.* This type of study involves collecting and analyzing data from several cases and can be distinguished from the single case study that may have subunits or subcases embedded within (such as students within a school). Instead of studying one good high school, for example, Lightfoot (1983) studied six. Her findings are presented first as six individual case studies (or "portraits" as she calls them); she then offers a cross-case analysis suggesting generalizations about what constitutes a good high school. The more cases included in a study, and the greater the variation across the cases, the more compelling an interpretation is likely to be. "By looking at a range of similar and contrasting cases, we can understand a single-case finding, grounding it by specifying *how* and *where* and, if possible, *why* it carries on as it does. We can strengthen the precision, the validity, and the stability of the findings" (Miles and Huberman, 1994, p. 29). The inclusion of multiple cases is, in fact, a common strategy for enhancing the external validity or generalizability of your findings (see Chapter Nine).

In summary, then, case studies can be identified by their disciplinary orientation, by their intent, or by some combination of the two. Thus in education, case studies are ethnographic evaluations, program descriptions, historical interpretations, sociological studies, and so on. While some case studies are purely descriptive, many more are a combination of description and interpretation or description and evaluation.

Strengths and Limitations of Case Studies

All research designs can be discussed in terms of their relative strengths and limitations. The merits of a particular design are inherently related to the rationale for selecting it as the most appropriate plan for addressing the research problem. One strength of an experimental design, for example, is the predictive nature of the research findings. Because of the tightly controlled conditions, random sampling, and use of statistical probabilities, it is theoretically possible to predict behavior in similar settings without actually observing that behavior. Likewise, if a researcher needs information about the characteristics of a given population or area of interest, a descriptive study is in order. Results, however, would be limited to describing the phenomenon rather than predicting future behavior.

Thus a researcher selects a case study design because of the nature of the research problem and the questions being asked. Case study is the best plan for answering the research questions; its strengths outweigh its limitations. The case study offers a means of investigating complex social units consisting of multiple variables of potential importance in understanding the phenomenon. Anchored in real-life situations, the case study results in a rich and holistic account of a phenomenon. It offers insights and illuminates meanings that expand its readers' experiences. These insights can be construed as tentative hypotheses that help structure future research; hence, case study plays an important role in advancing a field's knowledge base. Because of its strengths, case study is a particularly appealing design for applied fields of study such as education. Educational processes, problems, and programs can be examined to bring about understanding that in turn can affect and perhaps even improve practice. Case study has proven particularly useful for studying educational innovations, for evaluating programs, and for informing policy. Collins and Noblit (1978) note the strengths of this type of research, which they call *field studies,* for policy analysis:

> Field research better captures situations and settings which are more amenable to policy and program intervention than are accumulated individual attributes. Second, field studies reveal not static attributes but understanding of humans as they engage in action and interaction within the contexts of situations and settings. Thus inferences concerning human behavior are less abstract than in many quantitative studies, and one can better understand how an intervention may affect behavior in a situation. . . . Field studies are

better able to assess social change than more positivistic designs, and change is often what policy is addressing [p. 26].

The special features of case study research that provide the rationale for its selection also present certain limitations in its usage. Although rich, thick description and analysis of a phenomenon may be desired, a researcher may not have the time or money to devote to such an undertaking. And assuming time is available to produce a worthy case study, the product may be too lengthy, too detailed, or too involved for busy policy makers and educators to read and use. Some suggestions for dealing with reporting and disseminating case studies can be found in the literature (and are discussed in Chapter Ten), but the amount of description, analysis, or summary material is up to the investigator. Guba and Lincoln (1981, p. 377) note an additional limitation of case study narratives. "Case studies can oversimplify or exaggerate a situation, leading the reader to erroneous conclusions about the actual state of affairs." Furthermore, they warn, readers may think that case studies are accounts of the whole: "That is, they tend to masquerade as a whole when in fact they are but a part—a slice of life."

Qualitative case studies are limited, too, by the sensitivity and integrity of the investigator. The researcher is the primary instrument of data collection and analysis. This has its advantages. But training in observation and interviewing, though necessary, is not readily available to aspiring case study researchers. Nor are there guidelines in constructing the final report, and only recently have there been discussions about how to analyze the data collected. The investigator is left to rely on his or her own instincts and abilities throughout most of this research effort.

A further concern about case study research—and in particular case study evaluation—is what Guba and Lincoln (1981) refer to as "unusual problems of ethics. An unethical case writer could so select from among available data that virtually anything he wished could be illustrated" (p. 378). Both the readers of case studies and the authors themselves need to be aware of biases that can affect the final product. Clearly related to this issue of bias is the inherently political nature of case study evaluations. MacDonald and Walker (1977) observe that "educational case studies are usually financed by people who have, directly or indirectly, power over those studied and portrayed" (p. 187). Moreover, "at all levels of the system what people *think* they're doing, what they *say* they are doing, what they *appear* to others to be doing, and what in fact they *are* doing, may be sources of considerable discrepancy. . . . Any research which threatens to reveal these discrepancies threatens to create dissonance, both personal and political" (p. 186, emphasis in original).

Further limitations involve the issues of reliability, validity, and generalizability. As Hamel (1993, p. 23) observes, "the case study has basically been faulted for its lack of representativeness . . . and its lack of rigor in the collection, construction, and analysis of the empirical materials that give rise to this study. This lack of rigor is linked to the problem of bias . . . introduced by the subjectivity of the researcher" and others involved in the case. These issues, which will be discussed more fully in Chapter Nine, are the focus of much discussion in the literature on qualitative research generally.

Summary

Although most educators have encountered case studies in their professional studies or their professional work, the term *case study* is not used precisely; it has become a catchall category for studies that are clearly not experimental, survey, or historical. And to a large extent, the term has been used interchangeably with other qualitative research terms.

In this chapter, I have delineated the nature of qualitative case studies in education. Case studies can be defined in terms of the process of conducting the inquiry (that is, as case study research), the bounded system or unit of analysis selected for study (that is, the case), or the product, the end report of a case investigation. Further, qualitative case studies are particularistic, descriptive, and heuristic. Because a case study has these attributes, a researcher might choose this approach to illuminate a phenomenon. Case studies can also be understood in terms of their disciplinary framework, which commonly draws from anthropology, history, psychology, and sociology. Whether the studies describe, interpret, or evaluate a phenomenon or build theory are issues also considered. The chapter closes with a discussion of the strengths and limitations of this form of qualitative research.

Chapter Three

Designing the Study and Selecting a Sample

Rarely would anyone starting out on a trip just walk out the door with no thought of where to go or what to do. The same is true when beginning a research study. Each activity is best undertaken with some idea of what you want to do and, in the case of research, what you want to know; you need a question or focus to guide your inquiry and a plan for carrying it out. This plan, or map, is the research design that helps you get *"from here to there,* where *here* may be defined as the initial set of questions to be answered, and *there* is some set of conclusions (answers) about these questions" (Yin, 1994, p. 19, emphasis in original).

The set of questions to be answered is derived from what is technically known as the *theoretical framework* of your study. The theoretical framework defines the research problem. This chapter explains what a theoretical framework is and what the role of a literature review is in establishing this framework. Next explained is how to shape a research problem that is most appropriately dealt with through a qualitative research design. Once the research problem is defined, your next task is to select the sample to be studied—a process also covered in this chapter.

The Theoretical Framework

A colleague of mine once commented that if she could have figured out what a theoretical framework was early on, she could have cut a year off of her graduate studies! Indeed, the theoretical or conceptual framework of a study and where theory fits into a research study continue to mystify and frustrate many a novice (and sometimes experienced) researcher. Yet it is often the lack of a clearly articulated theoretical framework—or weak theorizing in general—that results in a study proposal or report being rejected by oversight committees and publication outlets. I hope this section of the chapter will help you avoid this common pitfall in designing qualitative studies.

Qualitative research is designed to inductively build rather than to test concepts, hypotheses, and theories. Because of this characteristic, many believe mistakenly that theory has no place in a qualitative study. Actually it would be difficult to imagine a study *without* a theoretical or (a term that can be used interchangeably) conceptual framework. As Becker (1993) points out, "We couldn't work at all if we didn't have at least an implicit theory of knowledge; we wouldn't know what to do first" (p. 221). The trick is to make this framework explicit.

Just what is a theoretical framework? The theoretical framework is derived from the orientation or stance that you bring to your study. It is the structure, the scaffolding, the frame of your study. Every study has one. There are several ways to identify what it is. First, what is your disciplinary orientation? Each of us has been socialized into a discipline with its own vocabulary, concepts, and theories. Since this book is addressed primarily to educators, I presume that you think in terms of educational concepts and theories. Of course education, like many applied fields, also draws upon other disciplines to inform its practice. For example, psychology and its various subfields, sociology, history, and anthropology strongly influence education.

This disciplinary orientation is the lens through which you view the world. It determines what you are curious about, what puzzles you, and hence, what questions you ask that in turn begin to give form to your investigation. Looking at the same classroom, for example, different researchers might ask different questions about it. An educator might ask questions about the curriculum, the instructional strategies, or the learning activities. A psychologist might be curious about the self-esteem or motivation of certain students, a sociologist about the social interaction patterns or roles that different participants assume, an anthropologist about the culture of the classroom—its rites and rituals.

That the same entity can be approached from different orientations is exemplified in a collection of essays on adult learning (Merriam, 1993). In the collection, Boucouvalas discusses adult learning from a psychological, and in particular, a transpersonal psychology perspective. She thus speaks of the phenomenon in terms of levels, states, and structures of consciousness, subliminal learning, and the like. Wilson, however, frames learning from a situated cognition perspective. This view assumes that learning is situated in the everyday world of human social activity, employs the "tools" (like maps, computers) in the immediate environment, and cannot be adequately understood apart from the context in which it occurs. In another chapter, Tisdell presents adult learning from a feminist pedagogy perspective. Here the focus is on understanding the nature of structured power relationships in society as they are manifest in the classroom and on facilitating women's empowerment in the learning environment. A qualitative research study could be designed from each of these perspectives. Each study would draw from a different literature base (transpersonal psychology, situated cognition, feminist pedagogy), would use concepts and terms unique to that orientation, and would state the research problem and study purpose to reflect the particular assumptions and concerns of that perspective.

One of the clearest ways to identify your theoretical framework is to attend to the literature you are reading that is related to your topic of interest. What are the titles of journals? What key words do you use to search databases for information? At the very least, you will be looking into the literature to see if the study you are thinking of doing has already been done. In your search, what are the recurring concepts, models, and theories? Who are the major writers, theorists, and researchers in this area? (See the following section on reviewing the literature for a fuller discussion of this process).

The framework of your study will draw upon the concepts, terms, definitions, models, and theories of a particular literature base and disciplinary orientation. This framework in turn will generate the "problem" of the study, specific research questions, data collection and analysis techniques, and how you will interpret your findings. Schultz (1988), writing about vocational education research, observes that "any research problem may be approached from more than one theoretical perspective. . . . The choice of a theoretical model/conceptual framework . . . will guide the research process in terms of the identification of relevant concepts/constructs, definition of key variables, specific questions to be investigated, selection of a research design, choice of a sample and sampling procedures, data collection strategies . . . data analysis techniques, and interpretation of findings" (p. 34).

All aspects of the study are affected by its theoretical framework. The theoretical framework in relation to the specific research problem to be investigated can be pictured as a set of interlocking frames. The outermost frame—the theoretical framework—is the body of literature, the disciplinary orientation that you draw upon to situate your study. This framework indicates to the reader the topic you are interested in. It also identifies what is known about the topic (citing appropriate literature), what aspect of the topic you are going to focus on, what is not known (the "gap" in the knowledge base), why it is important to know it, and the precise purpose of the study. All of this information is pulled from the larger frame of the study in order to construct the problem statement itself (see the section on problem statement in this chapter). Thus the problem statement is represented by a second frame that is firmly lodged in the larger framework. Finally, the exact purpose of the study is within the problem statement and can be pictured as the third, inner-most frame in this set of interlocking frames.

The theoretical framework, problem statement, and purpose can be illustrated in a study of reentry black women (Johnson-Bailey and Cervero, 1996). The authors begin by stating, "Racism and sexism as societal forces negatively impact the lives of Black women (Amott & Matthaei, 1991; Hacker, 1992) and are directly visible in Black women's lives as evidenced by their economic standing, their high mortality rate, and their low rate of educational attainment" (p. 142). We are introduced to the general topic and then more specifically to the academic setting: "Since academia does not exist in a vacuum, it is only logical to assume that the same forces are ever present within the classroom. So it is imperative that when the lives of Black women in college are studied that these concerns be addressed, particularly when, in the last twenty years, American colleges have experienced a dramatic influx of non-traditional students, many of whom are Black women" (p. 143). The research problem within the theoretical framework is then identified, as is the precise purpose of the study. "The problem, then, is that Black women as a group go unnoticed and unresearched, and their specific and individual needs remain unaddressed by academia. This study was designed to examine the educational narratives of reentry Black women in an effort to determine the ways that the dynamics of the larger society, which often negatively impact their lives, are played out in higher education" (p. 144). The problem and purpose are clearly embedded within the "theoretical framework" of "Black feminist thought and its resulting epistemology, whose theories and literature helped establish parameters for this research study" (p. 144).

In addition to determining how the problem and purpose are shaped, "our observations as researchers are framed in some ways rather than others, which makes perception itself theory-laden. Theory allows seeing what we would otherwise miss; it helps us anticipate and make sense of events" (Thornton, 1993, p. 68). That is to say that the things we observe in the field, the questions we ask of our participants, and the documents we attend to are determined by the theoretical framework of the study. It also determines what we do not see, do not ask, and do not attend to. "There must always be selection criteria and these are derived, in part at least, from theoretical assumptions, from ideas about what produces what" (Hammersley, Scarth, and Webb, 1985, p. 54). The sense we make of the data we collect is equally influenced by the theoretical framework. That is, our analysis and interpretation—our study's findings—will reflect the constructs, concepts, language, models, and theories that structured the study in the first place. In the study of reentry black women, for example, the findings are presented in terms of concepts of race, gender, class, and color from black feminist thought.

As Schwandt (1993, p. 7) states, "Atheoretical research is impossible." A theoretical framework underlies all research. Theory is present in all qualitative studies because no study could be designed without some question being asked (explicitly or implicitly). How that question is phrased and how it is worked into a problem statement reflect a theoretical orientation.

Confusion arises about this issue because qualitative research is inductive, leading to interpretive or analytical constructs, even to "theory." The argument could be made, however, that most qualitative research inherently shapes or modifies existing theory in that (1) data are analyzed and interpreted in light of the concepts of a particular theoretical orientation, and (2) a study's findings are almost always discussed in relation to existing knowledge (some of which is theory) with an eye to demonstrating how the present study has contributed to expanding the knowledge base. Even those who set out to develop a grounded theory (see Chapter One) do not enter the study with a blank mind, with *no* notion of what to think about or look for. "In fact, grounded theory is a complex process of both induction and deduction, guided by prior theoretical commitments and conceptual schemes. In this means of analysis, as well as in any other attempt to move from field notes to concepts and interpretations, the task is far from purely inductive and inferential" (Schwandt, 1993, p. 9). Further, the insights that form the basis of a grounded theory can come from existing theory as well as personal experiences and the experiences of others. In using existing theory as a source for new theory, the strategy "is to line up what one takes as theoretically possible or probable with what one is finding in the field" (Glaser and Strauss, 1967, p. 253). Strauss and Corbin (1994) go even further in acknowledging how much grounded theory has been "influenced by contemporary intellectual trends and movements, including ethnomethodology, feminism, political economy, and varieties of postmodernism," and that "additional ideas and concepts suggested by contemporary social and intellectual movements are entering analytically as *conditions* into the studies of grounded theory researchers" (p. 276, emphasis in original).

This section presents a case for theory permeating the entire process of qualitative research. The very questions you raise derive from your view of the world. In research, this view is lodged in a disciplinary base and can be identified through attending to the literature you review in preparation for the study. A discussion of how and why you review the literature follows.

Reviewing the Literature

It should be obvious that one way to identify and establish the theoretical framework of a qualitative study is to review the relevant literature. By *literature* I mean the theoretical or conceptual writing in an area (the "think" pieces) and the data-based research studies in which someone has gone out and collected and analyzed data. In practice, designing a study is not a linear process of reading the literature, identifying the theoretical framework, and then writing the problem statement. Rather, the process is highly interactive. Your question takes you to some of the literature, which sends you back to looking anew at the phenomenon of interest. In trying to shape the problem, you go back again to the literature, and so on. In essence, you carry on a dialogue with previous studies and work in the area.

Typically, the first question you ask in this dialogue is whether there *is* any literature on the topic. If so, does it confirm that you are onto a problem that needs researching, or has your idea already been researched to death? In a chapter aptly titled, "Terrorized by the Literature," Becker (1986b) speaks to everyone's fear of discovering that a "carefully nurtured idea was in print before they thought of it (maybe before they were born) and in a place they should have looked" (p. 136). Claiming that there is no literature on a topic can only mean that no one thinks the topic is worth studying, there is no way to study it, or, more than likely, you have searched too narrowly. In my experience there is always some related literature. An investigator who ignores prior research and theory risks pursuing a trivial problem, duplicating a study already done, or repeating others' mistakes. The goal of research—contributing to the knowledge base of the field—may then never be realized. According to Cooper (1984, p. 9), "the value of any single study is derived as much from how it fits with and expands on previous work as from the study's intrinsic properties." And if some studies seem more significant than others, it is "because the piece of the puzzle they solve (or the puzzle they introduce) is extremely important."

Why Review the Literature?

Investigators who do not take the time to find out what has already been thought or researched may be missing an opportunity to make a significant contribution to their field. Indeed, one function of the literature review is to provide the foundation for contributing to the knowledge base. No problem in education exists in isolation from other areas of human behavior. Consequently, there is always some research study, some theory, some thinking related to the problem that can be reviewed to inform the study at hand.

Besides providing a foundation—a theoretical framework—for the problem to be investigated, the literature review can demonstrate how the present study advances, refines, or revises what is already known. It is important for the researcher to know how his or her study deviates from what has already been done. A literature review can do more than set the stage for a study, however. The process can contribute to formulating the problem and answering specific design questions. Knowing what hypotheses have been advanced and tested previously, how terms have been defined, and what assumptions have been dealt with by other investigators can simplify the researcher's task; knowing what research designs have been used before, and with what success, can save time and money. For qualitative studies, researchers can benefit from knowing how well certain data collection techniques used in previous related studies may or may not have yielded meaningful data.

Previous research is often cited in support of the way the study is framed, how concepts are defined, and so on. Previous literature can also be drawn upon to make the case that the present study is necessary, urgent, and important to undertake.

Finally, a commanding knowledge of previous studies and writing on a topic offers a point of reference for discussing the contribution the current study will make to advancing the knowledge base in this area. The researcher literally situates his or her findings in the previous literature, pointing out the exact nature of the contribution.

In the typical report of a research study, a citation of previous literature—sometimes even the same citation—may appear in three places. First, previous literature and writing are cited in the introduction, perhaps judiciously quoted from, to build the case for doing the present study. A quote from a well-known authority about the importance of a problem and the need for research in the area will shore up the researcher's position. Underscoring the paucity of research on a topic by citing the only few existing studies is also persuasive.

The second place for a literature citation is in a section or chapter often called the "Literature Review," or "Previous Research."

Here the literature is synthesized and critiqued; the work that has been done on the topic, its strengths, and its shortcomings are highlighted. In an article-length report of a study, previous literature is often integrated into the development of the problem for study.

Third, the discussion of the findings of a study, found at the end of a research report, always contains references to the literature. In the discussion the researcher points out what the study contributes to the knowledge base of the field by showing how the study's findings extend, modify, or contradict previous work.

While there is little doubt that a literature review can strengthen a research study, determining the best time to conduct the review is a matter of some debate. Most writers would agree that the task of becoming familiar with the background of a topic is best undertaken early in the research process; a literature review's impact on problem formulation is an interactive process. At one end of a continuum is a researcher reviewing the literature to *find* a problem; at the other end is a researcher reviewing the literature to see if the problem already found has ever been studied. Somewhere in the middle is the investigator who has some notion about what he or she wants to research and consults the literature for help in focusing the problem. While a literature review helps in problem formulation regardless of design, in grounded theory studies in particular, there is a range of opinion as to when the literature should be consulted. Glaser (1978) feels it is best to wait until after data have been collected.

> In deductive research the analyst first reads the literature of the field to the fullest coverage possible, from which he deducts or synthesizes a framework, usually theoretical, to study and verify in his research. . . . He then collects the data according to the concepts of the framework. . . . Because of his initial scholarship and deduction his findings are directly woven into the literature of the field. . . .
>
> In our approach we collect the data in the field first. Then [we] start analyzing it and generating theory. When the theory seems sufficiently grounded and developed, *then* we review the literature in the field and relate the theory to it through the integration of ideas. . . . Thus scholarship in the same area starts after the emerging theory is sufficiently developed so the theory will not be preconceived by preempting concepts [p. 31].

Glaser is clear that even in inductive, grounded theory studies, it is essential to read widely. He suggests reading in substantive areas somewhat different from the research area at first, then reading in the researcher's own area as the project gets under way. The activity is then highly relevant, for the researcher can "skip and dip, thereby gaining greater coverage, since he now has a clear purpose for covering his field, which is to integrate his generated theory with the other literature in the field" (Glaser, 1978, p. 32). However, given the trade-offs of being unduly influenced by previous work versus the way in which an early review of the literature can enhance even a grounded theory study, most qualitative researchers would consult the literature earlier rather than later in the process.

Steps in Conducting a Literature Review

How is a literature review conducted? This topic is covered in more depth in other sources (Cooper, 1984; McMillan and Schumacher, 1984; Merriam and Simpson, 1995). Nevertheless, a summary of the process might be helpful. First, the scope of the search is determined by how well defined the research problem is, as well as the researcher's prior familiarity with the topic. If you as a prospective researcher have only a vague sense of a problem you want to investigate, a good way to start would be to conduct an overview of the topic. You can get information from subject encyclopedias, handbooks, and yearbooks. Major studies, theories, issues, and so on can be identified in this way. The next step is to check bibliographies, indexes, and abstracts that reference specific aspects of a topic. This step in the search is typically done by computer.

Once a set of references and abstracts has been collected, you must decide which full-length resources should be obtained. This selection can be made on the basis of the following criteria:

- Is the author of the source an authority on the topic, one who has done much of the empirical work in the area, or one who has offered seminal theory upon which subsequent research and writing has been based? If so, that author's work will be quoted by others and listed in bibliographies on the topic.

- When was the article or book or report written? As a rule, the most recent work in an area should be included in a review.
- What exactly was written about or tested? If a particular resource or research study is highly relevant to your present research interest, it should be included even if the "who" and "when" criteria are not met.
- What is the quality of the source? A thoughtful analysis, a well-designed study, or an original way of viewing the topic is probably a significant piece of literature. In historical or documentary analysis, the quality of primary and secondary sources is a major criterion for inclusion into the data base [Merriam and Simpson, 1995, pp. 39–40].

Once you have decided which sources you want to look at more closely, you must obtain the full document. This can be frustrating if your library does not carry thousands of journals or if you have to buy a dissertation. I suggest starting with the resources readily available; it may be that you will not need to track down the more obscure resources. In any case, be scrupulously diligent about recording the *full* bibliographic reference. If you write down a particularly good quote or idea, record the page number. Many a researcher has spent hours looking for the first initial, volume number, date, or page number of a reference! Begin developing an annotated bibliography. This will be something you can add to and draw from as you begin putting together the rationale for your study.

Knowing when to stop reviewing the literature is as important as knowing where and how to locate sources. There are two ways you can determine if you have done enough. One is to recognize that you have covered all of the relevant literature in the area. Your first glimpse of this end point happens when you turn to the reference list at the end of an article or report and discover that you are familiar with all of the references listed. You may even have read them all. When this happens two or three times, you can feel that you have accounted for most, if not all, the relevant literature. This is a saturation point. The second clue is a bit more subjective—you realize you *know* the literature. You can cite studies, people, dates, theories, historical trends, and so on. You have a command of the literature. It is time to quit.

The Review

A literature review is a narrative essay that integrates, synthesizes, and critiques the important thinking and research on a particular topic. Having collected and reviewed the relevant sources, the researcher still faces the task of writing up the review into a coherent narrative essay. There are probably as many organizing possibilities as there are authors. Most literature reviews are organized according to particular themes found in the literature reviewed. A review of the literature on learning styles, for example, might contain sections on conceptualizations of learning style, instruments that measure learning style, populations that have been used in learning style research, and so on. Sometimes reviews are organized chronologically, and "some reviews may evolve into a combined thematic and chronological organization" (Merriam and Simpson, 1995, p. 48). For example, "You might handle the early, though important, literature on the topic under a chronological heading . . . and then move on to relevant themes characteristic of the most recent work. Conversely, the bulk of the literature might be organized thematically with the most recent work under a heading such as 'recent developments'" (p. 48). Regardless of the organization, a crucial component of any literature review is the critical assessment of the research and literature included. The reader wants to know what you think of the literature, its strengths as well as its weaknesses, whether or not it constitutes a major breakthrough in the thinking on the topic, what it adds to the knowledge base, and so on.

In summary, a familiarity with previous research and theory in the area of study is necessary for situating your study in the knowledge base of the field. A review of the literature can also yield information that will be helpful when you make design decisions. Further, the literature is crucial to identifying the overall theoretical framework of your study, as well as shaping the problem statement.

The Research Problem

It would be a fruitless undertaking to embark on a research journey without first identifying a research problem. Most people understand what it means to have a "problem." A problem in the conventional sense is a matter involving doubt, uncertainty, or difficulty. A person with a problem usually seeks a solution, some clarification, or a decision. So too with a research problem. For Dewey (1933), a problem is anything that "perplexes and challenges the mind so that it makes belief . . . uncertain" (p. 13).

Where do you look for something that perplexes and challenges the mind? The most logical place for those of us in applied fields such as education is with our everyday practice. Look around. What is interesting to you that you do not quite understand? What puzzles you? What are you curious about? For example, you might observe that all your efforts to include certain students in classroom discussion have failed. You might wonder about any number of factors related to this situation. Is there something about these students that makes them reluctant to participate? Is it the methods you use to include them? Is there something about the classroom atmosphere? Your personality? Thus out of personal, practical experience can come research questions "suggested by observations of certain relationships for which no satisfactory explanation exists, routine ways of doing things that are based on authority or tradition lacking research evidence, or innovations and technological changes that need long-term confirmation" (McMillan and Schumacher, 1984, p. 49).

A research problem can also come from the literature, especially previous research or theory in an area. Nearly every research study has a section with suggestions for future research, many of which could be approached qualitatively. Something you read in your professional journals for a class assignment or even for leisure reading may give rise to a question that can be shaped into a research problem. Much of the theoretical literature in adult education, for example, states that adults are self-directed and therefore prefer to participate in planning, implementing, and evaluating their own learning. However, data-based studies of adult learners have revealed that some do not want or know how to take control of their own learning. Since these two notions are inconsistent, a problem arises. Is self-direction a precondition of adult learning, or is it one of the goals of an adult learning activity? What differentiates self-directed learners from those who are not? What about the context of learning that may or may not promote self-direction? Is self-direction, as opposed to say, collaborative learning, desirable?

Although not as common in qualitative research, a research problem can be derived from a theory by questioning whether a particular theory can be sustained in practice. Even architects of grounded theory (see Chapter One) concede that qualitative research can be used to elaborate and modify existing theory by the rigorous "matching of theory against data" (Strauss and Corbin, 1994, p. 273). For example, in studying male psychosocial development, Levinson and colleagues (1978) discovered that having a mentor was a crucial factor in men's realizing their young adulthood dreams and being successful at midlife. The mentor was approximately eight to fifteen years older, the relationship usually lasted from two to three years, and it was eventually necessary for the protégé to end the relationship in order to be his own man. A qualitative case study of a successful midlife man might be undertaken to test Levinson's theory of mentoring.

Problems can also emanate from current social and political issues. In the past, for example, "the women's movement raised questions about sex equity in general and in sex stereotyping of educational materials and practices. The civil rights movement led to research on the education of minority children and the effects of desegregation on racial attitudes, race relations, self-concept, achievement, and the like" (McMillan and Schumacher, 1984, p. 49). Recently, the changing demographic structure of American society has brought issues of multiculturalism and diversity to the attention of educators. Boshier's study (1992) of the ways in which the discourse around AIDS has been framed and the consequent implications for educators is yet another example of how current social and political issues might frame a research study.

The first task, then, in conducting a qualitative study is to raise a question about something that perplexes and challenges the mind. It has often been said that more art than rules is involved in research. In comparing the qualitative research to the art form of dance, Janesick (1994) says of this important first step, "All dances make a statement and begin with the question, What do I want to say in this dance? In much the same way, the qualitative researcher begins with a similar question: What do I want to know in this study? This is a critical beginning point. Regardless of point of view, and quite often because of our point of view, we construct and frame a question for inquiry" (p. 210).

The thing you are curious about, then, forms the core of the research problem, or the problem statement. It reflects your particular theoretical framework; more precisely, it represents a gap in the knowledge base. That there is nothing to fill the gap is determined by reviewing the literature and research on the question. In crafting the research problem, you move from general interest, curiosity, or doubt about a situation to a specific statement of the research problem. In effect, you have to translate your general curiosity into a problem that can be addressed through research.

The structure of a problem statement, which essentially lays out the logic of the study, can be compared to the funnel shape— broad at the top and narrow at the bottom. At the "top" you identify the general area of interest. Is it students with learning disabilities? Public school innovation? Learning to read? Instruction? Math anxiety? Adults in higher education? Shared governance? You acquaint the reader with what this topic is all about; you introduce key concepts, what has already been studied with regard to this topic, and why it is an important topic, that is, why anyone should care about it.

Moving along, you then narrow the topic, directing the reader toward the specific question you have. At this juncture you also point out the lack of information—the knowledge gap— with regard to this particular aspect of the topic. Perhaps nothing in the literature addresses your question, or there may be some research, but for reasons you make clear, it is inadequate or flawed in some important way. You have just led your reader down the funnel to the point where the need for the study is obvious. What needs to be done becomes the precise purpose of your study. Problem statements often conclude with the statement, "The purpose of this study is to . . ." Following is the problem statement from a study of power relations in graduate education classes. Note that the author begins broadly by locating the reader in the topic of interest, which reflects the theoretical framework of the study—in this case, feminist pedagogy. She then points out the gap in the literature related to the particular aspect of this topic she is interested in and concludes with a purpose statement:

Power relationships are present everywhere in society. There is a power disparity between racial minorities and the white majority,

between the poor and the wealthy, the uneducated and the educated, and women and men. To some extent, these power relations
are reproduced and maintained through the educational
process. . . . The power of both the hidden and overt curriculum to
contribute to the maintenance and reproduction of existing power
relationships is operative at every level of formal education from
nursery school to graduate school, even in higher education settings where critical thinking skills are promulgated and valued, and
emancipatory educational theories are developed and
discussed. . . .

While there is a body of literature that discusses the nature of
power relations in adult education (Collard & Law, 1989; Cunning-
ham, 1988, 1992; Hart, 1985, 1990), there has been a lack of data-
based research that specifically examines power relations in the
learning environment based on gender or race, or interlocking systems of privilege and oppression, such as gender and race, or gender and class. The purpose of this study was to determine how
power relations predominantly based on gender, but including
other interlocking systems of privilege and oppression, such as race
or ethnicity, class, and age, are manifested in classrooms composed
of adult students [Tisdell, 1993, pp. 203–204].

The purpose of Tisdell's study—to investigate how power relations manifest themselves in classrooms of adult students—is a
good illustration of the type of question best addressed by a qualitative design. She was not interested in conducting an experiment
or measuring the prevalence of power relations; rather, she won-
dered what the phenomenon looked like in graduate classes. To
answer this question she conducted a comparative case study in
which she observed all sessions of two courses, one with a male
instructor and one with a female instructor. She also interviewed
the instructors and a selection of students from each class.

Questions about process (why or how something happens)
commonly guide qualitative research, as do questions of understanding (what happened, what does it mean for those involved).
In another study, for example, the researcher was interested in top-
level women executives and how they learned to navigate and
advance in often inhospitable corporate environments (Bierema,
1996). She could have identified barriers and strategies from the
literature and from her personal experience and surveyed women

executives in Fortune 500 companies. Instead, she was interested in how the women themselves understood their experiences, and thus she designed a qualitative study to uncover those meanings.

The purpose statement is often followed by a set of research questions. These questions reflect the researcher's thinking on the most significant factors to study. They guide the inquiry, and they determine how data are to be collected. In qualitative research they often identify areas of inquiry for what to observe in a field observation, or what questions to ask in an interview. Research questions are similar to hypotheses in quantitative research; hypotheses are much more precise and indicate the nature of measurement and analysis involved. Research questions that guide a qualitative inquiry should not be confused with *the* question, curiosity, or puzzlement that gave rise to the study in the first place (and that is reflected in the problem statement and purpose of the study). For example, in Bierema's (1996) study of executive women, her overall question or purpose was to understand how these women learned enough about the culture to break through the glass ceiling. Questions that guided the study were, "What formal and informal learning do women experience to develop their understanding of organizational culture? What barriers do women encounter in their climb up the corporate ladder? What are executive women's strategies for coping and excelling in corporate environments?" (p. 149).

Sample Selection

Once the general problem has been identified, the task becomes to select the unit of analysis, the sample. Within every study there probably exist numerous sites that could be visited, events or activities that could be observed, people who could be interviewed, documents that could be read. The researcher thus needs "to consider where to observe, when to observe, whom to observe and what to observe. In short, sampling in field research involves the selection of a research site, time, people and events" (Burgess, 1982, p. 76).

The two basic types of sampling are probability and nonprobability sampling. Probability sampling (of which simple random sampling is the most familiar example) allows the investigator to generalize results of the study from the sample to the population from which it was drawn. Since generalization in a statistical sense is not a goal of qualitative research, probabilistic sampling is not necessary or even justifiable in qualitative research (see Chapter Nine for more discussion on generalizability). Thus nonprobability sampling is the method of choice for most qualitative research. Anthropologists, for example, have long maintained that nonprobability sampling methods "are logical as long as the fieldworker expects mainly to use his data not to answer questions like 'how much' and 'how often' but to solve *qualitative* problems, such as discovering what occurs, the implications of what occurs, and the relationships linking occurrences" (Honigmann, 1982, p. 84). Thus the most appropriate sampling strategy is nonprobabilistic—the most common form of which is called *purposive* (Chein, 1981) or *purposeful* (Patton, 1990). Purposeful sampling is based on the assumption that the investigator wants to discover, understand, and gain insight and therefore must select a sample from which the most can be learned. Chein (1981) explains, "The situation is analogous to one in which a number of expert consultants are called in on a difficult medical case. These consultants—also a purposive sample—are not called in to get an average opinion that would correspond to the average opinion of the entire medical profession. They are called in precisely because of their special experience and competence" (p. 440).

Patton (1990) argues that "the logic and power of purposeful sampling lies in selecting *information-rich cases* for study in depth. Information-rich cases are those from which one can learn a great deal about issues of central importance to the purpose of the research, thus the term *purposeful* sampling" (p. 169, emphasis in original).

To begin purposive sampling, you must first determine what selection *criteria* are essential in choosing the people or sites to be studied. LeCompte and Preissle (1993, p. 69) prefer the term *criterion-based selection* to the terms *purposive* or *purposeful* sampling. In criterion-based selection you "create a list of the attributes essential" to your study and then "proceed to find or locate a unit matching the list" (p. 70). The criteria you establish for purposeful sampling directly reflect the purpose of the study and guide in the identification of information-rich cases. You not only spell out the criteria you will use, but you say why the criteria are important. For example, in Bierema's (1996) study of executive women in corporate settings mentioned earlier, she decided that to ensure that the women were top-level executives, they would have to be from Fortune 500–type corporate environments (one criterion); they had to have achieved executive-level status, which meant that they would have responsibility for a business unit with supervisory, policy development, or organizational strategy responsibilities (a second criterion). Third, she reasoned that they had to have been with the same company for at least five years "to ensure that each participant understood the corporate culture" (p. 150).

Types of Purposeful Sampling

A number of writers have differentiated among different types of purposeful sampling (Goetz and LeCompte, 1984; Miles and Huberman, 1994; Patton, 1990). Some of the more common types are *typical, unique, maximum variation, convenience, snowball, chain,* and *network* sampling. Using a population of high school graduates for illustration, a discussion and example of each of these types follows.

A *typical* sample would be one that is selected because it reflects the average person, situation, or instance of the phenomenon of interest. "When the typical site sampling strategy is used," Patton (1990) writes, "the site is specifically selected because it is not in any major way atypical, extreme, deviant, or intensely unusual" (p. 173). Using a profile of the average or typical high school graduate, any who fit this profile could be included in a purposeful sample.

A *unique* sample is based on unique, atypical, perhaps rare attributes or occurrences of the phenomenon of interest. You would be interested in them *because* they are unique or atypical. With regard to high school graduates, you might select one who has become a professional athlete.

Maximum variation sampling was first identified by Glaser and Strauss (1967) in their book on grounded theory. A grounded theory, it was reasoned, would be more conceptually dense and potentially more useful if it had been "grounded" in widely varying instances of the phenomenon. Findings from even "a small sample of great diversity" yields "important shared patterns that cut across cases and derive their significance from having emerged out of heterogeneity" (Patton, 1990, p. 172). Sometimes this strategy involves "a deliberate hunt for negative" or disconfirming "instances or variations" of the phenomenon (Miles and Huberman, 1994, p. 29). Maximum variation sampling of high school graduates would involve identifying and seeking out those who represent the widest possible range of the characteristics of interest for the study.

Convenience sampling is just what is implied by the term—you select a sample based on time, money, location, availability of sites or respondents, and so on. While some dimension of convenience almost always figures into sample selection, selection made on this basis alone is not very credible and is likely to produce "information-poor" rather than information-rich cases (Patton, 1990, p. 183). A convenience sample of high school graduates might begin with your own teenagers and their friends.

Snowball, chain, or *network* sampling is perhaps the most common form of purposeful sampling. This strategy involves asking each participant or group of participants to refer you to other participants. As Patton (1990) says, this strategy involves identifying participants or "cases of interest from people who know people who know people who know what cases are information-rich, that is, good examples for study, good interview subjects" (p. 182). High school graduates would name other graduates who exemplify the characteristics of interest in the study.

Finally, some qualitative research designs incorporate an ongoing sample selection process commonly referred to as *theoretical sampling*. This type of sampling begins the same way as purposeful sampling, but the total sample is not selected ahead of time. Popularized by Glaser and Strauss (1967), "theoretical sampling is the process of data collection for generating theory whereby the analyst jointly collects, codes, and analyzes his data and decides what data to collect next and where to find them, in order to develop his theory as it emerges" (p. 45). The researcher begins with an initial sample chosen for its obvious relevance to the research problem. The data lead the investigator to the next document to be read, the next person to be interviewed, and so on. It is an evolving process guided by the emerging theory—hence, "theoretical" sampling. Analysis occurs simultaneously with identifying the sample and collecting the data. "The analyst who uses theoretical sampling cannot know in advance precisely what to sample for and where it will lead him. . . . It is never clear cut for what and to where discovery will lead. It is ongoing" (Glaser, 1978, p. 37). As data are being collected and theoretical constructs begin to evolve, the researcher might also look for exceptions (negative-case selection) or variants (discrepant-case selection) to emerging findings.

How Many in the Sample?

Invariably, the question of how many people to interview, how many sites to visit, or how many documents to read concerns—more likely haunts—the novice qualitative researcher. Unfortunately for those with a low tolerance for ambiguity, there is no answer. It always depends on the questions being asked, the data being gathered, the analysis in progress, the resources you have to support the study. What is needed is an adequate number of participants, sites, or activities to answer the question posed at the beginning of the study (in the form of the purpose statement). Lincoln and Guba (1985) recommend sampling until a point of saturation or redundancy is reached. "In purposeful sampling the size of the sample is determined by informational considerations. If the purpose is to maximize information, the sampling is terminated when no new information is forthcoming from new sampled units; thus *redundancy* is the primary criterion (p. 202, emphasis in original).

   If you are submitting a proposal to a funding agency, dissertation committee, or other oversight board for approval or support, you can offer a tentative, approximate number of units to be included (that is, people, sites, cases, activities, and so on), knowing full well that this will be adjusted in the course of the investigation. Patton (1990) recommends specifying a minimum sample size "based on expected reasonable coverage of the phenomenon given the purpose of the study" (p. 186).

The Sample in Case Studies

Unlike the other types of qualitative research presented in Chapter One (basic or generic qualitative study, ethnography, phenomenology, grounded theory), *two* levels of sampling are usually necessary in qualitative case studies. First, you must select "the case" to be studied. Then, unless you plan to interview, observe, or analyze *all* the people, activities, or documents within the case, you will need to do some sampling within the case.

As I discussed in Chapter Two, a case is a single unit, a bounded system. As Stake (1995) points out, sometimes selecting a case turns out "to be no 'choice' at all . . . It happens when a teacher decides to study a student having difficulty, when we get curious about a particular agency, or when we take the responsibility of evaluating a program. The case is given" (p. 3). Other times, we have a general question, an issue, a problem that we are interested in, and we feel that an in-depth study of a particular instance or case will illuminate that interest.

To find the best case to study, you would first establish the criteria that will guide case selection and then select a case that meets those criteria. For example, if your interest is in programs that are successful in addressing learning disabilities, you would establish criteria for what constitutes a successful program; then you would select a program that meets those criteria. This program would be the case. For multicase or comparative case studies you would select several "cases" based on relevant criteria. One of the criteria might be that you want as much variation as possible; hence, you would be employing a maximum variation sampling strategy in the selection of your cases. Using the successful learning disabilities program example, you might seek out programs that are successful in a wide range of socioeconomic neighborhoods or that address a wide range of disabilities or grade levels.

Thus the researcher first identifies the case—the bounded system, the unit of analysis—to be investigated. The case can be as varied as a second-grade classroom, a systemwide model science program, or a patient education clinic at a local hospital. Within every case there exist numerous sites that could be visited (as in the model science program), events or activities that could be observed, people who could be interviewed, documents that could be read. A sample *within* the case needs to be selected either before the data collection begins or while the data are being gathered (ongoing or theoretical sampling). Random sampling can be used within the case, and indeed, this is one strategy that can be employed for addressing validity (see Chapter Ten). More commonly, however, purposeful sampling as outlined earlier is used to select the sample within the case, just as it is used to select the case itself. However, a second set of criteria is usually needed to purposefully select whom to interview, what to observe, and which documents to analyze.

Thus the questions, concerns, and purposes of qualitative studies lead to forms of nonprobability sampling in determining the sample of instances, locations, people, and times to be included. Purposive or purposeful sampling usually occurs before the data are gathered, whereas theoretical sampling is done in conjunction with data collection. The size of the sample within the case is determined by a number of factors relevant to the study's purpose. In case studies, then, sample selection occurs first at the case level, followed by sample selection within the case. For both levels of sampling, criteria need to be established to guide the process. Using the successful learning disabilities program as an example, the criteria for selecting the program (the case) might be the following: the program will have been in existence for a minimum of five years; 80 percent of its students are able to join regular classes after one year in the program; the program deals with learning disabilities in reading and math only. Once the program has been selected, you will need to determine whom to interview (unless you plan to interview everyone) and what to observe. Criteria for selecting the interview sample might include all administrators, teachers who have been with the program at least five years, students representing various ages, length in the program, and particular learning disabilities.

Summary

I began this chapter by explaining that the theoretical framework of a study is the underlying structure upon which all other aspects of the study rest. Previous literature plays an important role in the formation of a study's theoretical framework and problem statement. I then reviewed the benefits of conducting a literature review, the steps in doing it, and the place of the review in the overall research process. Establishing the theoretical framework and reviewing the literature, which I discussed sequentially in the chapter are, in reality, quite intertwined. From a review of the literature a researcher discovers what research exists on a topic and how theory and previous research may help frame the study at hand. Likewise, a researcher is guided to a specific body of literature by the emerging problem, by issues that arise during data collection and analysis, and by the need to interpret findings in light of previous research.

Defining the research problem is a key step in any type of research. You can examine your own practice, review the literature, or look to current social problems for questions that can be shaped into a research problem. The statement of the problem presents the logic of the study and includes a very specific purpose statement. Selecting the sample is dependent upon the research problem. In qualitative research, the most appropriate sampling strategy is nonprobability sampling. Purposeful and theoretical sampling are well-known and widely used nonprobability sampling strategies in qualitative research. The chapter closes with a discussion of sample selection in case study research.

Part Two

Collecting Qualitative Data

Data are nothing more than ordinary bits and pieces of information found in the environment. They can be concrete and measurable, as in class attendance, or invisible and difficult to measure, as in feelings. Whether or not a bit of information becomes data in a research study depends solely on the interest and perspective of the investigator. The way in which rainwater drains from the land may be data to a soil scientist, for example, but not even noticed by the homeowner. Likewise, activity patterns in a school cafeteria, while holding no interest to students, staff, or faculty, may be of great interest to someone studying students' behavior outside the classroom.

Data conveyed through words have been labeled *qualitative,* whereas data presented in number form are *quantitative.* Qualitative data consist of "direct quotations from people about their experiences, opinions, feelings, and knowledge" obtained through interviews; "detailed descriptions of people's activities, behaviors, actions" recorded in observations; and "excerpts, quotations, or entire passages" extracted from various types of documents (Patton, 1990, p. 10).

Part Two is about collecting data through interviews, observations, and documents, or in Wolcott's (1992) "common, everyday terms" (p. 19), data collection is about asking, watching, and reviewing. It should be kept in mind, however, that "the idea that we 'collect' data is a bit misleading. Data are not 'out there' waiting collection, like so many rubbish bags on the pavement. For a start, they have to be noticed by the researcher, and treated as data for the purposes of his or her research. 'Collecting' data always involves selecting data, and the techniques of data collection . . . will affect what finally constitutes 'data' for the purposes of research" (Dey, 1993, p. 15). The data collection techniques used, as well as the specific information considered to be "data" in a study, are determined by the researcher's theoretical orientation, by the problem and purpose of the study, and by the sample selected (see chapters in Part One for a discussion of these factors).

Interviewing is probably the most common form of data collection in qualitative studies in education. In numerous studies it is the only source of data. Chapter Four focuses on interviews: the different types of interviews, good interview questions, and how to record and evaluate interview data; considerations of the interviewer and respondent interaction are also discussed.

Conducting observations is the topic of Chapter Five. The different roles an observer can assume, what to observe when on-site, how to record observations, and the content of fieldnotes are topics discussed in this chapter.

The third technique covered in Part Two is mining data from documents. *Documents* is a term used broadly in this book to refer to printed and other materials relevant to a study, including public records, personal documents, and physical artifacts. A distinction is also made between the common reference to documents as materials existing naturally in the context of the study versus researcher-generated documents.

The final chapter in Part Two explores the use of all three data collection strategies in case study research. Examples are drawn from three case studies, each representing a different facet of educational practice.

Chapter Four

Conducting Effective Interviews

Throughout the process of conducting a qualitative study, investigators continually make decisions, choose among alternatives, and exercise judgment. Once the research problem has been identified, the researcher must decide what information will be needed to address the problem and how best to obtain that information. Interviewing is a common means of collecting qualitative data. I will discuss the types of interviews in this chapter. Other topics include asking good questions, beginning the interview, recording and evaluating interview data, and the nature of the interaction between interviewer and respondent.

Interview Data

In all forms of qualitative research, some and occasionally all of the data are collected through interviews. The most common form of interview is the person-to-person encounter in which one person elicits information from another. Group or collective formats can also be used to obtain data, but group interviews need to account for group processes, a topic beyond the scope of this discussion (Fontana and Frey, 1994). However, both person-to-person and group interviews can be defined as a conversation—but a "conversation with a purpose" (Dexter, 1970, p. 136). The main purpose of an interview is to obtain a special kind of information. The researcher wants to find out what is "in and on someone else's mind" (Patton, 1990, p. 278). As Patton explains:

We interview people to find out from them those things we cannot directly observe. . . . We cannot observe feelings, thoughts, and intentions. We cannot observe behaviors that took place at some previous point in time. We cannot observe situations that preclude the presence of an observer. We cannot observe how people have organized the world and the meanings they attach to what goes on in the world. We have to ask people questions about those things. The purpose of interviewing, then, is to allow us to enter into the other person's perspective [p. 196].

Interviewing is necessary when we cannot observe behavior, feelings, or how people interpret the world around them. It is also necessary to interview when we are interested in past events that are impossible to replicate. For example, school psychologists might be interested in the reaction of students who witnessed a teacher being attacked at school. Likewise, a catastrophic event such as a nuclear accident or natural disaster cannot be replicated, but its effects on a community might be the focus of a qualitative case study investigation. Interviewing is also the best technique to use when conducting intensive case studies of a few selected individuals, as Bateson (1990) did in interviewing five women for her book, *Composing a Life*. Conversely, interviewing can be used to collect data from a large number of people representing a broad range of ideas. Rubin's study (1985) of friendship in which she interviewed three hundred men and women from diverse backgrounds is such an example. In short, the decision to use interviewing as the primary mode of data collection should be based on the kind of information needed and whether interviewing is the best way to get it. Dexter (1970) summarizes when to use interviewing. "Interviewing is the preferred tactic of data collection when . . . it will get *better* data or *more* data or data *at less cost* than other tactics!" (p. 11). I would add that interviewing is sometimes the *only* way to get data.

Types of Interviews

The most common way of deciding which type of interview to use is by determining the amount of structure desired. Figure 4.1 presents a continuum that is based on the amount of structure of an

Figure 4.1. Interview Structure Continuum.

Highly Structured/Standardized

- wording of questions predetermined
- order of questions predetermined
- oral form of a survey

Semistructured

- mix of more- and less-structured questions

Unstructured/Informal

- open-ended questions
- flexible, exploratory
- more like a conversation

interview. At one end of the continuum fall highly structured, questionnaire-driven interviews; at the other end are unstructured, open-ended, conversational formats. In highly structured interviews, sometimes called standardized interviews, questions and the order in which they are asked are determined ahead of time.

The most structured interview is actually an oral form of the written survey. The U.S. Census Bureau and marketing surveys are good examples of oral surveys. The problem with using a highly structured interview in qualitative research is that rigidly adhering to predetermined questions may not allow you to access participants' perspectives and understandings of the world. Instead, you get reactions to the *investigator's* preconceived notions of the world. Such an interview is also based on the shaky assumptions that respondents share a common vocabulary and that the questions "are equally meaningful to every respondent" (Denzin, 1970, p. 123). The major use of this highly structured format in qualitative research is to gather common sociodemographic data from respondents. That is, you may want to know everyone's age, income, history of employment, marital status, level of formal education, and so on. You may also want everyone to respond to a particular statement or to define a particular concept or term.

For the most part, however, interviewing in qualitative investigations is more open-ended and less structured. Less structured formats assume that individual respondents define the world in unique ways. Your questions thus need to be more open-ended. A less structured alternative is the semistructured interview. As is illustrated in Figure 4.1, the semistructured interview is halfway between the ends of the continuum. In this type of interview either all of the questions are more flexibly worded, or the interview is a mix of more and less structured questions. Usually, specific information is desired from all the respondents, in which case there is a highly structured section to the interview. But the largest part of the interview is guided by a list of questions or issues to be explored, and neither the exact wording nor the order of the questions is determined ahead of time. This format allows the researcher to respond to the situation at hand, to the emerging worldview of the respondent, and to new ideas on the topic.

At the other end of the continuum shown in Figure 4.1 are unstructured, informal interviews. These are particularly useful when the researcher does not know enough about a phenomenon to ask relevant questions. Thus there is no predetermined set of questions, and the interview is essentially exploratory. One of the goals of the unstructured interview is, in fact, learning enough about a situation to formulate questions for subsequent interviews. Thus the unstructured interview is often used in conjunction with participant observation in the early stages of a case study. It takes a skilled researcher to handle the great flexibility demanded by the unstructured interview. Insights and understanding can be obtained in this approach, but at the same time an interviewer may feel lost in a sea of divergent viewpoints and seemingly unconnected pieces of information. Totally unstructured interviewing is rarely used as the sole means of collecting data in qualitative research. In most studies the researcher can combine all three types of interviewing so that some standardized information is obtained, some of the same open-ended questions are asked of all participants, and some time is spent in an unstructured mode so that fresh insights and new information can emerge.

By way of illustrating the kinds of questions you might ask in each of the types of interviews—highly structured, semistructured, or unstructured—let us suppose you are studying the role of mentoring in the career development of master teachers. In a highly structured interview you might begin by giving each respondent a definition of mentoring and then asking the person to identify someone who is a mentor. In a semistructured interview you would be more likely to ask each teacher to describe his or her understanding of mentoring; or you might ask the teacher to think of someone who is a mentor. In an unstructured interview you might ask the respondent to share how he or she got to be a master teacher. More directly, but still rather unstructured, would be a question about the influences or factors that have helped to shape the respondent's career.

Asking Good Questions

The key to getting good data from interviewing is to ask good questions; asking good questions takes practice. Pilot interviews are crucial for trying out your questions. Not only do you get some practice in interviewing, you also quickly learn which questions are confusing and need rewording, which questions yield useless data, and which questions, suggested by your respondents, you should have thought to include in the first place.

Different types of questions will yield different information. The questions you ask depend upon the focus of your study. Using the example of mentoring in the career development of master teachers, if you want to know the role mentoring played in career development, you would ask questions about teachers' personal experience with mentoring and probably get a descriptive history. Follow-up questions about how they *felt* about a certain mentoring experience would elicit more affective information. You might also want to know their opinion as to how much influence mentoring has generally in a teacher's career.

The way in which questions are worded is a crucial consideration in extracting the type of information desired. An obvious place to begin is by making certain that what is being asked is clear to the person being interviewed. Questions need to be understood in familiar language. "Using words that make sense to the interviewee, words that reflect the respondent's world view, will improve the quality of data obtained during the interview. Without sensitivity to the impact of particular words on the person being interviewed, the answer may make no sense at all—or there may be no answer" (Patton, 1990, p. 312). Avoiding technical jargon and terms and concepts from your particular disciplinary orientation is a good place to begin. In a study of HIV-positive young adults, for example, participants were asked how they made sense of, or came to terms with, their diagnosis, not how they constructed meaning in the process of perspective transformation (the theoretical framework of the study) (Courtenay, Merriam, and Reeves, forthcoming).

Good Questions and Questions to Avoid

An interviewer can ask several types of questions to stimulate responses from an informant. Strauss, Schatzman, Bucher, and Sabshin (1981) offer a list of four major categories of questions: *hypothetical, devil's advocate, ideal position,* and *interpretive* questions. Each is defined in Table 4.1 and illustrated with examples from a case study of displaced workers participating in a Job Training and Partnership (JTPA) program.

Table 4.1. Four Types of Questions with Examples from a JTPA Training Program Case Study.

Type of Question	Example
• Hypothetical Question: asks what the respondent might do or what it might be like in a particular situation; usually begins with "What if" or "Suppose"	"Suppose it is my first day in this training program. What would it be like?"
• Devil's Advocate Question: challenges the respondent to consider an opposing view	"Some people would say that employees who lose their job did something to bring it about. What would you say to them?"
• Ideal Position Question: asks the respondent to describe an ideal situation	"What do you think the ideal training program would be like?"
• Interpretive Question: advances tentative interpretation of what the respondent has been saying and asks for a reaction	"Would you say that returning to school as an adult is different from what you expected?"

Hypothetical questions ask respondents to speculate as to what something might be like or what someone might do in a particular situation. Hypothetical questions begin with "What if" or "Suppose." Responses are usually descriptions of the person's actual experience. In the JTPA study, for example, the hypothetical question, Suppose it is my first day in this training program. What would it be like? elicited descriptions of what it was actually like for the participants.

Devil's advocate questions are particularly good to use when the topic is controversial and you want respondents' opinions and feelings. This type of question also avoids embarrassing or antagonizing respondents if they happen to be sensitive about the issue. The wording begins, "Some people would say," which in effect depersonalizes the issue. The response, however, is almost always the respondent's personal opinion or feeling about the matter. In the

JTPA example, the question, Some people would say that employees who lose their job did something to bring it about. What would you say to them? usually revealed how the respondent came to be unemployed and thus involved in the training program.

Ideal position questions elicit both information and opinion; these can be used with virtually any phenomenon under study. They are good to use in evaluation studies because they reveal both the positives and the negatives or shortcomings of a program. Asking what the ideal training program would be like in the JTPA example revealed things participants liked and would not want changed, as well as things that could have made it a better program.

Interpretive questions provide a check on what you think you are understanding, as well as provide an opportunity for yet more information, opinions, and feelings to be revealed. In the JTPA example, the interpretive question, Would you say that returning to school as an adult is different from what you expected? allowed the investigator to confirm the tentative interpretation of what had been said in the interview.

Some types of questions should be avoided in an interview. Table 4.2 outlines three types of questions to avoid and illustrates each from the JTPA study. First, avoid multiple questions—either one question that is actually a double question or a series of single questions that does not allow the respondent to answer one by one. An example of a double question is, How do you feel about the instructors and the classes in the JTPA training program? A series of questions might be, What's it like going back to school as an adult? How do instructors respond to you? What kind of assignments do you have? In both cases the respondent is likely to ask you to repeat the question(s), ask for clarification, or give a response covering only one part of the question—and that response may be uninterpretable. If, for example, an interviewee responded to the question, How do you feel about the instructors and the classes? with "They're OK—some I like, some I don't," you would not know whether instructors or classes were being referred to (in either part of the answer).

Leading questions should also be avoided. Leading questions reveal a bias or an assumption that the researcher is making, which

Table 4.2. Questions to Avoid.

Type of Question	Example
• Multiple Questions	How do you feel about the instructors and the classes?
• Leading Questions	What emotional problems have you had since losing your job?
• Yes-or-No Questions	Do you like the program? Has returning to school been difficult?

may not be held by the participant. These set the respondent up to accept the researcher's point of view. The question, What emotional problems have you had since losing your job? reflects an assumption that anyone losing a job will have emotional problems.

Finally, all researchers warn against asking yes-or-no questions. Any question that *can* be answered with a simple yes or no may in fact be answered just that way. Yes-or-no responses give you almost no information. For the reluctant, shy, or less verbal respondent, they offer an easy way out; they can also shut down or at least slow the flow of information from the interviewee. In the JTPA example, questions phrased in a yes-or-no manner, while at their core seek good information, can yield nothing. Thus asking, Do you like the program? may be answered yes or no; rephrasing it to, What do you like about the program? necessitates more of a response. The same is true of the question, Has returning to school been difficult? Asking, How have you found the experience of returning to school? mandates a fuller response.

A ruthless review of your questions to weed out poor ones before you actually conduct an interview is highly recommended. Ask the questions of yourself, challenging yourself to answer as minimally as possible. Also note whether you would feel uncomfortable honestly answering any of the questions. This review followed by a pilot interview will go a long way to ensure that you are asking good questions.

Probes

Probes are also questions or comments that follow up something already asked. It is virtually impossible to specify these ahead of time because they are dependent on how the participant answers the lead question. This is where being the primary instrument of data collection has its advantages, especially if you are a highly sensitive instrument. You make adjustments in your interviewing as you go along. You sense that the respondent is on to something significant or that there is more to be learned. Probing can come in the form of asking for more details, for clarification, for examples. Glesne and Peshkin (1992) point out that "probes may take numerous forms; they range from silence, to sounds, to a single word, to complete sentences" (p. 85). Silence, "used judiciously . . . is a useful and easy probe—as is the bunched utterance, '*uh huh, uh huh*,' sometimes combined with a nodding head. 'Yes, yes' is a good alternative; variety is useful" (p. 86, emphasis in original). As with all questions, not just probes, the interviewer should avoid pressing too hard and too fast. After all, the participant is being interviewed, not interrogated.

Following is a short excerpt (Weeks, n.d.) from an interview with a man in midlife who had been retained in grammar school. The investigator was interested in how being retained had affected the person's life. Note the follow-up questions or probes used to garner a better understanding of his initial reaction to being retained.

Interviewer: How did you feel about yourself the second time you were in first grade?

Respondent: I really don't remember, but I think I didn't like it. It was probably embarrassing to me. I think I may have even had a hard time explaining it to my friends. I probably got teased. I was probably defensive about it. I may even have rebelled in some childlike way. I do know I got more aggressive at this point in my life. But I don't know if being retained had anything to do with it.

Interviewer: How did you feel about your new first grade teacher?

Respondent: She was nice. I was very quiet for a while, until I got to know her.

Interviewer: How did you feel about yourself during this second year?

Respondent: I have to look at it as a follow-up to a period when I was not successful. Strictly speaking, I was not very successful in the first grade—the first time.

Interviewer: Your voice sometimes changes when you talk about that.

Respondent: Well, I guess I'm still a little angry.

Interviewer: Do you feel the retention was justified?

Respondent: (long pause) I don't know how to answer that.

Interviewer: Do you want to think about it for a while?

Respondent: Well, I did NOT learn anything in the first grade the first time, but the lady was nice. She was my Mom's best friend. So she didn't teach me anything, and she made me repeat. I had to be retained, they said, because I did not learn the material, but (shaking his finger), I could have. I could have learned it well. I was smart. . . .

The best way to increase your skill at probing is to practice. The more you interview, especially on the same topic, the more relaxed you become and the better you can pursue potentially fruitful lines of inquiry. Another good strategy is to scrutinize a verbatim transcript of one of your interviews. Look for places where you could have followed up but did not, and compare them with places where you got a lot of good data. The difference will most likely be from having maximized an opportunity to gain more information through gentle probing.

The Interview Guide

The interview guide, or schedule as it is sometimes called, is nothing more than a list of questions you intend to ask in an interview. Depending on how structured the interview will be, the guide may contain dozens of very specific questions listed in a particular order (highly structured) or a few topical areas jotted down in no particular order (unstructured) or something in between. As I noted earlier, most interviews in qualitative research are semistructured; thus the interview guide will probably contain several specific questions that you want to ask everyone, some more open-ended questions that could be followed up with probes, and perhaps a list of some areas, topics, and issues that you want to know more about but do not have enough information about at the outset of your study to form specific questions.

An investigator new to collecting data through interviews will feel more confident with a structured interview format where most, if not all, questions are written out ahead of time in the interview guide. Working from an interview schedule allows the new researcher to gain the experience and confidence needed to conduct more open-ended questioning. Most researchers find that they are highly dependent upon the interview guide for the first few interviews but that they soon can unhook themselves from constant reference to the questions and can go with the natural flow of the interview. At that point, an occasional check to see if all areas or topics are being covered may be all that is needed.

New researchers are often concerned about the order of questions in an interview. No rules determine what should go first and what should come later. Much depends upon the study's objectives, the time allotted for the interview, the person being interviewed, and how sensitive some of the questions are. Factual, sociodemographic-type questions can be asked to get the interview started, but if there are a lot of these, or if some of them are sensitive (for example, if they ask about income, age, or sexual orientation), it might be better to ask them at the end of the interview. By then the respondent has invested in the interview and is more likely to see it through by answering these questions.

Generally it is a good idea to ask for relatively neutral, descriptive information at the beginning of an interview. Respondents can be asked to provide basic descriptive information about the phenomenon of interest, be it a program, activity, or experience, or to chronicle their history with the phenomenon of interest. This information lays the foundation for questions that access the interviewee's perceptions, opinions, values, emotions, and so on. Of course it is not always possible to separate factual information from more subjective, value-laden responses. And again, the best way to tell whether the order of your questions works or not is to try it out in a pilot interview.

In summary, then, questions are at the heart of interviewing, and to collect meaningful data a researcher must ask good questions. The interviewer can make use of hypothetical, devil's advocate, ideal position, and interpretive questions. Multiple questions, leading questions, and questions that can be answered yes or no are to be avoided. The skillful use of probes can yield additional information about a topic.

Beginning the Interview

Collecting data through interviews involves, first of all, determining whom to interview. That depends on what the investigator wants to know and from whose perspective the information is desired. Selecting respondents on the basis of what they can contribute to the researcher's understanding of the phenomenon under study means engaging in purposive or theoretical sampling (discussed in Chapter Three). In a qualitative case study of a community school program, for example, a holistic picture of the program would involve the experiences and perceptions of people having different associations with the program—administrators, teachers, students, community residents. In Kline's (1981) case study of a back-to-industry program for postsecondary faculty, it was essential to interview both postsecondary faculty and industry officials. Unlike survey research in which the number and representativeness of the sample are major considerations, in this type of research the crucial factor is not the number of respondents but the potential of each person to contribute to the development of insight and understanding of the phenomenon.

How can such people be identified? One way is through initial on-site observation of the program, activity, or phenomenon under study. On-site observations often involve informal discussions with participants to discover those who should be interviewed in depth. A second means of locating contacts is to begin with a key person who is considered knowledgeable by others and then ask that person for referrals. Initial informants can be found through the investigator's own personal contacts, community and private organizations, advertisements in newspapers or public places, or random door-to-door or person-to-person contacts. Dexter (1970) warns against being misled by an eager but not particularly helpful informant. He suggests that the interviewer convey the idea that early interviews are part of a preliminary exploration that will lead to identifying key informants. This process can be accelerated by interviewing someone thoroughly familiar with the situation or, conversely, someone who is new enough to the situation to see how it compares to other situations (Denzin, 1970).

Taylor and Bogdan (1984) list five issues that should be addressed at the outset of every interview:

1. The investigator's motives and intentions and the inquiry's purpose
2. The protection of respondents through the use of pseudonyms
3. Deciding who has final say over the study's content
4. Payment (if any)
5. Logistics with regard to time, place, and number of interviews to be scheduled [p. 87–88]

Besides being careful to word questions in language clear to the respondent, the interviewer must be aware of his or her stance toward the interviewee. Since the respondent has been selected by the investigator on purpose, it can be assumed that the participant has something to contribute, has had an experience worth talking about, and has an opinion of interest to the researcher. This stance will go a long way in making the respondent comfortable and forthcoming with what he or she has to offer.

An interviewer should also assume neutrality with regard to the respondent's knowledge; that is, regardless of how antithetical to the interviewer's beliefs or values the respondent's position might be, it is crucial for the success of the interview to avoid arguing, debating, or otherwise letting personal views be known. Patton (1990) distinguishes between neutrality and rapport. "At the same time that I am neutral with regard to the content of what is being said to me, I care very much that that person is willing to share with me what they are saying. *Rapport is a stance vis-à-vis the person being interviewed. Neutrality is a stance vis-à-vis the content of what that person says*" (p. 317, emphasis in original).

Taylor and Bogdan also suggest several ways of maximizing the time spent getting an informant to share information. A slow-starting interview, for example, can be moved along by asking respondents for basic descriptive information about themselves, the event, or the phenomenon under study. Interviews aimed at constructing life-history case studies can be augmented by written narratives, personal documents, and daily activity logs that informants are asked to submit ahead of time. The value of an interview, of course, depends on the interviewer's knowing enough about the topic to ask meaningful questions in language easily understood by the informant.

Interviewer and Respondent Interaction

The interaction between interviewer and respondent can be looked at from the perspective of either party or from the interaction itself. Skilled interviewers can do much to effect positive interaction. Being respectful, nonjudgmental, and nonthreatening is a beginning. Obviously, becoming skilled takes practice; practice combined with feedback on performance is the best way to develop the needed skills. Role playing, peer critiquing, videotaping, and observing experienced interviewers at work are all ways novice researchers can improve their performance in this regard.

What makes a good respondent? Anthropologists and sociologists speak of a good respondent as an "informant"—one who understands the culture but is also able to reflect on it and articulate for the researcher what is going on. Key informants are able, to some extent, to adopt the stance of the investigator, thus becoming a valuable guide in unfamiliar territory. But not all good respondents can be considered key informants in the sense that anthropologists use the term. Good respondents are those who can express thoughts, feelings, opinions—that is offer a *perspective*—on the topic being studied. Participants usually enjoy sharing their expertise with an interested and sympathetic listener. For some, it is also an opportunity to clarify their own thoughts and experiences.

Dexter (1970) says there are three variables in every interview situation that determine the nature of the interaction: "(1) the personality and skill of the interviewer, (2) the attitudes and orientation of the interviewee, and (3) the definition of both (and often by significant others) of the situation" (p. 24). These factors also determine the type of information obtained from an interview. Let us suppose, for example, that two researchers are studying an innovative curriculum for first-year college students. One interviewer is predisposed to innovative practices in general, while the other favors traditional educational practices. One student informant is assigned to the program, while another student requests the curriculum and is eager to be interviewed. The particular combination of interviewer and student that evolves will determine, to some extent, the type of data obtained.

There has been much attention in recent literature to the subjectivity and complexity inherent in the interview encounter. Fontana and Frey (1994) write that scholarship has focused on "some of the assumptions and moral problems present in interviewing and with the controlling role of the interviewer" (p. 363). They note that in addition to race and gender, there has been increased attention to "the voices and feelings of the respondents," and to the interviewer-interviewee relationship. Others have raised questions about the ethical dimensions involved in the relationship (see Chapter Ten for a discussion of ethics), or focused on the complexities of language, or explored the challenges involved in establishing a collaborative research relationship (Munro, 1993).

Some of this discussion is framed in terms of insider-outsider status, especially with regard to visible social identities, most notably gender, race, age, and socioeconomic class (Cotterill and Letherby, 1994; Stanfield II, 1994; Olesen, 1994; Stacey, 1994; Munro, 1993). Seidman (1991, p. 76) discusses how "our experience with issues of class, race, and gender . . . interact with the sense of power in our lives." And, in turn, "the interviewing relationship is fraught with issues of power—who controls the direction of the interview, who controls the results, who benefits." Foster (1994), for example, explores the ambiguities and complexities of the interviewer-respondent relationship in her study of attitudes toward law and order among two generations. She analyzes her stance with regard to interactions with women versus men, the younger generation versus the older, the middle class versus the working class. Richman (1994), however, examines his relationships as a male sociologist studying a maternity ward.

Does a researcher need to be a member of the group being investigated to do a credible study? Is it preferable for women to interview women or for Hispanics to interview Hispanics? What about the intersection of race, gender, and class? Are people more likely to reveal information to insiders or outsiders? There are of course no right answers to any of these questions, only the pluses and minuses involved in any combination of interviewer and respondent. Seidman (1991) suggests that while being highly sensitive to these issues and taking them into account throughout the study, "interviewing requires interviewers to have enough distance to enable them to ask real questions and to explore, not to share, assumptions" (p. 77).

Thus the interviewer-respondent interaction is a complex phenomenon. Both parties bring biases, predispositions, attitudes, and physical characteristics that color the interaction and the data elicited. A skilled interviewer accounts for these factors in order to evaluate the data being obtained. Taking a stance that is nonjudgmental, sensitive, and respectful of the respondent is but a beginning point in the process.

Recording and Evaluating Interview Data

Of the three basic ways to record interview data, the most common by far is to tape record the interview. This practice ensures that everything said is preserved for analysis. The interviewer can also listen for ways to improve his or her questioning technique. Malfunctioning equipment and a respondent's uneasiness with being recorded are the drawbacks. Most researchers find, however, that after some initial wariness respondents tend to forget they are being taped. Occasionally interviews are videotaped. This practice allows for recording of nonverbal behavior, but it is also more cumbersome and intrusive than tape recording the interview.

A second way to record interview data is to take notes during the interview. Since not everything said can be recorded, and since at the outset of a study a researcher is not certain what is important enough to write down, this method is recommended only when mechanical recording is not feasible. Some investigators like to take written notes in addition to taping the session. The interviewer may want to record his or her reactions to something the informant says, to signal the informant of the importance of what is being said, or to pace the interview.

The third—and least desirable—way to record interview data is to write down as much as can be remembered as soon after the interview as possible. The problems with this method are obvious, but at times, writing or recording during an interview might be intrusive (when interviewing terminally ill patients, for example).

In any case, researchers must write their reflections immediately following the interview. These reflections might contain insights suggested by the interview, descriptive notes on the behavior, verbal and nonverbal, of the informant, parenthetical thoughts of the researcher, and so on. Postinterview notes allow the investigator to monitor the process of data collection as well as begin to analyze the information itself.

Ideally, verbatim transcription of recorded interviews provides the best database for analysis. Be forewarned, however, that even with good keyboard skills, transcribing interviews is a tedious and time-consuming project. You can of course hire someone to transcribe tapes for you. This can be expensive, and there are trade-offs in doing it. You do not get the intimate familiarity with your data that doing your own transcribing affords. Also, a transcriber is likely to be unfamiliar with terminology and, not having conducted the interview, will not be able to fill in places where the tape is of poor quality. If someone else has transcribed your tape, it is a good idea to read through the interview while listening to it in order to correct errors and fill in blanks. However, hiring someone to transcribe allows you to spend time analyzing your data instead of transcribing. I recommend that new and experienced researchers transcribe at least the first few interviews of any study, if at all possible. Exhibit 4.1 presents excerpts from a transcribed interview that was conducted as part of a study of consortia of higher education that had failed.

An alternative to fully transcribing an interview is the *interview log,* which I developed as a result of supervising graduate students who often cannot afford the time or cost of transcribing all their interview tapes. The strategy should be used sparingly and only late in a study.

The researcher begins by identifying at the top of the page the name, date, and other necessary details of the interview. The interviewer-researcher then plays the tape and takes notes on important statements or ideas expressed by the informant. Words or phrases or entire sentences are quoted exactly. These notes are coded to the tape counter so the exact location of such words can be accessed quickly at a later time. Tape position is recorded to the left of the words or phrases the researcher deems important. In a column to the far right is space for the researcher to add comments about what was said. The data on the interview log can later be

Exhibit 4.1. Sample Interview from a Case Study of
Failed Consortia of Higher Education.

Interviewer (I):   The first question I have is about the mission of [name of consortium]. My understanding is that it had three general areas in terms of mission: (1) the production of courses and materials for learning at a distance, (2) the promotion of external degree programs, and (3) the development of research on the adult learner and learning at a distance. Does that agree with your perceptions of [name of consortium]?

Respondent (R):   I think that was what they were trying to do. Now the extent to which they accomplished it is something else, but I do agree that that is what they were trying to do. It was an offshoot of some experiment in [state] but, in general, I would agree that that is what they were trying to do.

  I: From your perspective, what were the significant accomplishments of [name of consortium]?

  R: I think they did produce some very good programs. Very few, but what they did produce were top quality, and they did try to help the cooperating universities set up the programs in the states. For instance, we had a State Coordinator located at [another institution] and she represented both her institution and our own in setting up learning centers for the state. I suspect we never would have done that without the financial assistance of [the consortium] at the very beginning.

  I: What are the learning centers you referred to?

  R: Places where students could go to take examinations or view the television programs if they had missed them. These were primarily in [another institution's] extension facilities but there were expenses involved and [the consortium] provided funding for them. We still have them, and they never would have been started had it not been for [the consortium] so that is a real plus.

  I: So, in other words, if I am hearing you correctly, [the consortium] served as sort of a catalyst for certain activities that have continued since its demise?

  R: Yes.

  I: What were the shortcomings of [the consortium]?

  R: I think that their ideas were too grandiose. No real funding base that they could count on and the fact that their desire to develop good programs, and they were very good . . . they spent too much money! Now, presumably they couldn't have developed the good programs if they hadn't spent all this money. But I think so much money was

Exhibit 4.1. (continued)

spent on the programming that anything else they might have done just couldn't be done.

I: So was the focus too much on . . .

R: Production, yeah . . .

I: Why do you think [the consortium] was ultimately terminated?

R: Well, for one thing the leadership, but also the funding. I think when [name] tried to . . . the last straw was when he tried to turn it into a competing institution.

I: The transition to [name of] University?

R: Yeah, and people saw that as a possible threat.

I: How did [the consortium] transform into [name of] University?

R: I don't know, but I would suspect originally with [name]. Now I've not gone through these files that you have access to and there may be some indication there. I think that when [name] took over . . . well, before he took over, people weren't that hot on [the consortium] but they weren't unduly opposed to it. But he started changing it and it seemed to a lot of us anyway that he was trying to change it to something that was not what we were interested in.

I: Are there any things about the leadership that you can tell me specifically that may have contributed to the termination of [the consortium]?

R: I think if a person that is in charge of an organization does not realize, particularly when it's composed of a number of other organizations, if he does not realize we all have an equal say in it . . . if he thinks "I'm going to do something and I don't give a damn about what the member institutions want," it's going to fail because ultimately the leader, unless he or she has a complacent group of member institutions, can't do anything. And it may not be overt clashing; it may be foot-dragging. There are all sorts of ways to express your displeasure and because sometimes. . . . But [name] is a very interesting person. When he was at [institution] he tried to do some very interesting and innovative things, but somehow it didn't work. He's brilliant but that's not always enough. You have to know how to work with people. And if you have a really good idea, you'd better sell it to the people before you go outside and announce it.

Source: Offerman (1985). Reprinted with permission.

coded according to the emerging themes or categories from the data analysis phase of the study. (Strategies for analyzing qualitative data are covered in Chapters Seven and Eight.)

Exhibit 4.2 is a sample interview log using the same interview data found in Exhibit 4.1. Rather than transcribing the interview verbatim, however, the log captures the main points. Noting the tape position allows the researcher to access the original data quickly. One caveat with this alternative, however, is that the interview log is best used toward the end of a study when you are confirming tentative findings. If it is used too soon, important insights are easily overlooked; nor do you have the luxury of going back over the entire interview for instances of patterns you only recognized late in the study.

In addition to recording interview data for analysis, it is important to assess, as best you can, the quality of the data obtained. Several factors may influence an informant's responses, factors that may be difficult for the researcher to discern. The informant's health, mood at the time of interview, and so on may affect the quality of data obtained, as might an informant's ulterior motives for participating in the project (Whyte, 1982). Furthermore, all information obtained from an informant has been selected, either consciously or unconsciously, from all that he or she knows. What you get in an interview is simply the informant's perception.

While this personal perspective is, of course, what is sought in qualitative research, information may have been distorted or exaggerated. Such distortion can be detected by checking the plausibility of the account and the reliability of the informant (Whyte, 1982). "The major way to detect and correct distortion," according to Whyte, "is by *comparing an informant's account with accounts given by other informants*" (p. 116, emphasis in original). The researcher might also confirm the informant's account by checking documentary material or directly observing the situation (see Chapter Nine for a discussion of validity and reliability).

Summary

In qualitative research, interviewing is often the major source of the qualitative data needed for understanding the phenomenon under study. Interviews can range in structure from those in which

Exhibit 4.2. Sample Interview Log Using Interview in Exhibit 4.1.

Interviewee #8
Name of Consortium
Male, Dean of Continuing Education

Tape Position	Respondent's Comments	Researcher's Notes
074	Agrees tried to carry out three-part mission	
093	"Very few," but some top-quality programs; learning centers, persons, finances	Importance of people and financing in establishment of programs
109	Describes learning centers; "still have them"—"a real plus"	Some programs continue despite end of consortium
117		Consortium as catalyst
125	Ideas "too grandiose," "spent too much money," "no real funding base"	Funding is a crucial problem
134	"Production" focus	
144	Funding as well as leadership reasons for termination; "he tried to turn it into a competing institution"	Leadership important—can't become a "competing institution"
169	Change in focus created problem	Importance of individual administrator
179	Leadership problem: "you have to know how to work with people"; must consider member institutions	Leadership qualities needed in consortium

questions and the order in which they are asked are predetermined to totally unstructured interviews in which nothing is set ahead of time. Most common is the semistructured interview that is guided by a set of questions and issues to be explored, but neither the exact wording nor the order of questions is predetermined.

Asking good questions is key to getting meaningful data. Hypothetical, devil's advocate, ideal position, and interpretive questions can be used to elicit good data, while multiple and leading questions, as well as questions yielding yes-and-no answers, should be avoided. Follow-up questions or probes are an important part of the process. An interview guide contains the questions the researcher intends to ask.

Considering how to begin the interview and accounting for some of the complexities in the interaction between interviewer and respondent will result in a more informed analysis of the interview data. This chapter addressed those issues, along with some of the mechanics of recording interview data.

Chapter Five

Being a Careful Observer

Interviews are a primary source of data in qualitative research; so too are observations. Observations can be distinguished from interviews in two ways. First, observations take place in the natural field setting instead of a location designated for the purpose of interviewing; second, observational data represent a firsthand encounter with the phenomenon of interest rather than a secondhand account of the world obtained in an interview. In the real world of collecting data, however, informal interviews and conversations are often interwoven with observation. The terms *fieldwork* and *field study* usually connote both activities (observation and interviews) and, to a lesser degree, documentary analysis. That caveat notwithstanding, the primary focus of this chapter is on the activity of *observation*—the use of observation as a research tool, the problem of what to observe, the relationship between observer and observed, and the means for recording observations.

Observation in Research

Being alive renders us natural observers of our everyday world and our behavior in it. What we learn helps us make sense of our world and guides our future actions. Most of this observation is routine—largely unconscious and unsystematic. It is part of living, part of our commonsense interaction with the world. But just as casually conversing with someone differs from interviewing, so too does this routine observation differ from research observation. Observation is a *research* tool when it "(1) serves a formulated research purpose,

(2) is planned deliberately, (3) is recorded systematically, and (4) is subjected to checks and controls on validity and reliability" (Kidder, 1981b, p. 264).

Critics of participant observation as a data-gathering technique point to the highly subjective and therefore unreliable nature of human perception. Human perception is also very selective. Consider a traffic accident at a busy intersection. For each different witness to the accident there will be a different, perhaps even contradictory, account of what happened. However, the witnesses were not planning to systematically observe the accident, nor were they trained in observational techniques. These factors differentiate everyday observation from research-related observation. Patton (1990) contends that comparing untrained observers with researchers is like comparing what "an amateur community talent show" can do compared with "professional performers" (p. 202). Training and mental preparation are as important for researchers "to do their best" as they are for artists (p. 201). Wolcott (1992) also notes that the difference between "mere mortals" and qualitative researchers is that "qualitative researchers, like others whose roles demand selective attentiveness—artists and novelists, detectives and spies, guards and thieves, to name a few—pay special attention to a few things to which others ordinarily give only passing attention. Observers of any ilk do no more: We all attend to certain things, and nobody attends to them all" (pp. 22–23).

Just as you can learn to be a skilled interviewer, you can also learn to be a careful, systematic observer. Training to be a skilled observer includes "learning how to write descriptively; practicing the disciplined recording of field notes; knowing how to separate detail from trivia . . . and using rigorous methods to validate observations" (Patton, 1990, p. 201). You can practice observing in any number of ways—by being a complete observer in a public place, by being a participant observer in your work or social settings, or by watching films or videotapes. You can also apprentice yourself to an experienced field researcher, comparing his or her observations with yours. You might also read other people's accounts of the experience.

An investigator might want to gather data through observation for many reasons. As an outsider an observer will notice things that have become routine to the participants themselves, things that may lead to understanding the context. Observations are also conducted to triangulate emerging findings; that is, they are used in conjunction with interviewing and document analysis to substantiate the findings (see Chapter Nine). The participant observer sees things firsthand and uses his or her own knowledge and expertise in interpreting what is observed rather than relying upon once-removed accounts from interviews. Observation makes it possible to record behavior as it is happening.

Another reason to conduct observations is to provide some knowledge of the context or to provide specific incidents, behaviors, and so on that can be used as reference points for subsequent interviews. This is a particularly helpful strategy for understanding ill-defined phenomena. For example, in a study of respiratory therapists' critical thinking, Mishoe (1995) observed therapists as they worked in the clinical setting, and shortly thereafter she interviewed them. She was thus able to ask them what they were thinking with regard to specific behaviors she had witnessed on-site.

Finally, people may not feel free to talk about or may not want to discuss all topics. In studying a small educational unit, for example, the researcher might observe dissension and strife among certain staff members that an interview would not reveal. Observation is the best technique to use when an activity, event, or situation can be observed firsthand, when a fresh perspective is desired, or when participants are not able or willing to discuss the topic under study.

What to Observe

What to observe is determined by several factors. The most important is the researcher's purpose in conducting the study in the first place. In other words, the conceptual framework, the problem, or the questions of interest determine what is to be observed. As I noted in Chapter Two, a researcher's disciplinary orientation often determines how a problem is defined. An educator might observe a school because of an interest in how students learn, whereas a sociologist might visit the same school because of an interest in social institutions. Practical considerations also play a part in determining what to observe. Certain behavior is difficult to observe; a researcher must have the time, money, and energy to devote to observation and must be *allowed* to observe by those in the situation of interest.

Hawkins (1982) notes, "Impressions also influence the choice of what to observe. Researchers often begin a series of investigations by impressionistic, informal observation" (p. 22). These early impressions help determine subsequent patterns of observation. LeCompte and Preissle (1993) write that what to observe depends on the topic, the conceptual framework, "the data that begin to emerge as the participant observer interacts in the daily flow of events and activities, and the intuitive reactions and hunches that participant observers experience as all these factors come together" (p. 200).

What to observe is partly a function of how structured the observer wants to be. Just as there is a range of structure in interviewing, there is also a range of structure in observation. The researcher can decide ahead of time to concentrate on observing certain events, behaviors, or persons. A code sheet might be used to record instances of specified behavior. Less structured observations can be compared to a television camera scanning the area. Where to begin looking depends on the research question, but where to focus or stop action cannot be determined ahead of time. The focus must be allowed to emerge and in fact may change over the course of the study.

Nevertheless, no one can observe everything, and the researcher must start somewhere. Several writers (Goetz and LeCompte, 1984; Borg and Gall, 1989; Bogdan and Biklen, 1992; Patton, 1990; Taylor and Bogdan, 1984) present lists of things to observe, at least to get started in the activity. Here is a checklist of elements likely to be present in any setting:

1. *The physical setting:* What is the physical environment like? What is the context? What kinds of behavior is the setting designed for? How is space allocated? What objects, resources, technologies are in the setting? The principal's office, the school bus, the cafeteria, and the classroom vary in physical attributes as well as in anticipated behavior.
2. *The participants:* Describe who is in the scene, how many people, and their roles. What brings these people together? Who is allowed here? Who is not here who would be expected to be here? What are the relevant characteristics of the participants?
3. *Activities and interactions:* What is going on? Is there a definable sequence of activities? How do the people interact with the

activity and with one another? How are people and activities "connected or interrelated—either from the participants' point of view or from the researcher's perspective" (Goetz and LeCompte, 1984, p. 113)? What norms or rules structure the activities and interactions? When did the activity begin? How long does it last? Is it a typical activity, or unusual?

4. *Conversation:* What is the content of conversations in this setting? Who speaks to whom? Who listens? Quote directly, paraphrase and summarize conversations. If possible, use a tape recorder to back up your notetaking. Note silences and nonverbal behavior that add meaning to the exchange.

5. *Subtle factors:* Less obvious but perhaps as important to the observation are
   • Informal and unplanned activities
   • Symbolic and connotative meanings of words
   • Nonverbal communication such as dress and physical space
   • Unobtrusive measures such as physical clues
   • "What does *not* happen"—especially if it ought to have happened (Patton, 1990, p. 235, emphasis in original).

6. *Your own behavior:* You are as much a part of the scene as participants. How is your role, whether as an observer or an intimate participant, affecting the scene you are observing? What do you say and do? In addition, what thoughts are you having about what is going on? These become "observer comments," an important part of field notes.

Each participant observation experience has its own rhythm and flow. The duration of a single observation or the total amount of time spent collecting data in this way is a function of the problem being investigated. There is no ideal amount of time to spend observing, nor is there one preferred pattern of observation. For some situations, observation over an extended period of time may be most appropriate; for others, shorter periodic observations make the most sense given the purpose of the study and practical constraints.

The process of collecting data through observations can be broken into the three stages: entry, data collection, and exit. Gaining entry into a site begins with gaining the confidence and permission of those who can approve the activity. This step is more

easily accomplished through a mutual contact who can recommend the researcher to the "gatekeepers" involved. Even with an
advocate working on your behalf, it may be difficult to gain entry
to certain settings. In my experience, business and industry, some
government agencies, and some groups because of the sensitivity
or exclusivity of their mission (such as self-help groups, racial and
ethnic groups, and so forth) are difficult to gain entry to as an outsider. Bogdan and Biklen (1992) point out that most groups will
want answers to the following:

- What are you actually going to do?
- Will you be disruptive?
- What are you going to do with your findings?
- Why us?
- What will we get out of this? [p. 84–85]

Being prepared to answer these questions as candidly as possible, being persistent, and being able to adjust to modifications in
your original request will increase your chances of gaining entry.
Once entry has been gained, Taylor and Bogdan (1984) have some
comments for the first few days in the field:

- Observers should be relatively passive and unobtrusive, put
  people at ease, learn how to act and dress in the setting.
- Collecting data is secondary to becoming familiar with the setting.
- Keep the first observations fairly short to avoid becoming overwhelmed with the novelty of the situation.
- Be honest but not overly technical or detailed in explaining
  what you are doing.

They also suggest that the researcher establish rapport by fitting into the participants' routines, finding some common ground
with them, helping out on occasion, being friendly, and showing
interest in the activity.

Once you (the researcher) become familiar with the setting
and begin to see what is there to observe, serious data collection
can begin. There is little glamour and much hard work in this
phase of research. It takes great concentration to observe intently,

remember as much as possible, and then record in as much detail as possible what has been observed. Conducting an observation, even a short one, can be exhausting, especially in the beginning of a study. Everyone and everything is new; you do not know what will be important, so you try to observe everything; you are concerned about the effect you will have on the scene; you miss things while taking notes, and so on. It is probably best to do more frequent, shorter observations at first. The more familiar everything feels, the more comfortable you are in the setting, the longer you will be able to observe.

The overall time spent on the site, the number of visits, and the number of observations made per visit cannot be precisely determined ahead of time. At some point, time and money will run out, and new information will be scarce. Ideally, depletion of resources coincides with saturation of information. Leaving the field, however, may be even more difficult than gaining entry. It may mean "breaking attachments and sometimes even offending those one has studied, leaving them feeling betrayed and used" (Taylor and Bogdan, 1984, p. 67). Taylor and Bogdan recommend easing out or drifting off—that is, "gradually cutting down on the frequency of visits and letting people know that the research is coming to an end" (p. 68).

Relationship Between Observer and Observed

The researcher can assume one of several stances while collecting information as an observer; stances range from being a full participant—the investigator is a member of the group being observed—to being a spectator. Gold's (1958) classic typology offers a spectrum of four possible stances:

1. *Complete participant:* The researcher is a member of the group being studied and conceals his or her observer role from the group so as not to disrupt the natural activity of the group. The inside information obtainable by using this method must be weighed against the possible disadvantages—loss of perspective on the group, being labeled a spy or traitor when research activities are revealed, and the questionable ethics of deceiving the other participants.

2. *Participant as observer:* The researcher's observer activities, which are known to the group, are subordinate to the researcher's role as a participant. The trade-off here is between the depth of the information revealed to the researcher and the level of confidentiality promised to the group in order to obtain this information. Adler and Adler (1994, p. 380) call this an "active membership role" in which researchers are "involved in the setting's central activities, assuming responsibilities that advance the group, but without fully committing themselves to members' values and goals."

3. *Observer as participant:* The researcher's observer activities are known to the group; participation in the group is definitely secondary to the role of information gatherer. Using this method, the researcher may have access to many people and a wide range of information, but the level of the information revealed is controlled by the group members being investigated. Adler and Adler (1994, p. 380) differentiate this "peripheral membership role" from the active membership role just described. Here researchers "observe and interact closely enough with members to establish an insider's identity without participating in those activities constituting the core of group membership."

4. *Complete observer:* The researcher is either hidden from the group (for example, behind a one-way mirror) or in a completely public setting such as an airport or library.

More recent research has defined yet another possible stance of the researcher vis-à-vis participants—that of the *collaborative partner.* This role is closest to being a complete participant on the above continuum, but the investigator's identity is clearly known to everyone involved. Although defined variously within the areas of teacher research, feminist research, or action and participatory research, the defining characteristic of this stance is that the investigator and the participants are equal partners in the research process—including defining the problem to be studied, collecting and analyzing data, and writing and disseminating the findings. (For further discussion of this role see Olesen, 1994; Reinharz, 1992; Merriam and Simpson, 1995; McTaggart, 1991; Munro, 1993.)

Inherent in this continuum is the extent to which the investigation is overt or covert. Whether the researcher is a complete participant or a complete observer, the "real" activity is not known to those being observed. This situation leads to ethical questions related to the privacy and protection of research subjects—issues discussed more fully in Chapter Nine.

In reality, researchers are rarely total participants or total observers. Rather, they are what Gans (1982) calls a *researcher participant*—one "who participates in a social situation but is personally only partially involved, so that he can function as a researcher" (p. 54). Although the ideal in qualitative research is to get inside the perspective of the participants, full participation is not always possible. A researcher can never know exactly how it feels to be illiterate or mentally ill, for example. A question can also be raised as to just how much better it is to be an insider. Being born into a group, "going native," or just being a member does not necessarily afford the perspective necessary for studying the phenomenon. Jarvie (1982) notes that "there is nothing especially privileged about the observation of a parade made by those in it. Spectators are in a better position; television viewers in a still better one" (p. 68). However, Swisher (1986) was able to get reliable information about multicultural education from parents and teachers in a reservation community because she herself is a member of the community. Patton (1990) underscores the balance needed between insider and outsider in qualitative research. "Experiencing the program as an insider is what necessitates the participant part of participant observation. At the same time, however, there is clearly an observer side to this process. The challenge is to combine participation and observation so as to become capable of understanding the program as an insider while describing the program for outsiders" (p. 207).

As the researcher gains familiarity with the phenomenon being studied, the mix of participation and observation is likely to change. The researcher might begin as a spectator and gradually become involved in the activities being observed. In other situations an investigator might decide to join a group to see what it is actually like to be a participant and then gradually withdraw, eventually assuming the role of interested observer. For example, in recounting her field experiences in a home for the aged, Posner (1980) traces her movement from participant observer as a volunteer worker, to complete participant as a program director, to observer with minimum participation.

Participant observation is a schizophrenic activity in that the researcher usually participates but not to the extent of becoming totally absorbed in the activity. While participating, the researcher tries to stay sufficiently detached to observe and analyze. It is a marginal position and personally difficult to sustain. Gans (1982) captures the distress in being a researcher participant. "The temptation to become involved was ever-present. I had to fight the urge to shed the emotional handcuffs that bind the researcher, and to react spontaneously to the situation, to relate to people as a person and to derive pleasure rather than data from the situation. Often, I carried on an internal tug of war, to decide how much spontaneous participation was possible without missing something as a researcher" (p. 54).

The ambiguity of participant observation is one source of anxiety for the qualitative researcher. Gans cites three other sources that make this method of gathering data particularly difficult. There is, he writes, "the constant worry about the flow of research activities." And he goes on to ask, "Is one doing the right thing at the right time, attending the right meeting, or talking to the right people" (p. 58)? Another source of anxiety is "how to make sense out of what one is studying, how not to be upset by the initial inability to understand and how to order the constant influx of data" (p. 59). Finally, the inherent deception in participant observation leads to "a pervasive feeling of guilt" and "a tendency to overidentify with the people being studied" (p. 59).

Another concern is the extent to which the observer investigator affects what is being observed. In traditional models of research, the ideal is to be as objective and detached as possible so as not to "contaminate" the study. However, in qualitative research where the researcher is the primary instrument of data collection, subjectivity and interaction are assumed. The interdependency between the observer and the observed may bring about changes in both parties' behaviors. The question, then, is not whether the process of observing affects what is observed but how the researcher can identify those effects and account for them in interpreting the data. At the very least, participants who know they are being observed will tend to behave in socially acceptable ways and present themselves in a favorable manner. Further, participants will regulate their behavior in reaction to even subtle forms of feedback from the observer—as when notes are taken or behavior is attended to in a particular fashion. Finally, the mere presence of the observer in the setting can affect the climate of the setting, often effecting a more formal atmosphere than is usually the case.

The extent to which an observer changes the situation studied is not at all clear. Frankenberg (1982, p. 51) points out that in traditional anthropological studies the activities of an ethnographer (researcher) are not likely to change "custom and practice built up over years." It is more likely that the researcher will prove to be "a catalyst for changes that are already taking place." Others have suggested that the stability of a social setting is rarely disrupted by the presence of an observer (Reinharz, 1979). In any case, the researcher must be sensitive to the effects one might be having on the situation and account for those effects.

Recording Observations

What is written down or mechanically recorded from a period of observation becomes the raw data from which a study's findings eventually emerge. This written account of the observation constitutes *field notes,* which are analogous to the interview transcript. In both forms of data collection, the more complete the recording, the easier it is to analyze the data. How much can be recorded during an observation? The answer depends on the researcher's role and the extent to which he or she is a participant in the activity. On-site recording can thus range from continuous (especially for a total observer), to taking sketchy notes, to not recording anything at all during an observation. Although mechanical devices such as videotapes, film, or tape recorders can be used to record observations, the cost and obtrusiveness of these methods often preclude their use. It is much more likely that a researcher will jot down notes during an observation and wait until afterward to record in detail what has been observed. Thus, unlike an interviewer who can usually fall back on a tape recording of the session, a participant observer has to rely on memory to recount the session.

Even if the researcher has been able to take notes during an observation, it is imperative that full notes be written, typed, or dictated as soon after the observation as possible. It takes great self-discipline to sit down and describe something just observed. The observation itself is only half the work. "For the actual writing of notes may take as long or longer than did the observation! Indeed, a reasonable rule of thumb here is to expect and plan to spend as much time writing notes as one spent observing. . . . All the fun of actually being out and about monkeying around in some setting must also be met by cloistered rigor in committing to paper—and therefore to future usefulness—what has taken place" (Lofland, 1971, pp. 103–104).

Every researcher devises techniques for remembering and recording the specifics of an observation. It can be an intimidating part of qualitative research, however, and I advise beginning with short periods of observation; then practice recalling and recording data. Taylor and Bogdan (1984) offer some suggestions for recalling data. Later recall will be helped if *during* an observation investigators

- Pay attention.
- Shift from a "wide angle" to a "narrow angle" lens—that is, focusing "on a specific person, interaction, or activity, while mentally blocking out all the others" (p. 54).
- Look for key words in people's remarks that will stand out later.
- Concentrate on the first and last remarks in each conversation.
- Mentally play back remarks and scenes during breaks in the talking or observing.

Once the observation is completed, they suggest the following: leave the setting after observing as much as can be remembered; record field notes as soon as possible after observing; in case of a time lag between observing and recording, summarize or outline the observation; draw a diagram of the setting and trace movements through it; and incorporate pieces of data remembered at later times into the original field notes (Taylor and Bogdan, 1984). Bogdan (1972) also advises against talking to anyone about the observation before notes have been recorded. Finally, he suggests being more concerned with remembering the substance of a conversation than with producing a "flawless verbatim reproduction" (p. 42).

Field notes based on observation need to be in a format that will allow the researcher to find desired information easily. Formats vary, but a set of notes usually begins with the time, place, and purpose of the observation. It is also helpful to list the participants present or at least to indicate how many and what kinds of people are present—described in ways meaningful to the research. If the researcher is observing a school board meeting about a recent racial incident, for example, she or he could note the number of people present, whether they are parents, teachers, board members, or interested community residents, and the racial makeup of the group. A diagram of the setting's physical aspects might be included. Other hints for setting up field notes are to leave a wide margin on one side of the page or the other for later notes; double-space between segments of activity for ease of reading and data analysis; and use quotation marks when someone is directly quoted.

An important component of field notes is observer commentary; comments can include the researcher's feelings, reactions, hunches, initial interpretations, and working hypotheses. These comments are over and above factual descriptions of what is going on; they are comments on and thoughts about the setting, people, and activities. In raising questions about what is observed or speculating as to what it all means, the researcher is actually engaging in some preliminary data analysis. The joint collection and analysis of data is essential in qualitative research.

The content of field notes usually includes the following:

- Verbal descriptions of the setting, the people, the activities
- Direct quotations or at least the substance of what people said
- Observer's comments—put in the margins or in the running narrative and identified by underlining, bracketing, and the initials "OC"

Exhibit 5.1 presents an excerpt from field notes written after the researcher had observed a class session. The investigator was particularly interested in instruction and in the interaction between teacher and students. The topic for this session was the development and use of overhead transparencies. Note the diagram of the layout of the classroom, including where the observer is sitting ("Me" in the lower right); the observer's comments are interwoven throughout the recording. These are in italics and labeled "OC" to set them off from the observations.

Exhibit 5.1. Sample of Field Notes (Excerpts).

I got to the classroom about 10 minutes early so that I could observe how the classroom was laid out. I took a seat in the back and sketched a diagram of the class. There were still 5 minutes to go and no one had showed up yet, so I went out into the hall to wait for B. After a minute or so, B came along. I saw that B didn't have any materials and when I asked about it, B indicated that all the things needed were already in the classroom. We went in together. Only one student had arrived, but there were still a few minutes to go.

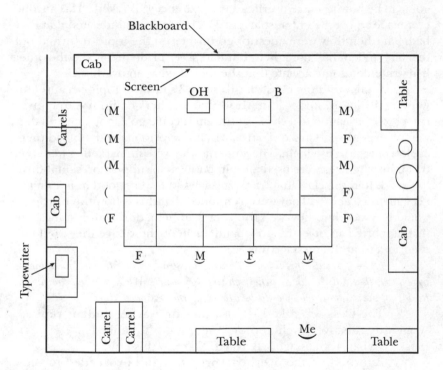

Another student arrived and started to chat about the first student's teaching activity that had taken place the day before. As they talked a few more students arrived, one of whom joined in the conversation. A few more students arrived. B was in the front of the classroom waiting to start the class. The conversation got onto the topic of lesson plans and the male in front of me asked what a lesson plan was. B asked him if he had gotten the handout on the topic, and after looking

Exhibit 5.1. (continued).

through his books, he said that he hadn't. B would get him a copy during the break. After noting that the class was small today, B asked if they had all picked a topic for the sample lesson that they would have to prepare materials for. Some indicated that they hadn't, and B asked them, "What are you interested in?" B told them that they would talk about it during lab time. Another student arrived. B asked the class again if anyone else had picked a topic. A student replied that she would teach multiplication.

B said that the class was going to start. The students quieted down and looked at her as she announced that the subject of today's lesson was going to be how to make overhead transparencies. B asked, "Has anyone ever made an overhead transparency?" A few students indicated that they had, but when they were questioned further on the topic, it turned out that one student had used them but had never made them, and the other had written on some acetate that she then used as an overhead.

B then told the class that this was B's favorite topic because this was a really good, low-cost method that teachers could use to convey complex information to a class. A little effort could go a long way, and they weren't expensive to make. There are a few ways to make them and there are lots of ways to use them. The students who were in marketing were told that transparencies were used a lot in business to support presentations.

B told the class that transparencies were very good in helping to get a message across. They were reminded that this is how their projects would be graded, in how well the overhead helped to convey a message that supported an objective, in what domain of knowledge they would be used, and what the message was.

OC—Up until this time, no one had asked any questions. The students were quiet; they didn't move in their chairs very much. While this was going on, the last of the students who would be attending the session arrived.

The class was asked what a domain was. A student replied, "Cognitive, affective, psychomotor." "Very good," B replied.

"What is a message?" B asked. No reply this time.

B turned on the overhead projector and proceeded to show some examples. The first one was a colorful slide of the planets.

OC—B must like planets. There is a model of the solar system, in similar colors, in B's office.

B pointed out that this particular slide would be useful in having students identify the planets and that the slide would not be very helpful in explaining planetary motion. The students were also shown an example of masking. (The names of the planets were masked by pieces of cardboard so that they could be revealed by the teacher, as required.)

OC—The students were attentive, but quiet, too quiet I thought. What's happening here is that the teacher is not asking enough questions. For example, B could have asked the students what the flaps were for, and why would you want to do such a thing. Instead of telling what the slide was good for, asking what it would be good for. Nice locus of control issue.

The second transparency's subject was the water cycle, a slide consisting of the main and two overlays. B explained how an overhead of this kind could be used to describe a process.

OC—The students were quiet, no questions.

The next transparency was used to describe a concept, in this case formal and informal balance. B explained that a slide should not be overly cluttered, which brought up the next example, a slide that had too much information on it. B next put up a slide that showed a computer, some modems, and a telephone and asked what the students thought of it. A few students replied that they did not understand it, whereupon B explained that it was a slide showing the electronic bulletin board for the college.

OC—It was probably B's intent to show the class a professional-looking slide, which it was. The content of the slide was, however, out of the experience of the students. This problem might have been gotten around by first explaining the content, and then asking the students what else they might have noticed about the slide, in order to bring up the subject of its professional look.

B asked the class to turn to page 23 of the workbook in order to see what the assignment for overhead transparencies will be. Each student was to make three transparencies relating to a lesson that had been devised by the student. They were to make one with the direct dye medium (the one with the notch), the second with the transfer sheet medium, and the third to be hand-drawn. The slides set would also have to demonstrate the techniques of masking, overlay, and color.

A student asked, "What's masking?" B then explained the concept of slow or controlled revelation. It was explained to the class that this technique is used when you don't wish to show the whole slide at once.

OC—It would have been nice to explain the relationship between masking and overlays.

B passed around a handout that described several techniques for building overheads with masking. B then asked the class if they would like a demonstration of how to make a slide using overlays. B had removed the overhead showing the requirements for the project.

A student asked, "What comes after masking?" B replied, "The use of color."

Exhibit 5.1. (continued).

B then started to show the class the technique for making a slide with two overlays. The slide that showed the water cycle was the subject. The main transparency was made and attached to the frame on all four sides with masking tape. The overlays were then made and attached to the frame on one side only. In B's example, the main was in red and the overlays in blue. B then went on to demonstrate how pieces of different-colored acetate may be used to add color to the slides. B indicated that these materials may be purchased in stores.

OC—*No one asks where.*

A student asked if the overlays need to be the same color. B replied that they can be anything the student wants.

Source: Brandt (1987). Reprinted with permission.

Ethnographers often maintain something called a *fieldwork journal*—an introspective record of the anthropologist's experience in the field. It includes his or her ideas, fears, mistakes, confusion, and reactions to the experience and can include thoughts about the research methodology itself. In addition to field notes and the fieldwork journal, ethnographers often write memos or "think papers" containing analysis and interpretation (Spradley, 1979). Qualitative researchers are more likely to use the integrated format described earlier, although some do keep a separate journal of the experience. That becomes a data source, and the researcher sometimes uses it when writing about the methodology. In a case study of a junior college that had received federal development funds, Malcolm (Malcolm and Welch, 1981) uses his own observer comments to describe his experiences with the methodology. On his first day on the site, he writes, "in anguish," on the back of a page of notes. "The memory load is tremendous! Recalling people and names, building layout and function, dialogue and argument. I had been afraid of my inability to observe and listen, but that problem, at least on this first day, pales in the face of memory load" (p. 75). Later, in a personal reaction to the methodology, he writes, "Despite intensive preparation for the study, I was surprised by a number of my reactions to the methodology. One was my conviction about the accuracy and validity of the results. . . . Other unexpected reactions related to the tremendous memory load and the constant demand to record the manifold aspects of each observation session, interview, and experience" (Malcolm and Welch, 1981, pp. 67–68).

Summary

Observation is a major means of collecting data in qualitative research. It offers a firsthand account of the situation under study and, when combined with interviewing and document analysis, allows for a holistic interpretation of the phenomenon being investigated. It is the technique of choice when behavior can be observed firsthand or when people cannot or will not discuss the research topic.

Fieldwork, as participant observation is often called, involves going to the site, program, institution, setting—the field—to observe the phenomenon under study. Unless it is public behavior the researcher wants to observe, entry must first be gained from those in authority. While on-site, the researcher is absorbed by what to observe, what to remember, what to record. This chapter presents some guidelines for these activities, such as what to observe, but ultimately the success of participant observation rests on the talent and skill of the investigator.

There are several stances an investigator can assume when conducting observations, from being a member of the group and a complete participant—an insider—to being a complete observer, unknown to those being observed; each stance has advantages and drawbacks. Regardless of the stance, an observer cannot help but affect and be affected by the setting, and this interaction may lead to a distortion of the situation as it exists under nonresearch conditions. The schizophrenic aspect of being at once participant and observer is a by-product of this method of data collection and is a problem not easily dealt with.

Finally, the observation is only half the process. Observations must be recorded in as much detail as possible to form the database for analysis. Field notes can come in many forms, but at the least they include descriptions, direct quotations, and observer comments.

Chapter Six

Mining Data from Documents

Interviewing and observing are two data collection strategies designed to gather data that specifically address the research question. Documents, however, are usually produced for reasons other than the research at hand and therefore are not subject to the same limitations. The presence of documents does not intrude upon or alter the setting in ways that the presence of the investigator often does. Nor are documents dependent upon the whims of human beings whose cooperation is essential for collecting good data through interviews and observations. Documents are, in fact, a ready-made source of data easily accessible to the imaginative and resourceful investigator. This chapter examines the nature of documents, various types of documents, their use in qualitative research, and their limitations and strengths. The last section of the chapter presents a look at a relatively new type of documents and data—those obtained on-line.

Nature of Documents

A number of terms are used to refer to sources of data in a study other than interviews or observations. I have chosen the term *document* as the umbrella term to refer to a wide range of written, visual, and physical material relevant to the study at hand. This term includes materials "in the broad sense of any communication"—for example novels, newspapers, love songs, diaries, psychiatric interviews, and the like (Holsti, 1969, p. 1). Documents, as the term is used in this chapter, also include what LeCompte and Preissle (1993) define as artifacts—"symbolic materials such as writing and signs and nonsymbolic materials such as tools and furnishings" (p. 216). Others use the term "available" materials or data. This means just about anything in existence prior to the research at hand. "The researcher may make use of letters or television transcripts, historical documents or journalistic accounts, tribal artifacts or works of art. He may analyze the records of corporations, police courts, or the U.S. Bureau of the Census. He may reexamine . . . the already completed studies of other scholars. As all these and diverse other materials accumulate, it may well be that increasing numbers of researchers will find that the data they need have already been gathered" (Selltiz, Jahoda, Deutsch, and Cook, 1959, pp. 240–241). Photographs, film, and video can also be used as data sources, as can physical evidence or traces (Webb and others, 1981; Harper, 1994). Although this chapter concentrates on written documents, the general discussion applies to all forms of data not gathered through interviews or observations.

Types of Documents

Public records, personal documents, and physical material are three major types of documents available to the researcher for analysis. Moreover, a researcher can create documents for the purpose of the investigation.

Public Records

Public records are "the ongoing, continuing records of a society" (Webb and others, 1981, p. 78). As Guba and Lincoln (1981) note, "The first and most important injunction to anyone looking for official records is to presume that if an event happened, some record of it exists" (p. 253). Public documents include actuarial records of births, deaths, and marriages, the U.S. census, police records, court transcripts, agency records, association manuals, program documents, mass media, government documents, and so on. Locating public records is limited only by the researcher's imagination and industriousness. Auster (1985), for example, demonstrates how to conduct a study of changing social expectations for family, career, gender roles, and sexual behavior through the sole data source of Girl Scout handbooks. Youth organization handbooks, she points out, "represent the intersection of biography and history" (p. 359), providing an excellent data source for studying changing social mores.

For those interested in educational questions, there are numerous sources of public documents—discussions of educational issues and bills in the *Congressional Record;* federal, state, and private agency reports; individual program records; and the statistical database of the Center for Educational Statistics. Since many case studies are at the program level, it is particularly important to seek out the paper trail for what it can reveal about the program—"things that cannot be observed," things "that have taken place before the evaluation began. They may include private interchanges to which the educator would not otherwise be privy. They can reveal goals or decisions that might be unknown to the evaluator" (Patton, 1990, p. 233). Ideally this paper trail includes "all routine records on clients, all correspondence from and to program staff, financial and budget records, organizational rules, regulations, memoranda, charts, and any other official or unofficial documents generated by or for the program" (p. 233). Such documents not only provide valuable information about the program itself, but they can also stimulate thinking "about important questions to pursue through more direct observations and interviewing" (p. 233).

If you were interested in studying the role of parent involvement in a neighborhood school, for example, you could look for public record documents in the form of the following: notices sent home to parents; memos between and among teachers, staff, and the parents' association; formal policy statements regarding parent involvement; school bulletin boards or other displays featuring aspects of parent involvement; newspaper and other media coverage of activities featuring parent involvement; and any official records of parent attendance or presence in the school.

Other sources of public information that are easily accessible but often overlooked include previous studies and data "banks" of information. However, in using these resources the researcher has to rely on someone else's description and interpretation of data rather than use the raw data as a basis for analysis. These meta-analyses, as they are called, are more common in quantitative research, although there has been some recent thinking as to how this strategy might apply to qualitative studies (LeCompte and Preissle, 1992; West and Oldfather, 1995). For large-scale or cross-cultural research, relying on previous studies may be the only realistic way to conduct the investigation.

An example of a data bank that is potentially useful in qualitative research, especially ethnographic studies (see Chapter One), is the Human Relations Area File (Murdock, 1983; Murdock and others, 1982). This file is a compilation of ethnographic studies of more than 350 societies; data are classified and coded by cultural group and also by more than 700 topics. Education is one broad topic under which such subtopics as elementary education, educational theory and methods, students, and vocational education can be found. The index is organized so that a researcher can retrieve documents related to the educational practices of one particular cultural group, or documents can be retrieved about a specific practice such as "student uprisings" across many cultures. Types of documents found in this file include ethnographer field notes, diary entries, reports to various agencies, books, newspaper articles, works of fiction about the culture, and photographs.

"Every literate society," writes Kidder (1981b), "produces a variety of material intended to inform, entertain, or persuade the populace" (p. 286). Popular media forms such as television, films, radio, newspapers, literary works, photography, cartoons, and the like are another source of "public" data. Mass communication materials are especially good sources for dealing with questions about some aspect of society at a given time, for comparing groups on a certain dimension, or for tracking cultural change and trends. They "concentrate on what is of current interest, and that concentration makes it possible to track many phenomena and index the growth and decline of public interest in them" (Webb and others, 1981, p. 120). Studies have been conducted, for example, on the roles of blacks in television, the presence of ageism in cartoons, and teenage culture in movies.

Personal Documents

In contrast to public sources of data, personal documents "refer to any first-person narrative that describes an individual's actions, experiences, and beliefs" (Bogdan and Biklen, 1992, p. 132). Such documents include diaries, letters, home videos, sermons, children's growth records, scrapbooks and photo albums, calendars, autobiographies, and travel logs. Selltiz, Jahoda, Deutsch, and Cook (1959) note that "the rationale for the use of personal documents is similar to that for the use of observational techniques. What the latter may achieve for overt behavior, the former can do for inner experiences: to reveal to the social scientist life as it is lived without the interference of research" (p. 325). Such documents can tell the researcher about the inner meaning of everyday events, or they may yield descriptions of "rare and extraordinary events in human life" (p. 327) such as can be found in Admiral Byrd's report of his experiences alone at the South Pole or Helen Keller's account of overcoming extraordinary physical handicaps.

Personal documents are a reliable source of data concerning a person's attitudes, beliefs, and view of the world. But because they are personal documents, the material is highly subjective in that the writer is the only one to select what he or she considers important to record. Obviously these documents are not representative or necessarily reliable accounts of what actually may have occurred. They do, however, reflect the participant's perspective, which is what most qualitative research is seeking. Burgess (1982) summarizes the nature of personal documents:

> The field researcher needs to consider: Is the material trustworthy? Is the material atypical? Has the material been edited and refined? Does the autobiographical material only contain highlights of life that are considered interesting? Furthermore, it could be argued that the material is automatically biased as only certain people produce autobiographies and keep diaries; there is self-selectivity involved in the sample of material available; they do not provide a complete historical record. Nevertheless, such material does provide a subjective account of the situation it records; it is a reconstruction of part of life. Furthermore, it provides an account that is based on the author's experience [p. 132].

An entire study can be based on personal documents. Abramson's (1992) case study of Russian Jewish emigration is based solely on his grandfather's diaries written over a twelve–year period. A well-known earlier study of Polish immigrant life relied heavily upon personal letters written between immigrants and relatives in Europe (Thomas and Znaniecki, 1927). Many of these letters were obtained by placing ads in local newspapers asking for them.

Physical Material

Physical material as a form of document, broadly defined, consists of physical objects found within the study setting. Anthropologists typically refer to these objects as *artifacts,* which include the tools, implements, utensils, and instruments of everyday living. Hodder (1994) includes artifacts and written texts that have physically endured over time as "mute material evidence" (p. 398) in the study of culture. In a study of students with physical disabilities, for example, specially designed or modified tools for learning (computers, sports equipment, and so on) could be included as part of the database.

Physical trace material is yet another potential source of information. Physical traces are defined as "any changes in the physical environment due to human actions" (Rathje, 1979, pp. 75–76). Examples of physical evidence being used in research studies are provided by Webb and others (1981, p. 2):

- One investigator wanted to know the relationship between reported and actual beer consumption. He obtained a "front door" measure by asking residents of houses how much beer they consumed each week and a "back door" measure by counting the beer cans in their garbage cans. The back door measure resulted in a considerably higher estimate of beer consumption.
- The degree of fear induced by a ghost-story-telling session can be measured by noting the shrinking diameter of a circle of seated children. . . .
- Library withdrawals were used to demonstrate the effect of the introduction of television into a community. Fiction titles dropped, nonfiction titles were unaffected. . . .
- A child's interest in Christmas was demonstrated by distortions in the size of Santa Claus drawings.
- Racial attitudes in two colleges were compared by noting the degree of clustering of blacks and whites in lecture halls.

Two basic means of studying physical traces are to note their erosion, which is the degree of wear, and to note their accretion, which is the degree of accumulation. The wear and tear on floor tiles in front of a museum exhibit as a sign of public interest is a well-known example of erosion (Webb and others, 1966); the accumulation of beer cans in the preceding list is a good example of accretion.

Because physical traces can usually be measured, they are most often suited for obtaining information on the incidence and frequency of behavior. They are also a good check on information obtained from interviews or surveys. In case study research, most physical trace measures are used to supplement data gathered through interviews and observations. A researcher might, for example, compare the wear and tear on computer terminals in a school program that purports to include computer literacy in its basic curriculum. Other advantages of using trace measures are noted by Rathje (1979, pp. 78–79):

- Trace measures record the results of actual behavior, not reported or experimental approximations.
- Trace measures are usually *nonreactive* and *unobtrusive*. Since they are applied after behavior has occurred they do not modify the behavior they seek to study.
- Material traces are ubiquitous and readily available for study.
- Because material traces are applied to inanimate objects, they usually require minimal cooperation and inconvenience from human subjects.
- Because the number of measures of traces depends upon the recorder's interest rather than informant patience, a variety of interrelated behaviors can often be studied at once.
- Because of the minimal inconvenience and expense to informants, trace measures can be used over long time periods as longitudinal monitoring devices.

Researcher-Generated Documents

Most commonly, when documents are included in a study, what is being referred to are public records, personal documents, and physical material *already present* in the research setting. Because they have not been produced for the research purpose, they often contain much that is irrelevant to the study; by the same token, they can contain clues, even startling insights, into the phenomenon under study. Most researchers find them well worth the effort to locate and examine.

Researcher-generated documents are documents prepared by the researcher or for the researcher by participants after the study has begun. The specific purpose for generating documents is to learn more about the situation, person, or event being investigated. The researcher might request that someone keep a diary or log of activities during the course of the investigation. Or a life history of an individual or historical account of a program might be solicited to illuminate the present situation.

A researcher's photographs are another example of this type of document. Such photographs, often taken in conjunction with participant observation, provide a "means of remembering and studying detail that might be overlooked if a photographic image were not available for reflection" (Bogdan and Biklen, 1992, p. 143). Preskill (1995) reports using photographs to document aspects of the organizational culture of a magnet high school; the photos were also used as resources in interviewing teachers and students—what Preskill calls "reading photographs" and "photographic interviewing" (p. 189). Photographs can also be taken by the participants. In a study of differing perceptions of white and African American Greek members of their university environment, researchers provided disposable cameras to participants to take photos exemplifying what their university experience meant (Perka, Matherly, Fishman, and Ridge, 1992). These photos and interviews asking participants to interpret the photos provided the data for analysis. (See Becker, 1986a, for more on photography in qualitative research).

Quantitative data produced by the investigator also fall into this category of documents. Projective tests, attitudinal measures, content examinations, statistical data from surveys on any number of topics—all can be treated as documents in support of a qualitative investigation. In a case study of a county health workers' training program, for example, data were collected from written questionnaires as well as through observation and interviews. Results of the survey became supporting documentary material for the observation and interview-based findings of the study (Dominick and Cervero, 1987).

In summary, then, documents include a broad range of materials available to the researcher who is creative in seeking them out. Literally millions of public and private documents, as well as physical traces of human behavior, can be used as primary or secondary sources of data. Further, documents can be generated by the researcher once the study has begun.

Using Documents in Qualitative Research

Using documentary material as data is not much different from using interviews or observations. Glaser and Strauss (1967) compare fieldwork with library research. "When someone stands in the library stacks, he is, metaphorically, surrounded by voices begging to be heard. Every book, every magazine article, represents at least one person who is equivalent to the anthropologist's informant or the sociologist's interviewee. In those publications, people converse, announce positions, argue with a range of eloquence, and describe events or scenes in ways entirely comparable to what is seen and heard during fieldwork" (p. 163).

Whether in fieldwork or library work, the data collection is guided by questions, educated hunches, and emerging findings. Although the search is systematic, both settings also allow for the accidental uncovering of valuable data. Tracking down leads, being open to new insights, and being sensitive to the data are the same whether the researcher is interviewing, observing, or analyzing documents. Since the investigator is the primary instrument for gathering data, he or she relies on skills and intuition to find and interpret data from documents.

Finding relevant materials is the first step in the process. As I mentioned, this is generally a systematic procedure that evolves from the topic of inquiry itself. A case study of a back-to-industry program for postsecondary faculty logically led the researcher to memos, background papers, advertising material, application forms, and final reports on the project (Kline, 1981). A qualitative study of classroom instruction would lead to documents in the form of instructors' lesson plans, student assignments, objects in the classroom, official grade reports and school records, teacher evaluations, and so on. Besides the setting itself, the logical places to look are libraries, historical societies, archives, and institutional files. Others have located personal documents like letters and diaries by placing advertisements in newspapers and newsletters (Taylor and Bogdan, 1984).

Selltiz, Jahoda, Deutsch, and Cook (1959) observe that finding pertinent documents hinges to some extent on the investigator's ability to think creatively about the problem under study. "The use of such data demands *a capacity to ask many different questions related to the research problem.* By definition, the purpose for which available records have been collected is different from the purpose for which the social scientist wishes to use them" (p. 318, emphasis in original). Thus the researcher must keep an open mind when it comes to discovering useful documents. Being open to any possibility can lead to serendipitous discoveries. Recent tobacco company exposés have been buttressed by the discovery of buried memos in which the addictive quality of nicotine is discussed; the famous Watergate tapes were literally stumbled upon during routine questioning of White House staff.

Once documents have been located, their authenticity must be assessed. Since they were not produced for the researcher, the investigator must try to "reconstruct the process by which the data were originally assembled by somebody else" (Riley, 1963). It is important to determine "the conditions under which these data were produced, what specific methodological and technical decisions may have been made, . . . and the consequent impact on the nature of the data now to be taken over" (p. 252). A news release to the general public serves a quite different purpose than an internal memo on the same issue. In evaluating artifacts—that is, objects used or produced by a particular cultural group—LeCompte and Preissle (1993) suggest that the researcher ask such questions as, What is the history of its production and use? How is its use allocated? Is its selection biased? How might it be distorted or falsified?

Determining the authenticity and accuracy of documents is part of the research process. Burgess (1982) writes that documents should not be used in isolation. It is the investigator's responsibility to determine as much as possible about the document, its origins and reasons for being written, its author, and the context in which it was written. Guba and Lincoln (1981), citing Clark (1967), list the questions a researcher might ask about the authenticity of documents:

- What is the history of the document?
- How did it come into my hands?
- What guarantee is there that it is what it pretends to be?
- Is the document complete, as originally constructed?
- Has it been tampered with or edited?
- If the document is genuine, under what circumstances and for what purposes was it produced?
- Who was/is the author?
- What was he trying to accomplish? For whom was the document intended?
- What were the maker's sources of information? Does the document represent an eyewitness account, a secondhand account, a reconstruction of an event long prior to the writing, an interpretation?
- What was or is the maker's bias?
- To what extent was the writer likely to want to tell the truth?
- Do other documents exist that might shed additional light on the same story, event, project, program, context? If so, are they available, accessible? Who holds them? [pp. 238–239]

An important distinction for historians that qualitative researchers might also attend to is whether documents are primary or secondary sources. Primary sources are those in which the originator of the document is recounting firsthand experience with the phenomenon of interest. The best primary sources are those recorded closest in time and place to the phenomenon by a qualified person. Given this definition, most personal documents and eyewitness accounts of social phenomena could be considered primary resources. Secondary sources are reports of a phenomenon by those who have not directly experienced the phenomenon of interest; these are often compiled at a later date. Interestingly, the same document could be classified as primary or secondary depending upon the purpose of the study. The diary of a loved one caring for someone with terminal cancer, for example, would be a primary source of data for a study on caretaking; it would be considered a secondary source of data for understanding how patients themselves cope with a terminal disease.

After assessing the authenticity and nature of documents or artifacts, the researcher must adopt some system for coding and cataloging them. If at all possible, written documents should be copied and artifacts photographed or videotaped. By establishing basic descriptive categories early on for coding, the researcher will have easy access to information in the analysis and interpretation stage. In a case study of a career enhancement award program, for example, applications for the award were part of the database (Zeph, 1991). The applications were coded according to the applicant's type of employment, dollar amount of request, sex, geographic location, and nature of the project proposed.

In qualitative case studies, a form of content analysis is used to analyze documents. Essentially, content analysis is a systematic procedure for describing the content of communications. Historians and literary critics have long used content analysis to analyze historical documents and literary works. Modern content analysis has most often been applied to communications media (newspapers, periodicals, television, film) and has had a strong quantitative focus. A major concern has been measuring the frequency and variety of messages and confirming hypotheses. Most research designs using content analysis are sequential in nature—"moving from category construction to sampling, data collection, data analysis and interpretation" (Altheide, 1987, p. 68). Data collection and coding are often carried out by novices using protocols and trained to count units of analysis.

Quantification need not be a component of content analysis, however. The nature of the data can also be assessed. Altheide (1987) describes how qualitative content analysis differs from conventional content analysis. "Ethnographic content analysis is used to document and understand the communication of meaning, as well as to verify theoretical relationships. Its distinctive characteristic is the reflexive and highly interactive nature of the investigator, concepts, data collection and analysis. . . . The investigator is continually central, although protocols may be used in later phases of the research. . . . The aim is to be systematic and analytic, but not rigid" (p. 68).

Limitations and Strengths of Documents

In judging the value of a data source, a researcher can ask whether it contains information or insights relevant to the research question and whether it can be acquired in a reasonably practical yet systematic manner. If these two questions can be answered in the affirmative, there is no reason not to use a particular source of data. Documents or artifacts have been underused in qualitative research, however. Glaser and Strauss (1967) attribute this underuse to the fact that researchers prefer to produce their own data, that the use of documents is too much like historical research, that researchers want "to see the concrete situation and informants in person" (p. 163), and that they distrust their own competency in using documentary materials.

Preferences for other sources of data may reflect a researcher's uncertainty about the potential of documents for yielding knowledge and insight. But the researcher's caution may also reflect some of the limitations inherent in this data source. Several limitations stem from the basic difference between this source and data gleaned from interviews or observations—that most documentary data have not been developed for research purposes. The materials may therefore be incomplete from a research perspective. In contrast to field notes, available materials may not "afford a continuity of unfolding events in the kind of detail that the theorist requires" (Glaser and Strauss, 1967, p. 182). Whether personal accounts or official documents are involved, the source may provide unrepresentative samples. "Often no one on the project keeps very good notes on processes, few memoranda are generated, and, even more often, the only writing that is done is in response to funders' requests for technical reports or other periodic statements about the progress of the program or project. If no documents exist, however, or if the documents are sparse and seem uninformative, this ought to tell the inquirer something about the context" (Guba and Lincoln, 1981, pp. 234–235).

Because documents are not produced for research purposes, the information they offer may not be in a form that is useful (or understandable) to the investigator. Furthermore, such data "may not fit present definitions of the concepts under scrutiny; they may lack correspondence with the conceptual model" (Riley, 1963,

p. 254). This is, of course, more of a problem when documents are used as secondary data sources to verify findings based on other data. If documents are used as part of the process of inductively building categories and theoretical constructs as in qualitative case studies, then their "fit" with preestablished concepts or models is less of a concern.

A third major problem with documentary materials is determining their authenticity and accuracy. Even public records that purport to be objective and accurate contain built-in biases that a researcher may not be aware of. For example, the incidence and frequency of crimes reported in police records may be a function of how certain crimes are defined and a particular department's procedures for reporting them. Personal documents are subject to purposeful or nonpurposeful deception. There is likely to be, for example, an underestimation of income in a personal income tax report versus an overestimation of expenses in a grant proposal. Distortion in personal documents may be unintentional in that the writer is unaware of his or her biases or simply does not remember accurately. Selltiz, Jahoda, Deutsch, and Cook (1959, p. 325) quote Augustine, who noted this problem of authenticity in his famous personal document, *Confessions*. "And when they hear me confessing of myself, how do they know whether I speak the truth?" Concern about authenticity applies to historical documents as well as to anonymous project reports and sources who wish to remain anonymous, such as "Deep Throat" of the 1974 Watergate case (Webb and others, 1981).

Despite these limitations, documents are a good source of data for numerous reasons. To begin with, they often meet Dexter's (1970) criteria for selecting a particular data collection strategy, that is, documents should be used when it appears they will yield "*better* data or *more* data . . . than other tactics" (p. 11). Many documents are easily accessible, free, and contain information that would take an investigator enormous time and effort to gather otherwise.

Furthermore, documents may be the *only* means of studying certain problems. Riley (1963) notes four situations in which documents are crucial to an investigation: (1) historical studies in which events can no longer be observed and informants may not recall or be available for recall; (2) cross-cultural studies in which settings are remote or inaccessible; (3) studies that rely on technical expertise such as a doctor's report; and (4) studies of intimate personal relationships that cannot be observed and that people are often reluctant to discuss.

The data found in documents can be used in the same manner as data from interviews or observations. The data can furnish descriptive information, verify emerging hypotheses, advance new categories and hypotheses, offer historical understanding, track change and development, and so on. Glaser and Strauss (1967) point to the usefulness of documents for theory building—a process that "begs for comparative analysis. The library offers a *fantastic range* of comparison groups, if only the researcher has the ingenuity to discover them" (p. 179, emphasis in original).

One of the greatest advantages in using documentary material is its stability. Unlike interviewing and observation, the presence of the investigator does not alter what is being studied. Documentary data are "objective" sources of data compared to other forms. Such data have also been called "unobtrusive." Webb and others' (1966) classic book on unobtrusive measures in its revised form is titled *Nonreactive Measures in the Social Sciences* (1981) because, they write, "we came to realize over the years that the original title was not the best one since it was the nonreactivity of the measures rather than their unobtrusiveness that was of major concern" (p. ix). Nonreactive measures include physical traces, official records, private documents, and simple and contrived observations.

Finally, documentary data are particularly good sources for *qualitative* case studies because they can ground an investigation in the context of the problem being investigated. Analysis of this data source "lends contextual richness and helps to ground an inquiry in the milieu of the writer. This grounding in real-world issues and day-to-day concerns is ultimately what the naturalistic inquiry is working toward" (Guba and Lincoln, 1981, p. 234).

Thus, like any other source of data, documents have their limitations and their advantages. Because they are produced for reasons other than research, they may be fragmentary, they may not fit the conceptual framework of the research, and their authenticity may be difficult to determine. However, because they exist independent of a research agenda, they are nonreactive, that is, unaffected by the research process. They are a product of the context in which they were produced and therefore grounded in the real world. Finally, many documents or artifacts cost little or nothing and are often easy to obtain.

On-Line Data Sources

Anyone who reads a newspaper has seen the term *information super-highway* applied to the Internet and heard about the explosive growth it has undergone in the last few years. From its humble beginnings as a communication tool exclusively for university professors and scientists (initially designed to withstand the results of a war), the Internet has become a standard resource for college students, businesses, and anyone else who has access to a computer with a modem.

In addition to providing a number of reference sources—albeit of uneven quality—the Internet supports interactions among people through various forms of computer-mediated communication. E-mail, listservs, usenet groups, chat rooms, and other interactive environments allow people who have never met to encounter one another and even establish relationships conducted primarily through on-line contacts. These interactions, still ill-defined within our society, are of obvious interest to qualitative researchers. In addition to being a focus for study in and of themselves, they provide multiple sources of data relating to other studies. What factors must be considered when accessing and analyzing these data sources?

In this section I will explore some of the issues associated with the use of on-line data sources. How are these sources similar to more familiar sources, such as documents, interviews, and observations? How are they different? What issues and concerns are raised by the effects of the media on the data-gathering process? What ethical considerations arise in this new research context?

These are not questions easily answered, nor are they the exclusive province of qualitative researchers. Articles in computer-related magazines and the popular press regularly discuss various effects of the Internet on society at large, ranging from explorations of the "multiple selves" possible on-line, to mentions of "on-line affairs" between people who have never seen one another in person, to news about religious groups using the Internet to build community, evangelize, and make sacred texts available to the public (Geller, 1996; McCorduck, 1996; Namuth and others, 1996). Even standard news magazines highlight issues related to cyberspace—the ambiguous destination to which the information superhighway leads. Since the changing electronic landscape outpaces the publication of specific maps or guides, this survey will merely outline a general range of concerns for discussion. For any particular area of study, the specific application of these considerations will vary.

On-Line Versus Off-Line Data

In qualitative research, the three basic ways to collect data have traditionally been through interviews, observations, and examinations of documents and artifacts (Merriam and Simpson, 1995). Many of the references and data sources available on-line reflect characteristics of these familiar data sources. Web pages, papers available through file transfer protocol, and various forms of "electronic paper" can be considered documents that are simply accessed on-line. Illustrations and programs—even games—available in static form to be downloaded by the user can be treated as artifacts. E-mail can be used to question individuals as in an interview, and researchers can observe the on-line interactions among individuals in a variety of formats.

To some extent then, on-line data collection offers an electronic extension of familiar research techniques, widening the scope of data available to the researcher. Certainly, many of the decisions faced in off-line situations emerge in parallel form in on-line research: whether to join an on-line community as a complete observer, a complete participant, or something in between; how to select a sample group; how to approach potential participants when initiating a study; how to gain trust; and so on.

However, on-line data collection has some important differences due to the nature of the medium through which it is conducted. These differences have a profound influence on the study that must not be ignored or trivialized. For example, individuals who do not have access to computers will be automatically excluded from the study. Is this appropriate for the study, or will demographic differences that correlate with computer access distort the findings?

Though the amount of information increases to an over-whelming degree, not all critical interactions are necessarily available for study. Members of a usenet group may also communicate through private e-mail messages that the researcher never sees (Schrum, 1996). Quantity of information is no guarantee of comprehensiveness.

In addition, each form of computer-mediated communication has a unique effect on the information it transmits. For example, an e-mail interview may have the same verbal content as one conducted in person, but it lacks inflection, body language, and the many other nuances that often communicate more vividly than words. Frequent users of e-mail recognize its limitations; new users are regularly warned that jokes and sarcasm do not travel well on-line, and they are taught "emoticons" that attempt to replicate the emotional richness common in speech. At the same time that some communication characteristics are curtailed or modified, others are artificially enhanced. The asynchronous nature of e-mail can add reflection time to an on-line interview that would be unavailable in a face-to-face session. Immediate reactions, strong emotional responses, and unguarded expressions are all lost to the researcher unless, after second thought, the participant chooses to make these transient first thoughts available—and is capable of articulating them in writing. These reactions could completely change the interpretation of a response. Conversely, a casual response may have an unexpected and unsettling permanency; e-mail exchanges long forgotten can resurface, sometimes in totally different and even misleading contexts.

Even as they become familiar with the evolving conventions of on-line expression, researchers need to remain alert to the variables of electronic communication. Participants in listservs and usenet groups have an entire terminology to describe certain types of exchanges, such as "flaming" (responding in a hostile manner), "trolling" (deliberately misleading), and "flame-baiting" (provoking flames from others) that occur as implicit meanings find new outlets.

In terms of group interactions, writing skills and computer literacy strongly influence how individuals are perceived on-line. Often someone will seem to have an entirely different character: a funny, charming person can seem caustic and sarcastic when the smile accompanying his words disappears. Another individual whose writing is mature and thoughtful may prove to have limited social skills when deprived of reflection time and forced to react spontaneously.

This discrepancy between real and on-line personalities occurs even when people are trying to be themselves—or at least an idealized version of themselves (Phillips and Barnes, 1995). It is compounded when individuals purposefully create different on-line personas, which is fairly frequent in some electronic environments. On-line interaction can vary widely, from scholarly communities in which individuals list their real names with their university affiliations and degrees, to fantasy games in which participants make up names and descriptions that reflect little of their off-line characteristics. Where does role-playing shade into deception? As Phillips and Barnes observe, "there is a great deal of opportunity to create fraud through role playing. . . . There is no way to corroborate the image you get. . . . Through text-only exchanges, you have no way to really know who you are talking to" (1995, pp. 39–40). Under these conditions, the assumption that the world is composed of multiple, changing realities—part of the qualitative paradigm—becomes at once a trivially self-evident observation and a magnified complication. Judging individuals by the way they choose to present themselves on-line is a risky business, and verification or triangulation may be far less reliable than in the "real world."

Even on-line documents and artifacts take on new qualities. The Web page cited today may be gone tomorrow or the content changed so radically as to be unrecognizable. Managing data assumes a new dimension when its stability can no longer be taken for granted. Version control, once only of concern to programmers and editors, emerges as a critical issue for anyone using the Internet as a reference or a resource.

This is a new territory, with unfamiliar rules that change as quickly as they are identified. My best advice for researchers is to recognize that the results of their research are strongly influenced by the characteristics of the data revealed, concealed, or altered because of the nature of the medium through which they are presented. Analyzing, describing, and discussing the potential effects of these characteristics will be an important aspect of research conducted from on-line data.

Effects of the Medium on Data Gathering

In addition to the differences between on-line and off-line data, differences caused by the manner in which data are gathered must be considered. In qualitative research, the researcher is the primary instrument for data collection and analysis. This factor is usually perceived as an advantage, because humans are both responsive and adaptive. At the same time, it carries the responsibility of assessing and reporting researcher biases that might have an impact on the study.

When collecting data from the Internet, the researcher is no longer the primary instrument for data collection; a variety of software tools must be used to locate, select, and process information. Like the researcher, these tools have inherent biases that may affect the study, but their biases may be very subtle—and often much more difficult for a researcher to detect and describe. As Norman (1993) observes, "different technologies afford different operations. That is, they make some things easy to do, others difficult or impossible. It should come as no surprise that those things that the affordances make easy are apt to get done, those things that the affordances make difficult are not apt to get done" (p. 106).

Software tools not only shape what is easy or difficult to do, but also shape the user's perception of what is possible, according to Carroll and Kellogg (1989), as cited in Kellogg and Richards (1995). "Software tools will also shape a user's 'policy' for handling information; after all, they determine which actions are possible to take towards a particular piece of information. A user's mental model of goals . . . possible to have vis-à-vis Internet information will arise, at least in part, from the functionality of the software" (pp. 13–14).

These passages raise critical concerns for qualitative researchers accessing data from the Internet: How are their tools shaping the task? Again this is a rapidly evolving area; the researcher's responsibility must be to describe tools and methods, as well as their potential effects on the work.

Ethical Issues

In any qualitative study, ethical issues relating to protection of the participants are of concern. In an on-line environment, these issues overlap the public debate about ownership of intellectual property, copyright, and free speech. The ability to read, save, copy, archive, and easily edit huge volumes of material written by faceless masses can lead a researcher to forget that these are the words of individuals. Even when the names are changed, some people are easily identified by the details of their messages. The highly public nature of some of the electronic environments in which people exchange ideas can lull researchers into forgetting the right to privacy that these individuals have, just as the seeming anonymity of electronic communication can lull individuals into revealing highly intimate details of their lives to anyone who happens to be reading their messages.

Schrum and Harris (1996), who are among the leaders in exploring the ethical implications of research conducted in the Internet's "virtual communities," frame a number of suggestions to researchers operating in this arena. They suggest that it is the researcher's responsibility to be informed about the basic tenets of ethical qualitative research, to inform participants about the research in a variety of accessible forms, and to respect the participants' ownership of materials they generate (Schrum and Harris, 1996, p. 19).

The term *participants* is commonly used by qualitative researchers to describe the individuals being studied. It is a carefully chosen identifier, with connotations of inclusion and willing cooperation. This single word captures a number of attitudes about research from the qualitative paradigm. It also serves as a litmus test concerning ethics. If this term cannot be accurately used—if *subjects* more appropriately describes the inclusion of unwilling or uninformed individuals under the researcher's scrutiny—then the researcher should honestly reevaluate the methods and procedures of the study.

The growing importance of on-line interaction makes it a natural arena for qualitative research. Three critical areas that the qualitative researcher must consider are the effects of the context on the data, the effects of software functionalities on the data-gathering process, and the effects the medium tends to have on ethical practice. Explicitly considering and describing the impact of these factors is a new responsibility of the qualitative researcher.

Summary

Documents, broadly defined to include public records, personal papers, physical traces, and artifacts, are a third major source of data in qualitative research. Although some documents might be prepared at the investigator's request (such as a respondent keeping a diary or writing a life history), most are produced independently of the research study. They are thus nonreactive and grounded in the context under study. Because they are produced for reasons other than the study at hand, some ingenuity is needed in locating documents that bear on the problem and then in analyzing their content. Congruence between documents and the research problem depends on the researcher's flexibility in construing the problem and the related questions. Such a stance is particularly fitting in qualitative studies, which, by their very nature, are emergent in design and inductive in analysis. Documents of all types can help the researcher uncover meaning, develop understanding, and discover insights relevant to the research problem.

Data gathering on-line is an emerging area of keen interest for qualitative researchers. However, a number of issues must be considered when using data from an on-line interaction; I reviewed some of these issues in this chapter.

Chapter Seven

Collecting Data in Case Studies

In previous chapters I discussed three data collection techniques—conducting interviews, observing, and analyzing documents. It is common for qualitative studies in education to employ only one, and at best two, of the three techniques for collecting data. In qualitative case studies, however, all three means of data collection are frequently used. Understanding the case in its totality, as well as the intensive, *holistic* description and analysis characteristic of a case study, mandates both breadth and depth of data collection. Data collection in a case study is a recursive, interactive process in which engaging in one strategy incorporates or may lead to subsequent sources of data. Drawing from three different studies, one on program planning with older adults, one on the role of human resource development in small businesses, and one on power and privilege in higher education classes, this chapter explores the interactive nature of data collection in case study research.

Three Case Studies: Problem and Sample Selection

The techniques you choose to use and the data you choose to collect using those techniques are determined by how you framed your study and selected the sample. Chapter Three explains how to identify your theoretical framework, state the problem and purpose of the study, and select a sample. This must all be done before you actually go out and collect data. Following is a brief overview of these first steps in the three case studies used here for illustration.

The theoretical framework of Harris's (1995) comparative case study of program planning in Learning in Retirement (LIR) institutes draws from the literature of curriculum design and program planning generally, and program planning with older adults in particular. The problem she identifies is that while there are numerous models of the program planning process, little is known about how it actually happens in context, and in particular, in the context of programs for older adults. The purpose of her study was to identify the program planning process of LIRs and see how contextual factors affect that process. As I discussed in Chapter Three, sample selection occurs at two levels in case study research. In Harris's study, five "cases" or sites were selected that met the following criteria: the LIRs had been in existence for at least four years; selections represented geographic diversity; and they were diverse in terms of type of institutional sponsorship. The five sites included a private research university in a highly populated urban area, a public state-supported university in a small rural community, a two-year church-affiliated college in a rural mountain community, a community college in a small rural town, and a state-supported university in a large metropolitan area.

Within each institute, or case, the LIR program coordinator (who was also the liaison between host institution and LIR), all planning committee members, and the main administrator of the host higher education institution (usually the president) were purposefully selected for interviews. A convenience sample of adult students was also selected. Observations of program planning committee meetings were conducted if meetings were held during on-site visits. Finally, all LIR documents in the form of mission statements, brochures, course schedules, and marketing materials were collected.

Rowden's (1994, 1995) study of the role of human resource development (HRD) in successful small businesses was grounded in the HRD and small business literature. The problem he identified was that while there were numerous studies of large Fortune 500 companies and annual surveys of the extent and nature of training and learning in the workplace, there was virtually no information on HRD in small businesses nor on how HRD may or may not contribute to the success of a company. The purpose of his study, then, became to investigate the role that HRD plays in the success of small businesses. An important consideration in the selection of cases was how "successful" was defined and just what constituted "small." First, manufacturing rather than service or retail companies were chosen because manufacturing companies usually include some of the service, sales, and marketing components characteristic of service and retail sectors and almost always have some form of training, whether it be on-the-job or classroom. Second, since 88 percent of manufacturing companies employ fewer than 200 workers, this number was used for defining "small." Third, "successful" was determined by survivability—whether companies had been in business for a minimum of ten years. Rowden (1994) says of this criterion, "While many arguments can be made as to the proper criteria for identifying successful companies, any small to mid-sized company that qualifies under the criteria of survivability should likewise qualify as a successful company under any other appropriate criteria" (p. 89). The three cases selected for the study included a paint manufacturing company employing an average of 66 workers; a solid-pine furniture manufacturing company with 109 employees; and a company engaged in the manufacture of commercial signs that employed 128.

Sample selection within each case, or business, proceeded much the same as in Harris's study. The business owner, the person in charge of training employees (no matter what the person's actual title was), and a random selection of middle-level managers and line employees were selected for interviewing. Several observations were conducted at each site, and pertinent documents were collected for analysis.

The third example is one I referred to earlier in this book— Tisdell's (1992, 1993) study of power relations in adult higher education classes. With her emphasis on gender and interlocking systems of power and privilege, Tisdell's theoretical framework drew from research on classroom interaction in higher education and feminist pedagogy. The problem she identified was a lack of data-based research that specifically examined power relations in the learning environment with particular reference to gender and other systems of privilege.

To see how these interlocking systems manifest themselves in adult higher education classrooms, Tisdell chose to conduct a comparative case study using two classrooms. She selected graduate classes to ensure that adult students beyond the usual college age of eighteen to twenty-two would be included. And since previous research had suggested that the gender of the instructor affects the nature of classroom interaction, she selected one class with a male instructor and one with a female instructor. So as not to increase the likelihood of greater participation of one gender over another, attention was given to the particular subject matter of the course. The two cases selected were two graduate classes in counseling education, one with a male instructor and one with a female instructor. Data collection involved observing nearly all sessions of both classes, interviewing both instructors after the first class session and again after the class was over, interviewing a volunteer sample of students from both classes at the end of the term, and reviewing textbooks, syllabi, and other class-related materials. Table 7.1 summarizes the theoretical framework, purpose statement, and case-level sample selection criteria for each study.

Data Collection in the Three Case Studies

As I noted earlier, data collection in case study research usually involves all three strategies of interviewing, observing, and analyzing documents. On-site investigation of the case involves observing what is going on, talking informally and formally with people, and examining documents and materials that are part of the context. As Patton (1990) points out, "Multiple sources of information are sought and used because no single source of information can be trusted to provide a comprehensive perspective. . . . By using a combination of observations, interviewing, and document analysis, the fieldworker is able to use different data sources to validate and cross-check findings" (p. 244).

Rarely, however, are all three strategies used equally. One or two methods of data collection predominate; the other(s) play a supporting role in gaining an in-depth understanding of the case. In Harris's, Rowden's, and Tisdell's studies, one method dominated, followed by a second and third method. Table 7.2 shows the emphasis of the three data collection methods in each study. As can be seen in the table, both Harris and Rowden relied most heavily upon interviewing for their case data, while for Tisdell, observations were the major source of data.

Table 7.1. Theoretical Framework, Study Purpose, and Case Selection Criteria in Three Case Studies.

Study	Theoretical Framework	Study Purpose	Case Selection Criteria
Harris (1995)	Curriculum design Program planning and older adults	To identify the program planning process in LIRs and the contextual factors that shape the process	• Established programs (in existence at least four years) • Geographic diversity • Diverse institutional sponsorship
Rowden (1994, 1995)	Human resource development and small businesses	To delineate the role of human resource development (HRD) in successful businesses.	• Extended period of being in business (at least ten years) • Manufacturing companies • Companies employing less than 200 workers
Tisdell (1992, 1993)	Adult classroom behavior and feminist pedogogy	To examine how power relationships predominately based on gender are manifested in adult higher education classes	• Graduate classrooms • Gender-neutral content • One male, one female instructor

**Table 7.2. Use of Data Collection
Techniques in Three Case Studies.**

Study	Interviewing	Observation	Document Analysis
Harris (1995)	1	3	2
Rowden (1995)	1	2	3
Tisdell (1993)	2	1	2

Perhaps because of the timing of her visits to the Learning in Retirement sites and the focus of the study (program planning), observations did not prove to be a major source of data in Harris's study; documents were more useful for gaining insight into the planning process. In both Rowden's and Tisdell's studies, documents were used to support emerging findings from interviews and observations. It might be pointed out that an unavoidable selection process occurs even *within* each of the strategies. No one can attend to all things in an observation or think of all possible questions that could be asked in an interview. At best, the researcher is guided by the focus of the study and by being open and sensitive to new ideas and insights as they emerge in the process. For the remainder of this section, examples of the interactive nature of data collection will be discussed for each of the case studies. It is also true that even while collecting data, the researcher is already beginning to analyze it, that is, noting something in an observation or a document or an interview to follow up on in subsequent data collection. Such a stance is not only appropriate in qualitative research, it is highly recommended (see Chapter Eight on beginning data analysis).

The Program Planning Process in LIR Institutes

Harris's (1995) study was informed by documents and observations before she visited any of the five sites. LIRs are related to Elderhostels (short-term residential college programs for older adults) through the Elderhostel Institute Network. This Network has the twofold mission of promoting the creation of new LIRs and of strengthening and supporting established LIRs. To those ends, the Network publishes monthly newsletters, manuals, and guides; it offers technical assistance and sponsors state and regional conferences. Harris had studied the documents from the Network and attended a regional conference on LIRs where she attended sessions, talked informally with participants, and examined additional documents, some of which were site-specific. Her site visits were thus informed by what she had learned in this preliminary phase of the study.

Harris's visit to the LIR institute at a private research university in a highly populated urban area included studying brochures and registration materials of the institute, touring the facilities used by the LIR, sitting through several classes, attending a planning session, and interviewing the director and other key people. As an example of the interactive nature of the data collection, what Harris noted in the brochure and observed in classes is followed up in the interview with the LIR director. Having noted that there were few art or sports-related classes listed in the course offerings, Harris asks about this in the interview with the director (DIR) in the following excerpts:

JH: Do you think there's a good diversity in the courses that you all plan?

DIR: Well, I hope so; I mean that's our idea. When we get about halfway through planning for a semester, for instance, we have kind of twenty classes nailed down. Then on my dandy curriculum committee list I will divide them into subject areas, and it usually becomes obvious that there's some glaring gaps. Like we have nothing in our history, or we don't have any language, or we're really heavy in literature. And that gives us a guidance for then how we're going to plan the remaining twenty, twenty-five classes.

JH: So there is a definite game plan when it comes to the diversity and types of classes?

DIR: Yeah, although there are no quotas. . . .

JH: And how about, one thing just because of my background, I don't see too much in the physical area or even the hands-on art. Is it because of lack of space or a different philosophy that you're coming out of?

DIR: Um, the art stuff is mostly a lack of space. . . .

JH: Okay, because just looking at it, I would have felt that, just looking at it that you wanted to keep it a little more [academic], and I think the majority of it you do, but you're not opposed. . . .

DIR: Well, there is a reason for that too, because if we were to do a lot of more hands-on, if we were to do, I don't know what, gardening and other things that you see in Community Education things. Then we're going to attract a student body who's attracted to that. It would be hard then to go back to a more academic kind of curriculum. . . .

JH: Do you think if somebody was looking at your institute here from the outside they would look at this group as academic elitists or not, if they didn't get to know the people?

DIR: Oh, I'm sure they would. . . . I wish they didn't, but we're a group here basically of leaders and of people who are really interested in intellectual sorts of things and I think there's a whole community of folks that want and come here just for that.

JH: Yeah, and that's your niche.

DIR: Yeah, that's our niche and so I'm trying not to be apologetic for it.

From this interchange, Harris was able to confirm what she had noticed in the program brochure—that the courses at this LIR were academically oriented and that this was the niche it had carved out for itself in a community with other sponsors of programs for older adults. This information also provided Harris with some insight into how the larger context of an LIR program shapes the program planning process.

In a second example of the interactive, recursive nature of data collection in a case study, at another site Harris attended an LIR board of directors meeting after having interviewed the president of the institute. In her field notes of this meeting, she notes that it was dominated by the president and curriculum director, both males, and that most everyone else, but especially the women, had little if any input into the discussion. At the close of the meeting,

Harris was approached by one of the women, a new member of the curriculum committee who had said nothing at the meeting, and asked to be interviewed. Note how Harris weaves in the previous interview and the observation as she confirms her hunch with this respondent (RES):

JH: How are ideas brought up?
RES: [It's] problematic. . . . I hate to say this, but I think that the curriculum committee is a male-dominated. . . .
JH: They said that themselves.
RES: Did they?
JH: Oh yeah. Yesterday that was one of the things that was brought out and your president said, "One of the things I really want to see here," he said, "67 percent of our group here is women and we need more topics about women; we need more women on the committee, etcetera," so he is very. . . .
RES: He's aware of that but he still controls it. Everything that the men suggest is okay by the men. And if you watched the dynamics of the group yesterday, for instance, I'm probably the only one of the women with a doctorate and when I suggested the thing with the library . . . I wish we could go on with that kind of thing. Because women are interested in lives of women and what they've done to fulfill themselves. . . . Well, I will push it again but I'm saying it was a dead balloon there.
JH: What you may have to do is call the other women on the committee ahead of time and say, ladies, you know, tell me if I'm seeing this right or wrong.
RES: I think maybe there's more networking with those men.
JH: [The men have been on the] committee a long time.
RES: For a long time . . . most of us women on the committee are pretty fulfilled with whatever we're doing. This isn't the only thing that we do. So for the men this might be their only output, you can see the age of the thing. In other words, I'm saying we probably haven't made the effort to really call on each other.

In yet another example, the values of the church-affiliated college in a rural mountain community expressed in the college's mission statement affected the curriculum planning of the LIR. As the curriculum chairperson stated, "We really do try to have at least one course that has to do with religion or philosophy, ethics, something of that sort. And I think we've kept to that pretty much. And that's not written anywhere, we just have the feeling that we would like to do that."

The Role of HRD in Successful Small Businesses

In determining how human resource development (HRD) or training contributed to the success of small manufacturing businesses, Rowden (1994, 1995) interviewed the CEO or president, administrative assistants, sales and technical managers, line supervisors, and line workers; he observed at staff meetings and training sessions and in the plants generally, and examined company policies, memos, bulletin boards, training materials, and the like. At all three manufacturing companies, it was necessary to conduct interviews with several key people before management felt comfortable with allowing him to sit in on meetings or training sessions or to observe operations on the shop floor. Once some trust was established, however, a more integrated pattern of data collection evolved.

One of the rationales for doing this study was the paucity of information about HRD in small businesses. Most small businesses do not have an identified function or role related to training and development, nor do they think of these activities as falling within the HRD designation; hence, in surveys and other reports, small businesses often relate having no human resource development or training activities. It became Rowden's task, then, to uncover what could be construed as HRD in these companies and then connect it to their apparent success. Observation and physical evidence thus frequently offered important clues to what was actually taking place with regard to HRD and how that affected the company's success.

One example of the detective-like work involved in data collection occurred at the paint and industrial coating manufacturing company. Rowden had already been told by the president, "I'm afraid we don't do very much [HRD or training]; I which we could. We're too busy trying to keep our heads above water. Some day when we settle down a bit, I hope we can put some time and money into training our people." However, Rowden (1994) wrote:

One begins to get a sense of some of the more formal development that takes place at the company when you enter the hallway just off the reception area. No less than 11 certificates or diplomas hang on the wall attesting to the technical competence of the lab personnel. In fact, recognition of formal training and development seems to pervade the entire organization. As one might expect, college diplomas hang on the walls in the offices of the president, technical services manager, and a couple of the sales people. What one might not expect is that a large variety of certificates hang on the walls of the employee lounge. One day, during a coffee break, a line worker was asked about the large number of certificates (about 25–30) hanging on the walls. She responded:

> She [the president] is real proud of any learning that we do and wants all of us to hang our diploma here for everyone to see. Sometimes we even have a little gathering at lunch to cheer someone that has finished something. They threw a little party where they brought in fried chicken for everybody the day I got that one [pointing to a copy of her GED certificate with an obvious swelling of pride] [p. 116].

As Rowden collected and analyzed more and more data, a finding began to surface that one of the ways training functions in the success of these companies is by making sure employees are integrated into the company's particular work practices or culture. A foreman from the furniture company explained, for example, that new employees go through an initial training period where they learn "how we do things and why and stuff like that." A document in the form of a memorandum from the vice president of manufacturing to new team leaders on the plant floor was added evidence. Quoting from the memorandum, Rowden (1994) writes that the vice president "spoke of 'making sure that all of your team is on the same page' and 'so all of them know what we are trying to accomplish.' She also spoke of providing 'assistance and coaching to those who need it regarding the new finishing process.' She closed the memo by reminding the supervisors that it was their responsibility to ensure that all their workers 'were up to speed on this new team thing . . . and work with your people some more if any of them still don't understand what we want'" (p. 157).

Rowden (1994) found further support for the notion of ensuring that even outside vendors train their workers in such a way as to promulgate the company culture. At a staff meeting at the sign company, the general manager instructed the head of the vinyl department to "make sure that when the people come out to show them how to operate that new computer program that they understand we want quality over speed. Some of them think all we want is to turn it out and don't care what it looks like" (p. 160).

Finally, in a graphic example of the interactiveness and interrelatedness of data collection methods in a case study, Rowden recorded in his field notes that he had observed an employee approach a line supervisor and say something; then the two of them left the plant floor, walked out of the building, and engaged in an animated discussion in the plant yard. Later, in an informal interview with the supervisor, Rowden asked about what he had seen. The supervisor reported that

> this was a process known as "going out under the tree." He explained that anytime anyone there had a problem that they wanted to discuss and did not want to be overheard or did not want an "official" record, they could invite the manager or even coworker to "go out under the tree to talk." There everyone could feel free to speak their mind without fear of reprisal or of hurting anyone's feelings. The workers had an informal guarantee that anything said out under the tree would never be used against them" [Rowden, 1996, p. 31].

This incident from an observation, along with the explanation from the interview, provided support for Rowden's contention that open communications in this company enhanced the quality of work life, which, in turn, supported the success of these small companies.

Power Relationships in Adult Higher Education Classes

The primary mode of data collection in Tisdell's (1992, 1993) study was classroom observations of nearly all sessions of two graduate classes in counseling education. Her role was as a nonparticipant observer introduced to each class as a doctoral student studying classroom social interaction patterns. The professors whom she interviewed both at the beginning and after the end of the term knew more precisely what she was investigating. Student volunteers were interviewed after the course was completed.

In teasing out how power relations manifest themselves in classrooms, Tisdell focused on gender but was also sensitive to the interlocking systems of privilege and oppression based on other factors such as race, class, and age. The interactions involving an American-born, Asian male student—Al—is a good example. Al identified his socioeconomic class as upper class, and he was extremely bright and quick-witted. So while his minority status as Asian American might have mitigated his power as a male, his upper-class origins as well as his intelligence resulted in his wielding a lot of power in class. Tisdell observed that in all small-group exercises that involved five or more people, Al sat either at the head of the table or on the table. She quotes directly from her field notes (1992, p. 248):

> Ruth, Carol, Sarah, and Karen sat on one side of the table in the order listed. Al sat *on* the table. I ask the group if they mind if I tape their discussion. They start making a joke of being taped and Al takes the tape recorder and says, "I got it, I got it. Want me to do my Elvis?' They joke about this and then begin the exercise. Al looks down from his position on the table at the four women, and they look up at Al when they make comments. . . . [Later in the exercise] After a short pause Carol looks up at Al, and directs the following question specifically to him as opposed to the other members of the group: 'What kinds of jobs do you think your children will have?'

The after-the-course interview with the professor of the class—Charles—confirmed Tisdell's observation of Al's multiple sources of power. Charles comments, "I thought they [Al's remarks] were offensive remarks often and just kind of shallow put downs on occasion and they were very gender-based . . . the dynamic there is [Al's] intelligence. . . . I think it's the respect we give intelligent people in academia. We give them all kinds of ground, and I think they gave him a lot of time" (Tisdell, 1992, p. 251).

The course on rehabilitation counseling taught by the woman instructor reinforced society's power relationships through some of the curriculum materials and instruction. The primary textbook for the class (copyright 1987) was sprinkled with sexist language.

For example, "A typical example would be a dock worker who develops a chronic back problem. Although ordered to change occupations by *his* physician . . . " (emphasis added) (Tisdell, 1992, p. 198). On one occasion, two female guest speakers working in a private rehab setting referred to all physicians and lawyers as "he." Two videos having to do with technology for people with disabilities were shown on another occasion. From her field notes Tisdell writes:

> One of the videos put out by General Motors was about the kind of adjustments that can be made to vans so that people with disabilities, particularly those with paraplegia or quadriplegia can drive. The video itself, which was actually about how to buy a van, did feature both males and females with disabilities, although the women were surprisingly silent. Only one woman had a speaking role at all in the entire video, and this was limited to a brief remark about the use of her feet. The rest of the speaking roles included both those who actually had disabilities and those narrating or explaining the procedure to custom design a van to fit a particular person's needs, were male.

> In the second video about children with disabilities using computers as a form of communication and for educational purposes, there were no females in the video at all. All the children featured in the video were boys, and three males who apparently work teaching the children with disabilities how to use computers were featured. A woman narrated the video; her voice was heard, but she was never pictured [pp. 201–202].

In both classes, Tisdell's observations were initially guided by the syllabus. For example, in the career counseling class with the male instructor, the syllabus had a section titled "Other Issues in Vocational Psychology," wherein topics and references were listed for subgroups of women, men, and racial minorities; however, the syllabus did not indicate how and when these topics would be integrated into the class. Field notes from class sessions were analyzed to see how these topics were manifest in the class. These observations were in turn referred to directly and indirectly in interviews with the instructor and students. Tisdell writes about a class session the last week of the term in which the instructor used his children to illustrate a point. In many previous stories mentioning his children, he had referred only to his two sons; this time a daughter is mentioned. Tisdell writes in her field notes an observer comment (OC)—"I am so surprised that CW has a daughter. I have never heard anything about her before." This observation caused Tisdell to go back to her field notes and try to determine to what extent Charles identified with and reinforced the males in his class. She finds some evidence for this and asks Charles about it: "I relate to them differently in therapy. I'm pretty aware of that. (pause) Well there weren't very many women in my family heritage so women were kind of prized but I don't know, I've never . . . I grew up in a very sexist household and I've grown a lot and I've become much more gender conscious but I still have those vestiges of what I grew up with" (quoted in Tisdell, 1992, p. 215).

As I noted earlier, nonparticipant observation was Tisdell's primary source of data. However, events, interactions, and activities observed during class were linked to documents such as the course syllabus and to data gathered in the instructor and student interviews. All three sources of data converged to provide a detailed description and analysis of how the power relations of society are reinforced and challenged in the classroom.

Summary

This chapter has served to draw together the previous three chapters on interviewing, field observation, and document analysis. These three techniques are the major means of collecting data in qualitative research. And, while we may assign scientific-sounding terms to these activities, as Wolcott (1992) says, what we are talking about is systematically "watching," "asking," and "reviewing" (p. 19). In some qualitative studies there is only one source of data; in case studies all three modes of data collection are typically employed. Further, the process is generally very interactive and holistic. You observe something on-site that you then ask about in an interview; or something may come to your attention in a document that manifests itself in an observation and perhaps informal conversation in the context of the observation.

I used three comparative case studies to illustrate this interactive nature of data collection and preliminary analysis. Harris's (1995) study of the program planning process in Learning in

Retirement institutes involved heavy use of interviews and documents, followed by observations. Interviews were also the main source of data in Rowden's (1994, 1995) study of the role of human resource development in successful small businesses. Observations also yielded quite a bit of important information, followed by company documents. In contrast, Tisdell's main sources of data were her observations of class sessions. Interviews were a secondary but important source of data, as were course-related materials.

In this chapter I tried to convey the holistic, comprehensive nature of data collection in qualitative case studies. While each technique can be studied and practiced by itself, in the real world of case study research, interviewing, observing, and examining documents merge in the process of understanding and describing the phenomenon of interest.

Analyzing and Reporting Qualitative Data

Choosing a qualitative research design presupposes a certain view of the world that in turn defines how a researcher selects a sample, collects data, analyzes data, and approaches issues of validity, reliability, and ethics. Part Three consists of four chapters that address the later stages of the research process, including two chapters on analyzing qualitative data, one chapter on producing valid and reliable knowledge in an ethical manner, and one chapter on writing the qualitative study report.

The book's separate chapters on data analysis and issues of validity, reliability, and ethics may be somewhat misleading; qualitative research is not a linear, step-by-step process. Data collection and analysis is a *simultaneous* activity in qualitative research. Analysis begins with the first interview, the first observation, the first document read. Emerging insights, hunches, and tentative hypotheses direct the next phase of data collection, which in turn leads to the refinement or reformulation of questions, and so on. It is an interactive process throughout that allows the investigator to produce believable and trustworthy findings. Unlike experimental designs in which validity and reliability are accounted for before the investigation, rigor in a qualitative research derives from the researcher's presence, the nature of the interaction between researcher and participants, the triangulation of data, the interpretation of perceptions, and rich, thick description.

It follows, then, that the final report of a qualitative study will look different from the final report of a conventional research design. In comparing the rhetoric of a quantitative study and a qualitative study of the same problem, Firestone (1987) notes that different strategies are used to persuade the reader of the authenticity of the findings. "The quantitative study must convince the reader that procedures have been followed faithfully because very little concrete description of what anyone does is provided. The qualitative study provides the reader with a depiction in enough detail to show that the author's conclusion 'makes sense'" (p. 19). The qualitative study reviewed by Firestone included "telling quotes from interviews, a description of agency staffing patterns, and excerpts from agency history. . . . The details are convincing," he writes, "because they create a gestalt that makes sense to the reader" (p. 19).

In the last four chapters of this book, readers will get a sense of the *interactive* nature of data collection, analysis, and reporting. The first chapter in Part Three introduces the reader to various data analysis strategies used in qualitative research and discusses the importance of simultaneously analyzing data as they are being collected. Also presented in Chapter Eight are practical guidelines for managing the data set, including a discussion of how computer programs can facilitate both data management and analysis. Chapter Nine is also devoted to data analysis. Explored in this chapter are levels of data analysis from simple description to theory building. A large segment of the chapter describes the process of extracting meaning from the data, especially with regard to the development of categories or themes that cut across the data. The final section of Chapter Nine examines data analysis as applied to case study research.

Throughout the analysis and reporting phases of qualitative research there is a tension between "descriptive excess" (Lofland, 1971, p. 129) and coming up with "reasonable conclusions and generalizations based on a preponderance of the data" (Taylor and Bogdan, 1984, p. 139). This tension extends to issues of validity and reliability—for the more grounded in supporting detail a researcher's findings are, the more credible and trustworthy they are. Chapter Ten explores the issues of internal validity, reliability, and external validity—the extent to which the findings of a qualitative study can be applied to other situations. There has probably been more discussion and debate about generalizability than any other single aspect of qualitative research. How to think about these issues, as well as concrete strategies for ensuring the trustworthiness of qualitative research, is the focus of Chapter Ten. Equally important are the ethical concerns that pervade the entire process of qualitative research, from conceptualization of the study to dissemination of findings. These are also discussed.

The final chapter in Part Three (and the final chapter of the book) is devoted to the writing of a qualitative research report. Covered are the preparation for writing, the content of the report and issues related to that content, and the dissemination of the findings. The chapter closes with some special considerations in writing the final report of a qualitative case study.

I present the chapters in this part of the book with the awareness that detailed instructions in analyzing and reporting qualitative research, though helpful, are merely guidelines in need of interpretation and application by the single most important component in qualitative research: the investigator.

Chapter Eight

Analytic Techniques and Data Management

Preceding chapters have explained how to gather data for a qualitative study through interviews, observations, and documents. In this chapter I will discuss managing those data and analyzing them as they are being collected. The separate chapters on data analysis may be misleading because collection and analysis should be a simultaneous process in qualitative research. In fact, the timing of analysis and the integration of analysis with other tasks distinguish a qualitative design from traditional, positivistic research. A qualitative design is emergent. The researcher usually does not know ahead of time every person who might be interviewed, all the questions that might be asked, or where to look next unless data are analyzed as they are being collected. Hunches, working hypotheses, and educated guesses direct the investigator's attention to certain data and then to refining or verifying hunches. The process of data collection and analysis is recursive and dynamic. But this is not to say that the analysis is finished when all the data have been collected. Quite the opposite. Analysis becomes more intensive as the study progresses, and once all the data are in.

First, I will give brief descriptions of different strategies for data analysis and follow with a discussion of the interactive nature of data collection and analysis. The final section is devoted to data management and the role of computers in qualitative research.

Data Analysis Strategies

Historically, data analysis in qualitative research has been something like a mysterious metamorphosis. The investigator retreated with the data, applied his or her analytic powers, and emerged but-terfly-like with "findings." Only recently have a number of publi-cations been devoted to describing and explaining the process of qualitative data analysis—resources that can be of help to researchers struggling to make sense out of their data (for exam-ple, Strauss, 1987; Strauss and Corbin, 1990, Dey, 1993; Miles and Huberman, 1994; Coffey and Atkinson, 1996). Nevertheless, there is little doubt that the process is highly intuitive; a researcher can-not always explain where an insight (that may later be a finding) came from or how relationships among data were detected. The best that any book can do, including this one, is to introduce op-tions for how to proceed, delineate strategies that have worked for the author, and provide illustrative examples. The real learning can only take place in the doing. With that caveat in mind, the first section of this chapter presents brief overviews of several data anal-ysis techniques.

Some data analysis strategies are identified with different theo-retical traditions or disciplines; others have emerged as general approaches to any qualitative data. The ones selected here for dis-cussion are commonly found in educational research. They are ethnographic analysis, narrative analysis, phenomenological analy-sis, and the constant comparative method. Two lesser-used tech-niques—content analysis and analytic induction—are also discussed.

Ethnographic Analysis

As I noted earlier, an ethnographic study focuses on the culture and social regularities of everyday life. Rich, thick description is a de-fining characteristic of ethnographic studies. "The analysis task," then, "is to reach across multiple data sources (recordings, artifacts, diaries) and to condense them, with somewhat less concern for the conceptual or theoretical meaning of these observations" (Miles and Huberman, 1994, p. 8). Anthropologists sometimes make use of preexisting category schemes to organize and analyze their data. The *Outline of Cultural Materials* developed by Murdock (Murdock and others, 1982) lists nearly eighty descriptive categories, each with up to nine subcategories by which readers can code data. This is a particularly useful scheme for comparing different cultures. Lofland and Lofland (1995) also suggest categories and subcategories for organizing aspects of society. Their four broad categories deal with (1) the economy; (2) demographics such as social class, sex, ethnicity, and race; (3) "basic situations of human life" (p. 104), including family, education, and health care; and (4) the environment, both "natural" and "built" (p. 104).

While *educational* ethnographies may make use of these category schemes, more often a classification scheme is derived from the data themselves. The scheme can employ terms commonly found in the culture itself (an emic perspective) or terms constructed by the ethnographer (an etic perspective). If the topics or variables within the scheme are seen to be interrelated, a typology may be created. *Typologizing* is defined by Lofland and Lofland (1995) as "the process of charting the possibilities that result from the conjunction of two or more variables" (p. 126, emphasis in original). Tesch (1990) elaborates on how relationships in the data can be displayed: "These relationships are often depicted in diagrams, such as grids or other structured boxes, outline- or tree-shaped taxonomies, . . . flow charts, decision tables, overlapping circles, starburst charts (with one term in the center and the related terms around the periphery), causal chains or networks, or anything else the researcher can invent" (p. 82). In an ethnographic study, these classification systems or "cognitive maps" (Werner and Schoepfle, 1987, p. 24) are used to order data regarding sociocultural patterns. Comparing elements within a classification system can lead to tentative hypotheses and explanations.

Narrative Analysis

At the heart of narrative analysis is "the ways humans experience the world" (Connelly and Clandinin, 1990, p. 2). As a research technique, the study of experience is through stories. Emphasis is on the stories people tell and on how these stories are communicated—on the language used to tell the stories. As Johnson-Bailey and Cervero (1996) note in their narrative analysis of reentry black women, as these women told their stories, "every utterance, even repetitions and noises" (p. 145), was regarded as part of the data to be analyzed.

First-person accounts of experience form the narrative "text" of this research approach. Whether the account is in the form of autobiography, life history, interview, journal, letters, or other materials that we collect "as we compose our lives" (Clandinin and Connelly, 1994, p. 420), the text is analyzed using the techniques of a particular discipline or perspective. Sociological and sociolinguistic models of narrative analysis emphasize the structure of the narrative and its relationship to the social context. "The processes of understanding, recalling and summarizing stories" (Cortazzi, 1993, p. 100)—in short, memory—characterizes the psychological approach. Anthropologists would be interested in how story narratives vary across cultures, as well as in "the cultural patterning of customs, beliefs, values, performance and social contexts of narration" (Cortazzi, 1993, p. 100). Literary models emphasize grammar, syntax, narration, and plot structure. In addition, ideological perspectives such as those embodied in feminist theory, critical theory, and postmodernism can be used to interpret life history narratives. Depending on the researcher, any of these frames can be applied to educational processes and situations (see Cortazzi, 1993; Hatch and Wisniewski, 1995; Josselson and Lieblich, 1995). As Coffey and Atkinson (1996) observe, "there are no formulae or recipes for the 'best' way to analyze the stories we elicit and collect. Indeed, one of the strengths of thinking about our data as narrative is that this opens up the possibilities for a variety of analytic strategies" (p. 80).

Phenomenological Analysis

Lodged as it is in the philosophy of phenomenology (see Chapter One), this type of analysis attends to ferreting out the essence or basic structure of a phenomenon. Several specific techniques—such as epoche, bracketing, imaginative variation, first- and second-order knowledge, and so on—are used to analyze experience. *Epoche,* for example, is the process "the researcher engages in to remove, or at least become aware of prejudices, viewpoints or assumptions regarding the phenomenon under investigation. . . . This suspension of judgment is critical in phenomenological investigation and requires the setting aside of the researcher's personal viewpoint in order to see the experience for itself" (Katz, 1987, p. 37). Imaginative variation has to do with trying to see the object of study—the phenomenon—from several different angles or perspectives. As Moustakas (1990, pp. 97–98) explains, "the task of Imaginative Variation is to seek possible meanings through the utilization of imagination, varying the frames of reference, employing polarities and reversals, and approaching the phenomenon from divergent perspectives, different positions, roles, or functions. The aim is to arrive at structural descriptions of an experience, the underlying and precipitating factors that account for what is being experienced. . . . How did the experience of the phenomenon come to be what it is?" A version of phenomenological analysis is called *heuristic inquiry* (Moustakas, 1990). Heuristic inquiry is even more personalized than phenomenological inquiry in that the researcher includes an analysis of his or her own experience as part of the data.

The Constant Comparative Method

The constant comparative method of data analysis was developed by Glaser and Strauss (1967) as the means of developing grounded theory. A grounded theory consists of categories, properties, and hypotheses that are the conceptual links between and among the categories and properties. Because the basic strategy of the constant comparative method is compatible with the inductive, concept-building orientation of all qualitative research, the constant comparative method of data analysis has been adopted by many researchers who are not seeking to build substantive theory.

The basic strategy of the method is to do just what its name implies—constantly compare. The researcher begins with a particular incident from an interview, field notes, or document and compares it with another incident in the same set of data or in another set. These comparisons lead to tentative categories that are then compared to each other and to other instances. Comparisons are constantly made within and between levels of conceptualization until a theory can be formulated.

The constant comparative method of data analysis will be explained in detail in the next chapter.

Content Analysis and Analytic Induction

Two less common data analysis techniques in qualitative research are content analysis and analytic induction. To some extent, both of these techniques are used implicitly in any inductive analysis of qualitative data. In one sense, all qualitative data analysis is content analysis in that it is the *content* of interviews, field notes, and documents that is analyzed. Although this content can be analyzed qualitatively for themes and recurring patterns of meaning, content analysis historically has been very quantitative in nature. Manning and Cullum-Swan (1994, p. 464) define its historical use as "a quantitatively oriented technique by which standardized measurements are applied to metrically define units and these are used to characterize and compare documents." The units of measurement in this form of content analysis center on communication, especially the frequency and variety of messages. In its adoption for use in qualitative studies, the communication of meaning is the focus. Analysis is inductive: "Although categories and 'variables' initially guide the study, others are allowed and expected to emerge throughout the study" (Altheide, 1987, p. 68). Essentially, quantitative content analysis looks for insights in which "situations, settings, styles, images, meanings and nuances are key topics" (Altheide, 1987, p. 68). The process involves the simultaneous coding of raw data and the construction of categories that capture relevant characteristics of the document's content.

Analytic induction, also called discrepant- or negative-case analysis (Kidder, 1981a), has its roots in sociology (Robinson, 1951; Katz, 1983; Denzin, 1978). Essentially, the process is one of continual refinement of hypotheses as the researcher finds instances that do not match the original hypothesis. Eventually a hypothesis evolves that explains all known cases of the phenomenon. The object is to achieve a perfect fit between the hypothesis and the data. In its purest form, analytic induction is a rigorous process of successively testing each new incident or case against the most recently formulated hypothesis or explanation of the phenomenon under study. The basic steps in the process are as follows (from Robinson, 1951):

- You begin your study with a tentative hypothesis or explanation of the phenomenon under study.
- You purposefully select an instance of the phenomenon to see if the hypothesis fits the case.
- If it does not fit the hypothesis, you reformulate the hypothesis; if it fits the hypothesis, you select additional cases to test against the hypothesis.

- You purposefully seek cases that apparently do not fit the explanation as formulated (negative or discrepant cases); "the discovery of one negative case disproves the explanation and requires a reformulation" (Borg and Gall, 1989, p. 405).
- The process continues until the reformulation covers all cases studied or no negative cases can be found.

While analytic induction in its most rigorous form is not often employed in qualitative research, the idea of testing tentative explanations (or hypotheses) in ongoing data collection is used.

Analysis During Data Collection

Picture yourself sitting down at the dining room table, ready to begin analyzing data for your modest qualitative study. In one pile to your left are three hundred or so pages of transcripts of interviews. In the middle of the table is a stack of field notes from your on-site observations, and to the right of that is a box of documents you collected, thinking they might be relevant to the study. You review what the purpose of your study is and questions that guided the inquiry. Now what do you do? Where do you start? How do you come up with say, twenty or even thirty pages of findings from hundreds of pages of data? You begin by reading a transcript, and then another. You realize you should have asked the second participant something that came up in the first interview. You quickly feel overwhelmed; you begin to feel that you are literally drowning in the data. It is doubtful that you will be able to come up with any findings. You have undermined your entire project by waiting until *after* all the data are collected before beginning analysis.

In a more enlightened scenario, you sit down at the dining room table with nothing more than the transcript of your first interview, or the field notes from your first observation, or the first document you collected. You review the purpose of your study. You read and reread the data, making notes in the margins to comment on the data. You write a separate memo to yourself capturing your reflections, tentative themes, hunches, ideas, and things to pursue that are derived from this first set of data. You note things you want to ask, observe, or look for in your next data collection activity. After your second interview, you compare the first set of data with the second.

This comparison informs the next data collected, and so on. Months later, as you sit down to analyze and write up your findings, you have a set of tentative categories or themes—answers to your research questions from which to work. You are organizing and refining rather than beginning data analysis.

Data analysis is one of the few facets, perhaps the only facet, of doing qualitative research in which there is a right way and a wrong way. As illustrated in the scenario just described, the right way to analyze data in a qualitative study is to do it *simultaneously* with data collection. At the outset of a qualitative study, the investigator knows what the problem is and has selected a sample to collect data in order to address the problem. But the researcher does not know what will be discovered, what or whom to concentrate on, or what the final analysis will be like. The final product is shaped by the data that are collected and the analysis that accompanies the entire process. Without ongoing analysis, the data can be unfocused, repetitious, and overwhelming in the sheer volume of material that needs to be processed. Data that have been analyzed while being collected are both parsimonious and illuminating.

Simultaneous data collection and analysis occurs both in and out of the field. That is, you can be doing some rudimentary analysis while you are in the process of collecting data, as well as between data collection activities as illustrated in the second scenario. Bogdan and Biklen (1992) offer ten helpful suggestions for analyzing data as they are being collected.

1. Force yourself to make decisions that narrow the study. "You must discipline yourself not to pursue everything . . . or else you are likely to wind up with data too diffuse and inappropriate for what you decide to do. The more data you have on a given topic, setting, or subjects, the easier it will be to think deeply about it and the more productive you are likely to be when you attempt the final analysis" (p. 155).

2. Force yourself to make decisions concerning the type of study you want to conduct. "You should try to make clear in your own mind, for example, whether you want to do a full description of a setting or whether you are interested in generating theory about a particular aspect of it" (p. 155).

3. Develop analytic questions. "Some researchers bring general questions to a study. These are important because they give

focus to data collection and help organize it as you proceed. . . . We suggest that shortly after you enter the field, you assess which questions you brought with you are relevant and which ones should be reformulated to direct your work" (p. 155).

4. Plan data collection sessions according to what you find in previous observations. "In light of what you find when you periodically review your field notes, plan to pursue specific leads in your next data collection session" (p. 157).

5. Write many "observer's comments" as you go. "The idea is to stimulate critical thinking about what you see and to become more than a recording machine" (p. 158).

6. Write memos to yourself about what you are learning. "These memos can provide a time to reflect on issues raised in the setting and how they relate to larger theoretical, methodological, and substantive issues" (p. 159).

7. Try out ideas and themes on subjects. "While not everyone should be asked, and while not all you hear may be helpful, key informants, under the appropriate circumstances, can help advance your analysis, especially to fill in the holes of description" (p. 161).

8. Begin exploring literature while you are in the field. "After you have been in the field for a while, going through the substantive literature in the area you are studying will enhance analysis" (p. 161). This reading "should provide you with stimulation rather than be a substitute for thinking" (p. 162).

9. Play with metaphors, analogies, and concepts. "Nearsightedness plagues most research. . . . Ask the question, 'What does this remind me of?'" (p. 162). "Another way to expand analytic horizons is to try to raise concrete relations and happenings observed in a particular setting to a higher level of abstraction" (p. 163).

10. Use visual devices. Trying to visualize what you are learning about the phenomenon can bring clarity to your analysis. Such representations can range from "primitive doodling" to sophisticated computer-generated models (p. 164).

Data collection and analysis is indeed an ongoing process that can extend indefinitely. There is almost always another person who could be interviewed, another observation that could be conducted, another document to be reviewed. When should you stop this phase of the investigation and begin intensive data analysis?

How do you know when you have collected enough data? The answer depends on some very practical as well as theoretical concerns. Practically, you may have depleted the time and money allocated to the project or run out of mental and physical energy. Ideally, the decision will be based more on the following criteria:

> *Exhaustion of sources* (although sources may be recycled and tapped multiple times); *saturation of categories* (continuing data collection produces tiny increments of new information in comparison to the effort expended to get them); *emergence of regularities*—the sense of "integration" (although care must be exercised to avoid a false conclusion occasioned by regularities occurring at a more simplistic level than the inquirer should accept); and *over-extension*—the sense that new information being unearthed is very far removed from the core of any of the viable categories that have emerged (and does not contribute usefully to the emergence of additional viable categories) [Lincoln and Guba, 1985, p. 350].

Managing Your Data

Some system for organizing and managing data needs to be devised early in your study. This involves coding, a term that has unfortunately further mystified the already mysterious process of data analysis. Coding is nothing more than assigning some sort of shorthand designation to various aspects of your data so that you can easily retrieve specific pieces of the data. The designations can be single words, letters, numbers, phrases, or combinations of these. Coding occurs at two levels—identifying information about the data and interpretive constructs related to analysis. The coding scheme can be quite simple, as in identifying a theme that can be illustrated with numerous incidents, quotes, and so on. Or it can be quite complex, with multilevels of coding for each incident (Strauss, 1987; Strauss and Corbin, 1990).

With regard to the first level of coding, each interview, set of field notes, and document needs identifying notations so that you can access them as needed in both the analysis and the write-up of your findings. This basic organization is easy to overlook, because at the time you are collecting some data, you will feel there is no way you could ever forget where and when an incident took place or the characteristics of the person you just interviewed. However, ten interviews later you are quite likely to have forgotten identifying characteristics of your earlier participants. Months later you will have forgotten quite a bit about all of your data. Hence, as you collect your data it is important to code it according to whatever scheme is relevant to your study. For example, in the study of how HIV-positive young adults make sense of their diagnosis (Courtenay, Merriam, and Reeves, forthcoming), each interview was coded with a pseudonym and the age, sex, race, family, and employment status of the participant, along with the date when first diagnosed. This allowed the researchers to access a particular interview transcript or to pull out several transcripts from the total set on any of the above dimensions or combinations of dimensions—women diagnosed less than three years ago, for example.

You also need to keep track of your thoughts, musings, speculations, and hunches as you engage in analysis. This kind of information might be interwoven with your raw data (as in observer comments in field notes), or it may be in separate files or memos. This information is actually rudimentary analysis, and you will need to access it to build on as you move between the emerging analysis and the raw data of interviews, field notes, and documents. More intensive analysis of the data can involve complex coding schemes. Dey (1993) points out that one of the problems with the term *coding* is the "rather mechanical overtone quite at odds with the conceptual tasks involved in categorizing data. This arises from the association of coding with a . . . set of rules governing the assignment of codes to data, thereby eliminating error and of course allowing recovery of the original data simply by reversing the process (i.e. decoding). Qualitative analysis, in contrast, requires the analyst to create or adapt concepts relevant to the data rather than to apply a set of pre-established rules" (p. 58). He warns that while "we may retain 'coding' as a term for replacing full category names by brief symbols, . . . we should not confuse this with the analytic process of creating and assigning the categories themselves" (p. 58).

You can of course, do all of this organizing by hand, and some qualitative researchers do. Another option for managing your data is to use a computer software program designed for qualitative research. A third option is a mix of manual and computer management. At the very least, transcripts and field notes will most likely have been transcribed, and the hard copy will have a computer file backup. Several word processing programs are sophisticated enough to be adapted to data management. Indeed, both the accessibility and popularity of computers in qualitative research is growing. The following section provides an overview of the possibilities, strengths, and limitations of computers in qualitative research.

Computers and Qualitative Data

The computer has a great capacity for organizing massive amounts of data, as well as facilitating communication among members of a research team. For example, data can be sent directly from an observation site to a central location where other researchers can read the field notes and compare them with their own. Ongoing analysis can be conducted among several researchers almost simultaneously through the use of computers. And by putting data on disks, "we are creating new databases that have the potential to be easily accessible and usable for secondary analysis. This could not only increase the reliability of our studies, but allow a whole new level of secondary analysis. Data from several different field projects could be compared easily" (Conrad and Reinharz, 1984, p. 8).

The use of computers in qualitative data analysis has increased dramatically in recent years. Whether the researcher is working collaboratively or individually, the computer has facilitated data management to the point that a researcher has a choice of programs designed for this purpose. However, as qualitative researchers grope for appropriate software tools to facilitate the research process, it is important to keep in mind that software programs offer real advantages in terms of speed and support for the research process, but they may also shape it in unanticipated ways.

This section provides a general introduction to computer-assisted qualitative research. First, I will provide an overview of the purposes for which software may be used in qualitative research and follow with a discussion of the types of programs currently available to support these purposes. Programs fall into two main divisions: standard commercial software adapted to support qualitative research, and programs specifically developed with qualitative research in mind. After discussing the software, I will summarize concerns about the impact of its use—concerns already identified by a number of researchers. Predictions about future developments for researchers considering the use of software will conclude the section.

Data Management and Theory Building

Whether a researcher is adapting a standard commercial program to qualitative research or using a program developed specifically for that purpose, data management is likely to be the first concern. Reid (1992) divides data management into three phases: data preparation, data identification, and data manipulation. Data preparation involves typing notes, transcribing interviews, and otherwise entering the data from which the researcher will be working. In addition, it might include minor editing or formatting. Its purpose is merely to create a clean record from which to work. Often, a standard word processor is the software of choice for this phase, even if the data are later to be used in conjunction with another program (Reid, 1992; Richards and Richards, 1994; Stanley and Temple, 1995; Weitzman and Miles, 1995). Data identification is intended "to divide text data into analytically meaningful and easily locatable segments" (Reid, 1992, p. 126). During data manipulation, these segments may be searched for, sorted, retrieved, and rearranged. Tesch (1990) discusses specific computer functions related to these research mechanics.

Reid stresses that the computer does not analyze qualitative data, it only manages it (p. 127). However, data management is no small aspect of analysis. First, it is difficult to cleanly separate "data management" from "data analysis" in qualitative research. For example, *code-and-retrieve* is a commonly used approach (both with and without computer assistance), corresponding to the phases that Reid calls *data identification* and *data manipulation*. Coding involves labeling passages of text according to content, and retrieving is providing a means to collect similarly labeled passages (Richards and Richards, 1994). As Thomas and Lyn Richards point out, this process is the beginning of theory building: even deciding on categories (codes) involves decisions about what concepts and ideas are being developed and explored (Richards and Richards, 1994).

Second, simply making this function less tedious provides new avenues for analysis. The development of the spreadsheet provides a useful comparison. Initially, it served as a glorified calculator that ran computations automatically. However, simply making calculations easier permitted the user to run multiple "what if" scenarios, exploring the results of different assumptions. Examples of scenarios include, If the mortgage rate were 1 percent higher but the down payment were lower, how would overall costs be affected? And, How about .5 percent lower, with double the down payment? Inspecting these scenarios provided a powerful decision-making tool that was created as a result of simply automating a previously tedious process. Automating tedious aspects of qualitative analysis will no doubt result in similar breakthroughs in the ways we examine data and observe the possible links and connections among the different pieces.

Thus it is not surprising that the second major development in computer software for qualitative research is software developed for the specific purpose of exploring data in support of theory emergence. For the most part, current software is developed by qualitative researchers who also program (or have associates who do), and it incorporates functions they believe support the emergence of theory, such as indexing systems and sophisticated search patterns.

However, the potential of filtering rules, expert systems, and artificial intelligence is just beginning to be considered and applied, with a mingling of hope and wariness (Hesse-Biber, 1995; Mangabeira, 1995; Richards and Richards, 1994; Weitzman and Miles, 1995). Researchers are using computer tools to explore theory building, hypothesis examination, and triangulation in new ways (Araujo, 1995; Dey, 1995; Hesse-Biber and Dupuis, 1995; Huber, 1995; Kelle and others, 1995; Kuckartz, 1995; Prein, Kelle, Richards, and Richards, 1995; Prein and others, 1995; Ragin, 1995; Richards and Richards, 1995; Roller, Mathes, and Eckert, 1995; Sibert and Shelly, 1995). This is an emerging area, filled with great possibilities and concerns.

Before discussing these concerns and potentials in depth, a brief description of current programs and their uses is in order.

Overview of Programs

This section will not attempt to review software in detail. However, some general observations will be valid, even when the details of the programs change.

Two major types of software can be considered in computer-assisted qualitative research. The first is standard office software—word processors, databases, and the like—that users adapt to qualitative research, often developing their own idiosyncratic working methods through trial and error. These software products have a number of advantages. They are readily available, they are produced and tested to commercial standards, and they are familiar enough to have minimal learning curves. However, they are not specifically designed with qualitative research in mind, and they lack some desirable features, which I will discuss in more detail later in the chapter.

Applications specifically designed to support the qualitative research process are the second type of software to consider. There is a wide range; each program has features that its designer felt essential to qualitative research. These features are the primary advantages of these packages. Disadvantages include usability issues common to products with limited audiences (for example, poor interface design that makes access to functionality difficult), lack of compatibility with other commercial programs, and steep learning curves.

Office Software

Word processors such as WordPerfect or Microsoft Word are probably the most familiar of the "office software" programs. This very familiarity makes them the first choice of many qualitative researchers. In fact, the strengths of a standard word processor are often unmatched in more specialized software, particularly in the area of text editing features. Whatever the specific program, certain functions can be expected, including line numbering, word searching, search and replace, and the ability to check spelling and create macros (keyboard shortcuts that initiate a longer sequence of actions). Stanley and Temple (1995) outline a working procedure for word processors, and Reid (1992) provides a number of step-by-step descriptions of rather advanced data management techniques that can be accomplished with word processors using only the most basic functions. More advanced features such as foot-noting, annotating, indexing, hypertext linking, and embedding graphic and media files extend the capability of word processing features (Richards and Richards, 1994).

However, the current generation of word processors have their limitations. Their search functions are not suited to enormous files or to large numbers of codes. In addition, today's word processors cannot search for combinations of data characteristics. A major weakness of word processors is their inability to perform Boolean searches to isolate specific instances of multiple conditions. They also do not provide strong management tools to track assigned data characteristics (such as codes), or support any quasi-statistical functions that may be needed (Reid, 1992; Richards and Richards, 1994; Stanley and Temple, 1995; Weitzman and Miles, 1995). If these features are essential, it may be wise to examine other software choices.

Other commercial software sometimes adapted for qualitative research needs are databases, hypertext programs, and some design software with linking capabilities. Several authors discuss how these programs might be used (Richards and Richards, 1994; Weitzman and Miles, 1995). These programs are less familiar than word processors to most people, and it may be as difficult to explore their capabilities and adapt them to qualitative research as to learn a program dedicated to qualitative research.

Qualitative Software

The number of software programs specifically designed for qualitative research has burgeoned in recent years, especially since the advent of the personal computer. Awareness of these programs is also on the rise; even researchers unfamiliar with the use of *The Ethnograph, QUALPRO, NUDIST,* and so on, recognize the names. Since the diversity of qualitative research software reflects the methodological diversity of qualitative research itself (Tesch, 1990), the difficulty for most researchers is in selecting the most appropriate program or programs to learn. Unfortunately, at this point in software evolution there is no ideal package that incorporates most of the capabilities, or even a standard array of features. In addition to variation in functionality, there is a wide range in the flexibility and user-friendliness of the systems.

Fortunately, reviews of programs are also becoming readily available, and these reviews usually address the methodological roots of a program as well as detailing its functional strengths and weaknesses (Prein, Kelle, and Bird, 1995; Tesch, 1990; Weitzman and Miles, 1995). Tesch's (1990) text is a classic example, almost evenly divided between descriptions of specific programs and an insightful analysis of qualitative methods that provides the foundation for her software evaluations. Building on Tesch's work, Weitzman and Miles (1995) provide a comprehensive review of qualitative software. In addition to consulting resources such as these, one might also contact the software developers for updated information and demos (if available) and interview colleagues about their reactions to these products.

As well as providing specific product reviews on a large number of programs, Weitzman and Miles (1995) also pose a thoughtful and comprehensive list of considerations to help narrow the range of choices. Before selecting a qualitative program with which to work, it would be a good idea to assess your own theoretical orientation, the types of data and projects with which you expect to work, and your resources—not to mention your computer skills. Other authors also discuss issues to be considered before selecting software (Fielding and Lee, 1995; Stanley and Temple, 1995). A number of researchers have even provided accounts of firsthand experience with some of these programs, describing their successes, frustrations, lessons learned in practice, and in some cases, assessments of the impact of the software on analysis (Armstrong, 1995; LeCompte, Preissle, and Tesch, 1993; Lee and Fielding, 1995; Mangabeira, 1995; Richards, 1995; Sprokkereef, Lakin, Pole, and Burgess, 1995; Stanley and Temple, 1995; Weaver and Atkinson, 1995). These accounts are particularly instructive if you are contemplating using one of the programs described.

Many reviewers categorize software programs in conceptually useful ways. Weitzman and Miles (1995) loosely divide the twenty-four programs they reviewed into five family clusters: text-retrievers, textbase managers, code-and-retrieval programs, code-based theory-builders, and conceptual network-builders. The word *loosely* is applied because the authors acknowledge that most programs are a blend of these general types (p. 16). Richards and Richards use a similar, but not identical, system: code-and-retrieval software, rule-based theory-building systems, logic-based systems, index-based systems, and conceptual network systems (Richards and Richards, 1994). Yet another categorization is built around task structures: data preparation and storage; segmenting, coding, and collating; establishing linkages; and transferal and display (LeCompte, Preissle, and Tesch, 1993).

Each of these categorizations is an attempt to broadly define certain types of functionality now available in different software programs designed for qualitative data analysis. Text-retrievers, textbase managers, and code-and-retrieval programs all focus on the aspects that Reid (1992) would characterize as data management: entry, organization, and manipulation of data. It can be argued that these programs merely automate the "cut-and-paste" techniques familiar to many researchers. However, as Weitzman and Miles (1995) point out, this automation offers distinct advantages: "Code-and-retrieve programs—even the weakest of them—are a quantum leap forward from the old scissors-and-paper approach: They're more systematic, more thorough, less likely to miss things, more flexible, and much, much faster" (p. 18). These functions provide a useful aid to theory building, but the special features and routines in the programs they have designated as "code-based theory builders" and "conceptual network-builders" go even further. Their range of capabilities may help the user make connections between codes to develop higher-level categorizations, or support the development or testing of propositions (Araujo, 1995; Dey, 1995; Hesse-Biber and Dupuis, 1995; Huber, 1995; Kelle and Laurie, 1995; Kuckartz, 1995; Prein, Kelle, Richards, and Richards, 1995; Prein and others, 1995; Ragin, 1995; Richards and Richards, 1995; Roller, Mathes, and Eckert, 1995; Sibert and Shelly, 1995; Weitzman and Miles, 1995).

Ironically, these very capabilities concern many researchers. The next section discusses some of the concerns that researchers have identified related to the use of computer-assisted qualitative research.

Issues in the Use of Qualitative Software

Concerns about the use of computers to assist in the analysis of qualitative data have been expressed by many authors, even those who strongly support such use (Agar, 1991; Akeroyd, 1991; Allatt and Benson, 1991; Cordingley, 1991; Fielding and Lee, 1995; Hesse-Biber, 1995; LeCompte, Preissle, and Tesch, 1993; Kelle and Laurie, 1995; Lonkila, 1995; Lee and Fielding, 1991; Mangabeira, 1995; Pfaffenberger, 1988; Richards, 1995; Richards and Richards, 1991, 1994; Seidel, 1991; Seidel and Kelle, 1995; Stanley and Temple, 1995; Tesch, 1990; Weitzman and Miles, 1995). Some of the concerns focus simply on practical issues common to any computer application: how to choose the best program, what trade-offs exist between ease of use and the power of the program; portability of data to and from other programs and across platforms, and so on. However, deeper concerns surround the relationship of this new tool to the process of research itself: How will computer-assisted qualitative research differ from research designs that do not involve computers? What unintended and possibly undesirable consequences accompany the capabilities these programs offer?

The most frequently mentioned concerns fall into several broad categories: that the tools will warp qualitative research or change its nature; that they will distance the researcher from the data or introduce errors; and that they will be used inappropriately. Each of these concerns is discussed more fully in the next section.

Software tools will shape a researcher's choice of methods; those easy to do on the computer will be chosen over those difficult to do. They may impose a certain set of procedures, a chronology, or an undesirable rigidity of approach. They may blur the lines between quantitative and qualitative in an unacceptable manner. Developers may fail to understand the range of demands in different approaches to qualitative research, building tools that are either too limiting or that invite overemphasis on one form of exploration. Freidheim (1984) also notes the potentially "serious cost of electronic filing" (p. 95), if the file management system determines the choice of topic or type of analysis. There is also the danger of curtailing data analysis, if all the information is filed neatly on disks rather than on pieces of paper in front of the investigator. Finally, by having to determine a data filing system early on, category construction or theory building may be brought to closure prematurely (Freidheim, 1984).

The second issue is that computer use may distance the user from the data. This can occur either because the program representations of data make it difficult to discern context or because it creates abstractions that lose important detail. Because the computer can automate large-scale changes, multiple errors may be introduced, perhaps resulting in data distortions that go undetected by the user. (On the other hand, the computer can allow greater simultaneous access to multiple data points and thus increase the ability to make connections.) Lyman (1984) also points out that the writing and reading of field notes is an intimate process that is often self-revelatory. Introducing a computer into the process interjects a different medium and thus a different relationship between the researcher and the data. This new relationship is more mechanical and impersonal, perhaps blocking insight that might otherwise emerge. Some of the richness of qualitative data may also be lost if the researcher begins substituting technical language and quantification for description and metaphor.

There is also the concern that the unthinking or inappropriate application of computer tools will result in poor research. Tesch (1990) worries that facility with computers may tempt researchers to "design the entire analysis process around the functions a computer makes available" (p. 303). Information about how programs work and the impact they have on research is not always available. If users do not sufficiently conceptualize the interaction between their analysis and the program, they may be prone to naive, unthinking application of the tool. Since novices may be particularly prone to this error, determining how and when to teach the use of these tools is a further consideration.

Two additional concerns are also emerging as researchers experiment with existing software. The first involves a heightened awareness of the ethics of participant privacy, given the power of this medium (Akeroyd, 1991). The second relates to how use of this software affects research teams, particularly when levels of research knowledge and computer literacy do not coincide (Richards, 1995; Sprokkereef, Lakin, Pole, and Burgess, 1995; Weitzman and Miles, 1995).

These are not lightweight issues: tools do shape tasks. The old proverb "If all you have is a hammer, everything looks like a nail" applies to computer-assisted hammers as well as standard ones. At the same time, a researcher risks becoming a Luddite by rejecting powerful tools out of hand. The most productive approach is to articulate and discuss concerns, to observe research results in practice, and to continue to thoughtfully assess the impact of these new tools. Researchers who plan to use software should identify their criteria for software selection, maintain a critical awareness of the effects of those tools in use, and report their influences, just as study limitations are now reported. Fortunately, pioneers in the area of computer-assisted qualitative research are setting a positive example in their critical reflection on the interactions of these tools and the research process (Akeroyd, 1991; Allatt and Benson, 1991; Araujo, 1995; Cordingly, 1991; Dey, 1995; Fielding and Lee, 1995; Hesse-Biber and Dupuis, 1995; Huber, 1995; Kelle, 1995; Kelle and Laurie, 1995; Kelle and others, 1995; Kuckartz, 1995; Lonkila, 1995; Prein, Kelle, Richards, and Richards, 1995; Prein and others, 1995; Ragin, 1995; Richards and Richards, 1995; Roller, Mathes, and Eckert, 1995; Seidel and Kelle, 1995; Sibert and Shelly, 1995).

New Developments

Wish lists of characteristics that researchers would like to see in future iterations of qualitative research programs are long. They include multitasking, improved coding and chunking abilities, improved ability to handle both qualitative and quantitative research from the same cases, multimedia annotation tools, improved coordination with other software programs, better orientation to the data, more powerful search and retrieval functions, easy audit trail creation, accommodation of related factual information not contained in the original text, and improved support for collaboration among members of a research team (Agar, 1991; Cordingley, 1991; Richards and Richards, 1994; Weitzman and Miles, 1995). Weitzman and Miles link additional recommendations to different qualitative research approaches and to different needs for data display (Weitzman and Miles, 1995). Overall, there is consensus that the array of current software is still uneven; useful features found in one program may be unavailable in another. One often-repeated wish is for a technological baseline—a standard array of basic features common to all qualitative software.

This wish will probably be realized as the qualitative software market matures. At this point, the proliferation of diverse software is typical of the early stages of technological development, when needs and capabilities are still being identified. Moore summarizes this basic marketing model and adds salient observations about the characteristics of the target market at different points in the cycle (Moore, 1991). In the introductory stage in a standard marketing cycle for technical products, multiple products are created, each with unique characteristics. As the market develops, these products will copy one another's strengths; at the same time, the number of products available will be reduced. For qualitative software this stage is already beginning; the clusters or families into which different reviewers divide the programs they discuss mark a certain level of merging and overlapping functionality. As these programs build on their successes and incorporate each others' best features, some of them will fall by the wayside. In a fully mature market, two or three well-developed products can be expected that will have similar functionalities (such as WordPerfect and Microsoft Word) and that leap-frog each other in terms of added features. This is, of course, assuming that the market does mature; a certain level of acceptance and diffusion is necessary to support continuing software development. As Tesch (1990) warns, "As long as qualitative researchers are reluctant to use the programs, only a few enthusiasts will continue to provide them. Any expectations about improvements or even breakthroughs in the future are likely to be foiled" (p. 304). A critical mass of acceptance is required for any innovation to succeed (Rogers, 1995).

According to Moore, at each stage of development, user expectations of the software will evolve as the product matures. In the introductory phase, the only people who can even attempt to use these products are technically sophisticated; they like technology, enjoy solving technical problems, and thus will tolerate software problems that less technically oriented users would not. The next group is less enchanted by the technology than the results it offers. They are less engaged in solving software problems but still patient with them. After all, they are involved in cutting-edge development, and that is part of the price a researcher must pay to be a leader.

In sharp contrast, the next group, the early mainstream, expects thoroughly tested and reliable software. Though they may be as technologically sophisticated as earlier groups, their attitude differs. They are primarily interested in getting a job done, and they want functional tools to do it with. They also expect user support for any problems they have. Many technological products fail to make the transition to this audience's expectations.

At later points in the cycle, late adopters and laggards have even higher expectations of product stability, ease of use, and support—and less understanding of the program's strengths and limitations. They are often resistant to technology, use it reluctantly, and are therefore less able to make critical assessments about it.

This model traces a common pattern in software development. Though this is not the only possible path, it is a likely scenario as more and more researchers embrace computer-assisted qualitative research. Understanding the phase that computer-assisted qualitative research is in will help in identifying the concerns and challenges facing the field as it evolves.

Summary

Beginning data analysis involves considering first the different strategies available to the qualitative researcher. In this chapter I have briefly reviewed several such strategies—ethnographic analysis, narrative analysis, phenomenological analysis, the constant comparative method, content analysis, and analytic induction. Resources were also cited for those interested in pursuing any of these options in more depth.

Getting started in data analysis also involves the recognition that it is best done in conjunction with data collection. A rich and meaningful analysis of the data will not be possible if analysis is begun after all data are collected. Further, the chances of a researcher being overwhelmed and rendered impotent by the sheer magnitude of data in a qualitative study will be greatly reduced if analysis begins early.

Finally, a researcher must consider how to organize and manage the voluminous amount of data typical of most qualitative studies. A discussion of data management included the role computers can play in both data management and data analysis.

Chapter Nine

Levels of Analysis

Data analysis is the process of making sense out of the data. And making sense out of data involves consolidating, reducing, and interpreting what people have said and what the researcher has seen and read—it is the process of making meaning. Data analysis is a complex process that involves moving back and forth between concrete bits of data and abstract concepts, between inductive and deductive reasoning, between description and interpretation. These meanings or understandings or insights constitute the *findings* of a study. Findings can be in the form of organized descriptive accounts, themes, or categories that cut across the data, or in the form of models and theories that explain the data. Each of these forms reflects different analytical levels, ranging from dealing with the concrete in simple description to high-level abstractions in theory construction.

The first section of this chapter focuses on data analysis related to descriptive accounts, category construction, and theory building. These levels of analysis occur in case study research as well as other types of qualitative research. However, multiple or comparative case study research has its own "levels" in the sense that there is "within-case" data analysis as well as "cross-case" analysis. The last section of this chapter is a discussion of data analysis in case study research.

Levels of Analysis

The most basic presentation of a study's findings is a descriptive account; even that description requires thinking through what will be included and what will be left out from the hundreds of pages of data collected for the study. Data are compressed and linked together in a narrative that conveys the meaning the researcher has derived from studying the phenomenon. While description is an important component of all forms of qualitative research, few studies are limited to this level of analysis. LeCompte and Preissle (1993), for example, believe that ethnographers who "simply describe what they saw . . . fail to do justice to their data. By leaving readers to draw their own conclusions, researchers risk misinterpretation. Their results also may be trivialized by readers who are unable to make connections implied, but not made explicit, by the researcher" (p. 267).

Category Construction

Moving beyond basic description to the next level of analysis, the challenge is to construct categories or themes that capture some recurring pattern that cuts across "the preponderance" (Taylor and Bogdan, 1984, p. 139) of the data. These categories or themes are "concepts indicated by the data (and not the data itself). . . . In short, conceptual categories and properties have a life apart from the evidence that gave rise to them" (p. 36). Devising categories is largely an intuitive process, but it is also systematic and informed by the study's purpose, the investigator's orientation and knowledge, and the meanings made explicit by the participants themselves. Typically, guidelines for category construction found in the literature are very general "and their applications are subject to the situational demands of a given study" (Constas, 1992, p. 255).

Categories and subcategories (or properties) are most commonly constructed through the constant comparative method of data analysis. As I explained in Chapter Eight, at the heart of this method is the continuous comparison of incidents, respondents' remarks, and so on, with each other. Units of data—bits of information—are literally sorted into groupings that have something in common. A *unit of data* is any meaningful (or potentially meaningful) segment of data; at the beginning of a study the researcher is uncertain about what will ultimately be meaningful. A unit of data can be as small as a word a participant uses to describe a feeling or phenomenon, or as large as several pages of field notes describing a particular incident. According to Lincoln and Guba (1985) a unit must meet two criteria. First, it should be heuristic—that is, the unit should reveal information relevant to the study and stimulate the reader to think beyond the particular bit of information. Second, the unit should be "the smallest piece of information about something that can stand by itself—that is, it must be interpretable in the absence of any additional information other than a broad understanding of the context in which the inquiry is carried out" (p. 345).

The task is to compare one unit of information with the next in looking for recurring regularities in the data. The process is one of breaking data down into bits of information and then assigning "these bits to categories or classes which bring these bits together again if in a novel way. . . . In the process we begin to discriminate more clearly between the criteria for allocating data to one category or another. Then some categories may be subdivided, and others subsumed under more abstract categories" (Dey, 1993, p. 44).

For a simple but vivid example of how to take raw data and sort them into categories, consider the task of sorting two hundred food items found in a grocery store. These two hundred food items in a research study would be bits of information or units of data upon which to base an analysis. By comparing one item with another, the two hundred items could be classified into any number of categories. Starting with a box of cereal, for example, you could ask whether the next item, an orange, is like the first. Obviously not. There are now two piles into which the next item may or may not be placed. By this process you can sort all the items into categories of your choice. One scheme may separate the items into the categories of fresh, frozen, canned, or packaged goods. Or you could divide them by color, weight, or price. More likely, you would divide the items into common grocery store categories: meat, dairy, produce, canned goods, and so on. These categories would be fairly comprehensive classes, each of which could be further subdivided. Produce, for example, includes the subcategories of fruits and vegetables. Fruits include citrus and noncitrus, domestic and exotic. All these schemes emerge logically from the "data"—the food items. The names of the categories and the scheme you use to sort the data will reflect the focus of your study.

The Step-by-Step Process

Category construction *is* data analysis, and all of the caveats about this process I discussed in the previous chapter should be kept in mind, the most important being that data analysis is done in con-

junction with data collection. There is, however, a growing preoc-
cupation with analysis in proportion to collection as the study progresses. And once all of the data are in, there is generally a period
of intensive analysis when tentative findings are substantiated,
revised, and reconfigured.

Category construction begins with reading the first interview
transcript, the first set of field notes, the first document collected
in the study. As you read down through the transcript, for example,
you jot down notes, comments, observations, and queries in the
margins. These notations are next to bits of data that strike you as
interesting, potentially relevant, or important to your study. Think
of yourself as having a conversation with the data, asking questions
of it, making comments to it, and so on. "The notes serve to isolate
the initially most striking, if not ultimately most important, aspects
of the data" (LeCompte, Preissle, and Tesch, 1993, p. 236).

After working through the entire transcript in this manner, you
go back over your marginal notes and comments and try to group
those comments and notes that seem to go together. This is akin
to sorting items in the grocery store example. Keep a running list
of these groupings attached to the transcript or on a separate
paper or memo to yourself. At the beginning of an inquiry, this list
is likely to be fairly long because you do not yet know what will surface across the rest of the data. You also will not yet know which
groupings might be subsumed under others.

Moving to your next set of data (transcript, field notes, or document), you scan it in exactly the same way as just outlined. You
do this, keeping in mind the list of groupings that you extracted
from the first transcript, checking to see if they are also present in
this second set. You also make a separate list of comments, terms,
and notes from this set and then *compare* this list with the one
derived from the first transcript. These two lists should then be
merged into one master list of concepts derived from both sets of
data. This master list constitutes a primitive outline or classification system reflecting the recurring regularities or patterns in your
study. These patterns and regularities become the categories or
themes into which subsequent items are sorted.

It should be clear that categories are abstractions derived from
the data, not the data themselves. To paraphrase Glaser and Strauss
(1967), these categories have a life of their own apart from the data

from which they came. Categories are conceptual elements that "cover" or span many individual examples of the category. This is illustrated in Figure 9.1.

The shaded background boxes represent incidents of the category from which the category was derived. The position of the category vis-à-vis the data is represented by the lighter ellipse in the figure.

Naming the Categories

The names of your categories can come from at least three sources: the researcher, the participants, or sources outside the study such as the literature. The most common situation is when the investigator comes up with terms, concepts, and categories that reflect what he or she sees in the data. In the second approach, the data

Figure 9.1. Deriving Categories from Data.

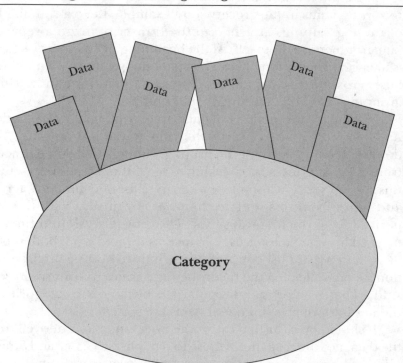

can be organized into a scheme suggested by the participants themselves. "This approach requires an analysis of the verbal categories used by participants and/or staff in a program to break up the complexity of reality into parts. It is a fundamental purpose of language to tell us what is important by giving it a name and therefore separating it from other things with other names" (Patton, 1990, p. 393). Patton gives the example of teachers' classification of dropouts into "chronics" and "borderlines" (p. 394). Bogdan and Biklen (1992) found that parents were classified by professional staff as "good parents," "not-so-good parents," or "troublemakers" (p. 169).

In addition to the participants' own categories, classification schemes can be borrowed from sources outside the study at hand. Applying someone else's scheme requires that the categories be compatible with the purpose and theoretical framework of the study. The database is scanned to determine the fit of a priori categories, and then the data are sorted into the borrowed categories.

There is some danger in using borrowed classification schemes, however. As Glaser and Strauss (1967) point out, "Merely selecting data for a category that has been established by another theory tends to hinder the generation of new categories, because the major effort is not generation, but data selection. Also, emergent categories usually prove to be the most relevant and the best fitted to the data. . . . Working with borrowed categories is more difficult since they are harder to find, fewer in number, and not as rich; since in the long run they may not be relevant, and are not exactly designed for the purpose, they must be respecified" (p. 37).

Several important guidelines can be used to determine the efficacy of categories derived from the constant comparative method of data analysis:

• Categories should *reflect the purpose of the research*. In effect, categories are the *answers* to your research question(s). One of Rowden's (1994) findings (or categories) regarding the role of human resource development (HRD) in successful small companies was that HRD activities serve to preserve the market niche of these companies. This category, "preserve the market niche," was one "answer" to the study's question of how human resource development functions in the success of small businesses.

• Categories should be *exhaustive*; that is, you should be able to place all data that you decided were important or relevant to the study in a category or subcategory.

• Categories should be *mutually exclusive*. A particular unit of data should fit into only one category. If the exact same unit of data can be placed into more than one category, more conceptual work needs to be done to refine your categories.

• Categories should be *sensitizing*. The naming of the category should be as sensitive as possible to what is in the data. An outsider should be able to read the categories and gain some sense of their nature. The more exacting in capturing the meaning of the phenomenon, the better. For example, the category "leadership" does not reveal as much as the category "charismatic leadership." In another example, "defiant behavior" is not as sensitizing as "defiance of adult authority figures."

• Categories should be *conceptually congruent*. This means that the same level of abstraction should characterize all categories at the same level. In the grocery store example described earlier, the items should not be sorted according to produce, canned goods, and fruit. While produce and canned goods are at the same conceptual level, fruit is a type of produce and should form a subcategory of produce.

Conceptual congruence is probably the most difficult criterion to apply. Investigators are usually so immersed in their data and their analysis that it is hard for them to see whether or not a set of categories make sense together. One of the best strategies for checking all the criteria against your category scheme is to display your set of categories in the form of a chart or table. This can be as simple as a list of one-word categories. In a study of the structure of simple reminiscence (Merriam, 1989), for example, the categories or findings were displayed in a list consisting of four terms—selection, immersion, withdrawal, and closure. Data displays can also be quite complex (Miles and Huberman, 1994). The point is that by laying out the basic structure of your findings in front of you, you can see how well all of the parts fit together. Also, by writing out the purpose statement at the top of your display, you can immediately see whether the categories are answers to the research question.

How Many Categories?

The number of categories a researcher constructs depends on the data and the focus of the research. In any case, the number should be manageable. In my experience, the fewer the categories, the greater the level of abstraction, and the greater ease with which you can communicate your findings to others. A large number of categories is likely to reflect an analysis too lodged in concrete description. Guba and Lincoln (1981) suggest four guidelines for developing categories that are both comprehensive and illuminating. First, the number of people who mention something or the frequency with which something arises in the data indicates an important dimension. Second, the audience may determine what is important—that is, some categories will appear to various audiences as more or less credible. Third, some categories will stand out because of their uniqueness and should be retained. And fourth, certain categories may reveal "areas of inquiry not otherwise recognized" or "provide a unique leverage on an otherwise common problem" (p. 95).

Several guidelines can help a researcher determine whether a set of categories is complete. First, "there should be a minimum of unassignable data items, as well as relative freedom from ambiguity of classification" (Guba and Lincoln, 1981, p. 96). Moreover, the set of categories should seem plausible given the data from which they emerge, causing independent investigators to agree that the categories make sense in light of the data. This strategy helps to ensure reliability and is discussed further in Chapter Ten.

Systems for Placing Data into Categories

Once you are satisfied with the set of categories derived from the data, the categories can be fleshed out and made more robust by searching through the data for more and better units of relevant information. The mechanical handling of the data at this stage of the analysis warrants some attention. Four basic strategies for organizing all the data in preparation for further analysis or for writing the results of the study include using index cards, file folders, information retrieval cards, and computer programs.

Each unit of information can be put onto a separate *index card* and coded according to any number of categories ranging from situational factors (who, what, when, where) to categories representing emerging themes or concepts. You could also first code the units in the margins of the interview transcripts, field notes, or documents. Photocopies can be made of the pages where you have made comments or notations or have identified tentative categories. Each photocopied unit of information is then placed on an index card; these can be sorted into piles by constantly comparing the information on one card with the information on the next. The piles are labeled, and the cards within that pile are coded accordingly. Once all the cards have been coded, cards relevant to a certain category can be retrieved by the code on the card.

A variation of the index card method is the use of *information retrieval cards*. At least two commercially available systems are available that can be used to sort data (Werner and Schoepfle, 1987). McBee or Indecks cards are large, index-type cards with numbered holes around the margins. First, the researcher pastes a photocopied unit of data on a card or types data onto a card. Second, the data are assigned a number representing a category. Third, the researcher punches out the corresponding numbered hole found on the margin of the card. A large rod, somewhat like a knitting needle, can then be passed through the same numbered hole on all of the cards; lifting and shaking the needle full of cards allows the coded and punched cards to fall out. When this has been done for all categories, all the data pertaining to specific, coded categories are grouped. This technique allows the cards to be left in random order, since all relevant information is coded by using the holes at the edge of the card.

If *file folders* are used, a photocopy of the entire database or case record is made. Working page by page as outlined earlier in this chapter, the researcher writes notations in the margins, including tentative categories or themes emerging from the raw data. The photocopied pages are then cut up, and coded sections are placed into file folders labeled by category or theme. Each unit of data needs to be coded not only by category but by its original page number and possibly by other identifying codes such as respondent's name and so on. If need be, each cut-up piece of information can be located later in the master copy.

Numerous *computer programs* have been developed to store, sort, and retrieve qualitative data. Some researchers have also devised systems using powerful word processing packages or database programs. Interview transcripts, observation notes, and so on are entered verbatim into the computer. The program then numbers each line of the database. The researcher uses a hard copy of the numbered database to analyze the data, making notes in the margins and developing themes or categories. Going from the hard copy back to the computer file, categories and their corresponding line numbers are entered. The researcher can then retrieve and print, by category, any set of data desired. Multiple levels of coding are possible for the same unit of information. (See Chapter Eight for more discussion of computers in qualitative research).

No doubt every researcher devises his or her own scheme for handling qualitative data. The four strategies for sorting data just presented allow for the easy retrieval of data and for cross-analysis of coded categories. Cross-analysis is especially important in a level of analysis that goes beyond a categorical or taxonomic integration of the data toward the development of theory. The development of theory is the most sophisticated level of data analysis and is discussed in the next section.

Developing Theory

Several levels of data analysis are possible in a qualitative case study. At the most basic level, data are organized chronologically or sometimes topically and presented in a narrative that is largely, if not wholly, descriptive. Moving from concrete description of observable data to a somewhat more abstract level involves using concepts to describe phenomena. Rather than just describing a classroom interaction, for example, a researcher might cite it as an instance of "learning" or "confrontation" or "peer support," depending on the research problem. This is the process of systematically classifying data into some sort of schema consisting of categories, themes, or types. The categories describe the data, but to some extent they also interpret the data. A third level of analysis involves making inferences, developing models, or generating theory. It is a process, Miles and Huberman (1994) write, of moving up "from the empirical trenches to a more conceptual overview of the landscape. We're no longer just dealing with observables, but also with unobservables, and are connecting the two with successive layers of inferential glue" (p. 261).

Thinking about data—*theorizing*—is a step toward developing a theory that explains some aspect of educational practice and allows a researcher to draw inferences about future activity. Theorizing is defined as "the cognitive process of discovering or manipulating abstract categories and the relationships among those categories" (LeCompte, Preissle, and Tesch, 1993, p. 239). It is fraught with ambiguity. "The riskiness of going beyond the data into a never-never land of inference" is a difficult task for most qualitative researchers because they are too close to the data, unable to articulate how the study is significant, and unable to shift into a speculative mode of thinking (p. 269). Theorizing about data can also be hindered by thinking that is linear rather than contextual. Patton (1990) notes the temptation to "fall back on the linear assumptions of quantitative analysis," which involves specifying "isolated variables that are mechanically linked together out of context" (p. 423). Such noncontextual statements "may be more distorting than illuminating. It is the ongoing challenge, paradox, and dilemma of qualitative analysis that we must be constantly moving back and forth between the phenomenon of the program and our abstractions of that program, between the descriptions of what has occurred and our analysis of those descriptions, between the complexity of reality and our simplifications of those complexities, between the circularities and interdependencies of human activity and our need for linear, ordered statements of cause-effect" (pp. 423–424).

Nevertheless, data often seem to beg for continued analysis past the formation of categories. A key here is when the researcher knows that the category scheme does not tell the whole story—that there is more to be understood about the phenomenon. This often leads to trying to link the conceptual elements—the categories—together in some meaningful way. One of the best ways to try this out is to visualize how the categories work together. Even a simple diagram or model using the categories and subcategories of the data analysis can effectively capture the interaction or relatedness of the findings. In Johnson-Bailey and Cervero's (1996) study of black reentry women, for example (see Chapter Three), her categories of silence, negotiation, and resistance were the strategies the black women in their study used to survive or succeed in formal education. However, these strategies were used both inside and outside the classroom, and they intersected with systems of race, gender, class, and color. Figure 9.2 shows a model displaying these interrelationships.

Johnson-Bailey and Cervero (1996) explain it as follows:

> The issues of race, gender, class, and color are depicted in the background surrounding the circle to indicate powerful forces which are ever-present in society. The center circle overlaps the smaller circles which represent the different segments of society: school, workplace, community, and family. The obstacles they encountered in school were no different than those experienced in the other three areas. To cope with old dilemmas, the women relied on familiar strategies (silence, negotiation, and resistance)

Figure 9.2. Linking Categories and Concepts in a Model of Reentry Black Women's Experience.

Rentry of Black Women

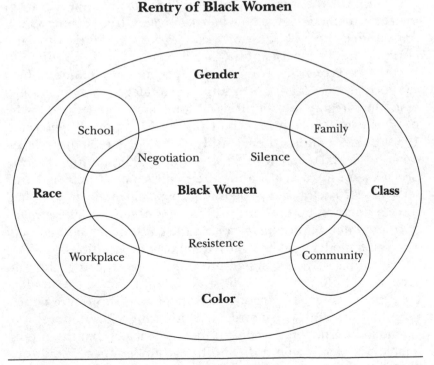

Source: Johnson-Bailey and Cervero (1996, p. 153). Reprinted with permission.

they had used throughout their lives, to respond to the direct impact of racism, sexism, classism, and colorism in these four social sites [p. 154].

Speculation is a key to developing theory in a qualitative study. Speculation involves "playing with ideas probabilistically. It permits the investigator to go beyond the data and make guesses about what will happen in the future, based on what has been learned in the past about constructs and linkages among them and on comparisons between that knowledge and what presently is known about the same phenomena. These guesses are projections about how confidently the relationships found or explanations developed can be expected to obtain in the future" (Goetz and LeCompte, 1984, p. 173).

The qualitative investigator who wishes to derive theory from data can turn to Glaser and Strauss (1967) and Strauss (1987) for assistance. They have devised a strategy for developing substantive theory—theory that applies to a specific aspect of educational practice. Since the theory is grounded in the data and emerges from them, the methodology is called *grounded theory* (see Chapter One). A grounded theory begins with categories. In addition to categories, a theory consists of two other elements—properties and hypotheses. Properties are also concepts but ones that describe a category; properties are not examples of a category but dimensions of it. The category "career malaise," for example, is defined by the properties of "boredom," "inertia," and "trapped" (Merriam, 1980). In a grounded theory study of the epistemological development of Malaysian women, Reybold (1996) found that the process was one of negotiating their culture with their personal sense of self. The category, "defining a personal model of self," had three properties representing how this was done: outright *adoption* of cultural definitions; *adaptation* of the culture; or *construction* of a personal model that disregarded cultural expectations.

Hypotheses are the suggested links between categories and properties. In Reybold's (1996) study of epistemological development cited earlier, she hypothesizes that family support of education for girls and women, diverse learning experiences, and extended international opportunities, are factors that foster epistemological development. In another grounded theory study of a faculty's participation in in-service workshops, for example, the researcher cited "workshop credibility" as one of several categories explaining faculty participation (Rosenfeldt, 1981). A property that helped to define workshop credibility was called "identification with sponsoring agent." The author hypothesized that "workshop participation will depend on the extent to which faculty members identify with the workshop sponsors. Namely, the greater the identification of the potential participants with the sponsoring agent, the greater the likelihood that professors will participate in a given workshop" (Rosenfeldt, 1981, p. 189). Such hypotheses emerge simultaneously with the collection and analysis of data. The researcher tries to support tentative hypotheses while at the same time remaining open to the emergence of new hypotheses. "Generating hypotheses requires evidence enough only to establish a suggestion—not an excessive piling up of evidence to establish a proof" (Glaser and Strauss, 1967, pp. 39–40).

The development of categories, properties, and tentative hypotheses through the constant comparative method (Glaser and Strauss, 1967) is a process whereby the data gradually evolve into a core of emerging theory. This core is a theoretical framework that guides the further collection of data. Deriving a theory from the data involves both the integration and the refinement of categories, properties, and hypotheses. As the theory solidifies, "major modifications become fewer and fewer as the analyst compares the next incidents of a category to its properties. Later modifications are mainly on the order of clarifying the logic, taking out non-relevant properties, integrating elaborating details of properties into the major outline of interrelated categories" (p. 110). In short, more data can be processed with fewer adjustments because the theory emerges "with a smaller set of higher level concepts" (p. 110).

At this point, "with reduction of terminology and consequent generalizing . . . the analyst starts to achieve two major requirements of theory: (1) *parsimony* of variables and formulation, and (2) *scope* in the applicability of the theory to a wide range of situations" (pp. 110–111, emphasis in original). Besides parsimony and scope, the emergent theory can be evaluated in terms of its overall explanatory power, by how well the generalizations are supported, by how well integrated the elements are, and by whether there is a logical consistency to every dimension of the theory.

Those who build theory in an applied field such as education need also be concerned with how well the theory fits the substantive area to which it will be applied, whether laypersons will be able to understand and use the theory, and whether the person who uses the theory will "have enough control in everyday situations to make its application worthwhile" (p. 245).

While building theory in the manner described by Glaser and Strauss is largely an inductive process, there are times throughout the investigation when a deductive strategy is used. Tentative categories, properties, and hypotheses continually emerge and must be tested against the data—that is, the researcher asks if there are sufficient data to support a certain category or hypothesis. If so, the element is retained; if not, it is discarded. Thus the researcher is continually shifting back and forth between deductive and inductive modes of thinking. For Glaser and Strauss (1967) the difference is one of emphasis. "Verifying as much as possible with as accurate evidence as feasible is requisite while one discovers and generates his theory—but *not* to the point where verification becomes so paramount as to curb generation" (p. 28).

In summary, data analysis is a process of making sense out of data. It can be limited to determining how best to arrange the material into a narrative account of the findings. More commonly, researchers extend analysis to developing categories, themes, or other taxonomic classes that interpret the meaning of the data. The categories become the findings of the study. When categories and their properties are reduced and refined and then linked together by tentative hypotheses, the analysis is moving toward the development of a theory to explain the data's meaning. This third level of analysis transcends the formation of categories, for a theory seeks to explain a large number of phenomena and tell how they are related. In a nice summary of the process, Dey (1993) compares qualitative data analysis to climbing a mountain to see the view.

> First of all, we must insist that our mountain rises above the plain world of common sense to afford a more "scientific"
> perspective. . . . We can allow our mountain to be of any size and shape; the small hill of a short undergraduate project, or the precipitous peak of a large-scale research project. . . . for the most part

much the same tasks are required of both. The mountain is climbed bit by bit, and while we are climbing, we focus on one step at a time. But the view we obtain is more than the sum of the sequence of steps we take along the way. Every so often, we can turn and look to the horizon, and in doing so we see the surrounding country from a fresh vantage point. . . . This climb, with its circuitous paths, its tangents and apparent reversals, and its fresh vistas, reflects the creative and non-sequential character of the analytic process. Progress may be slow and laborious, but it can be rewarded with some breath-taking revelations [pp. 53–54].

Data Analysis in Case Studies

While the basic strategy for analyzing data outlined earlier in this chapter and in Chapter Eight applies to all types of qualitative research, some features of case studies affect data analysis. First, a case study is an intensive, holistic description and analysis of a single, bounded unit. Conveying an understanding of the case is the paramount consideration in analyzing the data. Stake (1995) explains:

> Keeping in mind that it is *the case* we are trying to understand, we analyze episodes or text materials with a sense of correspondence [by which Stake means "consistency within certain conditions"]. We are trying to understand behavior, issues, and contexts with regard to our particular case. . . . We try to find the pattern or the significance through direct interpretation, just asking ourselves "What did that mean?" For more important episodes or passages of text, we must take more time, looking them over again and again, reflecting, triangulating, being skeptical about first impressions and simple meanings [p. 78, emphasis in original].

In case studies, communicating understanding—the goal of the data analysis—is linked to the fact that data have usually been derived from interviews, field observations, and documents. In addition to a tremendous amount of data, this range of data sources may present disparate, incompatible, even apparently contradictory information. The case study researcher can be seriously challenged in trying to make sense out of the data. Attention to data management is particularly important under these circumstances.

To begin the more intensive phase of data analysis in a case study, all the information about the case should be brought together—interview logs or transcripts, field notes, reports, records, the investigator's own documents, physical traces, and reflective memos. All this material needs to be organized in some fashion so that data are easily retrievable. Yin (1994) calls this organized material the *case study data base,* which he differentiates from the case study report. In a similar fashion, Patton (1990) differentiates the *case record* from the final *case study.* "The case record pulls together and organizes the voluminous case data into a comprehensive primary resource package. The case record includes all the major information that will be used in doing the case analysis and case study. Information is edited, redundancies are sorted out, parts are fitted together, and the case record is organized for ready access either chronologically and/or topically. The case record must be complete but manageable" (p. 386–387). The case study database (or record) then, is the data of the study organized so the researcher can locate specific data during intensive analysis.

The various procedures for deriving meaning from qualitative data described in this and the preceding chapter apply to the single case study. While the final write-up or case report may have a greater proportion of description than other forms of qualitative research in order to convey a holistic understanding of the case, the level of interpretation may also extend to the presentation of categories, themes, models, or theory. (For discussion of the final report, see Chapter Eleven).

Multiple or comparative case studies involve collecting and analyzing data from several cases. Instead of studying one good high school, for example, Lightfoot (1983) studied six. Her findings are presented first as six individual case studies (or "portraits" as she calls them); she then offers a cross-case analysis leading to generalizations about what constitutes a good high school.

In a multiple case study, there are two stages of analysis—the within-case analysis and the cross-case analysis. For the *within-case analysis,* each case is first treated as a comprehensive case in and of itself. Data are gathered so the researcher can learn as much about the contextual variables as possible that might have a bearing on the case. The data of the single qualitative case are analyzed as described here and in Chapter Eight. Once the analysis of each case is completed, *cross-case analysis* begins. A qualitative, inductive, multicase study seeks to build abstractions across cases. The researcher attempts "to build a general explanation that fits each of the individual cases, even though the cases will vary in their details" (Yin, 1994, p. 112). The researcher attempts to see "processes and outcomes that occur across many cases, to understand how they are qualified by local conditions, and thus develop more sophisticated descriptions and more powerful explanations" (Miles and Huberman, 1994, p. 172). Miles and Huberman warn that "cross-case analysis is tricky. Simply summarizing superficially across some themes or main variables by itself tells us little. We have to look carefully at the complex configuration of processes within each case, understand the local dynamics, before we can begin to see patterning of variables that transcends particular cases" (pp. 205–206).

As with the single case study, one of the challenges in a multicase study is in the *management* of the data; the researcher probably has considerably more raw information and must find ways to handle it without becoming overwhelmed. Cross-case studies are also likely to involve a team of investigators, each studying an assigned site. Clearly then, coordination of both personnel and data is called for. Indeed, ongoing collaboration in data analysis is essential in large-scale studies. Also essential are coordinated systems for recording data. Miles and Huberman (1994) have developed numerous methods for analyzing data from several cases or sites. The methods range from simple to complex, from descriptive to explanatory, and all involve devising matrices and other visual aids for displaying data across sites.

Ultimately, cross-case analysis differs little from analysis of data in a single qualitative case study. The level of analysis can result in little more than a unified description across cases; it can lead to categories, themes, or typologies that conceptualize the data from all the cases; or it can result in building substantive theory offering an integrated framework covering multiple cases.

A variation of cross-case or cross-site studies is the *case survey*. This is a form of secondary analysis in that the case studies have already been conducted and are available to the researcher. They function as databases to answer new questions or confirm new interpretations. Stenhouse (1978) proposed establishing a repository of case records in education so that these databases can be easily accessed by researchers. The Human Relations Area File (HRAF) I mentioned in Chapter Six is an anthropological database containing numerous ethnographic case studies. And in some ways, the Educational Resources Information Center (ERIC) functions as a repository, since it contains thousands of documents, reports, and studies in education. It does not separate case studies from other materials, however, so it would take some effort to identify case studies in particular.

The purpose of a case survey is to aggregate "diverse case studies together under a common conceptual framework so that findings will be cumulative . . . to identify what it is we already 'know,' what it is we do not know, and what it is we suspect" (Lucas, quoted in Guba and Lincoln, 1981, p. 247). The basic strategy for conducting a case survey differs somewhat from data analysis in cross-case studies. First, the researcher must determine the criteria by which cases are to be selected for analysis. This step requires "a tight definition of the phenomenon under investigation" (Guba and Lincoln, 1981, p. 250). Second, case surveys tend to be quantitative in nature, although they need not be. West and Oldfather (1995) suggest an innovative way to do a cross-case comparison of qualitative case studies. Pooled case comparison allows the comparison of "separate but similar studies *ex post facto*; like overlaying of one transparency on another, this method highlights both the uniqueness and the commonality of participants' experiences and allows us to understand each study more fully" (p. 454). Raw data from separate studies of similar phenomena are "pooled" into a data set for a fresh analysis.

In summary, data analysis in case studies must account for some of the identifying features of this particular type of qualitative research, including the focus on understanding and the typically broad range of data available for analysis. In a multiple case study, a within-case analysis is followed by a cross-case analysis.

Summary

The analysis of qualitative data can range from organizing a narrative description of the phenomenon, to constructing categories or themes that cut across the data, to building theory. Each of these levels of analysis calls upon the investigator's intuitive as well as analytical powers. The process can certainly be enhanced by employing techniques that have helped others, such as using data displays, as well as devising a systematic approach to the task. One particular approach, that of the constant comparative method of data analysis, was used in this chapter to demonstrate how to construct meaning from qualitative data.

I covered in some detail the ins and outs of category construction. The step-by-step process includes naming the categories, determining the number of categories, and figuring out systems for placing data into categories. Using categories as the basic conceptual element, I discussed how analysis can be extended to theory building. Finally, I discussed data analysis in case study research, with particular attention to within-case and cross-case analysis.

Chapter Ten

Dealing with Validity, Reliability, and Ethics

All research is concerned with producing valid and reliable knowledge in an ethical manner. Being able to trust research results is especially important to professionals in applied fields, such as education, in which practitioners intervene in people's lives. No classroom teacher, for example, will want to experiment with a new way of doing things without some confidence in its potential success. But how can consumers of research know when research results are trustworthy? They are trustworthy to the extent that there has been some accounting for their validity and reliability, and the nature of qualitative research means that this accounting takes different forms than in more positivist, quantitative research. In this chapter I will explore the issues of validity and reliability and offer practical suggestions for dealing with these concerns in qualitative research.

Ensuring validity and reliability in qualitative research involves conducting the investigation in an ethical manner. While well-established guidelines for the ethical conduct of research date back to the late 1940s, only recently has attention been given to the ethical concerns unique to qualitative research. I will conclude the chapter by considering the ethical questions that are likely to arise in qualitative research.

Validity and Reliability

In order for practitioners in a field such as education to learn about their practice and to conduct the business of teaching children and adults, research studies of all types are regularly undertaken. To have any effect on either the practice or the theory of education, these studies must be rigorously conducted; they need to present insights and conclusions that ring true to readers, educators, and other researchers. Cronbach (1975) emphasizes the practical, action-oriented goal for research in a social science such as education versus the amassing of empirical generalizations and laws in the physical sciences. In his view two types of practical contributions are possible. Researchers can "assess local events accurately, to improve short-run control" or they can "develop explanatory concepts, concepts that will help people use their heads" (p. 126). Valid and reliable qualitative research can meet both of these goals.

The applied nature of educational inquiry thus makes it imperative that researchers and others have confidence in the conduct of the investigation and in the results of any particular study. Assessing the validity and reliability of a qualitative study involves examining its component parts, as you might in other types of research. As Guba and Lincoln (1981, p. 378) point out, in an experimental study you can "talk about the validity and reliability of the instrumentation, the appropriateness of the data analysis techniques, the degree of relationship between the conclusions drawn and the data upon which they presumably rest, and so on." It is "not a whit different" in a qualitative case study—"were the interviews reliably and validly constructed; was the content of the documents properly analyzed; do the conclusions of the case study rest upon data?"

Coming at the same questions of validity and reliability from another perspective, Firestone (1987) explores how the quantitative and qualitative paradigms employ different rhetoric to persuade consumers of their trustworthiness. "The quantitative study must convince the reader that procedures have been followed faithfully because very little concrete description of what anyone does is provided. The qualitative study provides the reader with a depiction in enough detail to show that the author's conclusion 'makes sense'" (p. 19). Further, "the quantitative study portrays a world of variables and static states. . . . By contrast the qualitative study describes people acting in events" (p. 19).

Thus regardless of the type of research, validity and reliability are concerns that can be approached through careful attention to a study's conceptualization and the way in which the data were

collected, analyzed, and interpreted, and the way in which the findings are presented. Different types of research are based on different assumptions about what is being investigated, however, and
different designs seek to answer different questions. If, as in the
case of qualitative research, *understanding* is the primary rationale
for the investigation, the criteria for trusting the study are going
to be different than if discovery of a law or testing a hypothesis is
the study's objective. What makes experimental studies scientific
or rigorous or trustworthy "is the researcher's careful design of
contexts of production for phenomenon (experiments) and the
processes of measurement, hypothesis-testing, inference and interpretation and the like. What makes the case study work 'scientific'
is the observer's critical presence in the context of occurrence of
phenomena, observation, hypothesis-testing (by confrontation and
disconfirmation), triangulation of participants' perceptions, interpretations and so on" (Kemmis, 1983, p. 103).

Many writers on the topic argue that qualitative research, which
is based on different assumptions about reality and a different
worldview, should consider validity and reliability from a perspective congruent with the philosophical assumptions underlying the
paradigm. This may even result in naming the concepts themselves
differently (Lincoln and Guba, 1985). More recent writing from
postmodern, poststructural, constructivist, and critical perspectives
(Alcoff, 1991; Donmoyer, 1996; Guba and Lincoln, 1994; Lenzo,
1995; Lincoln, 1995) calls for the careful thinking through of
totally different conceptualizations of validity and reliability. Lincoln (1995) suggests that the emerging criteria for quality in interpretive inquiry be based on considering the relational aspects of
the research process (for example, the knower and the known). In
so doing, the distinction between quality or rigor and ethics "collapses" (p. 275).

In speaking of narrative inquiry, Connelly and Clandinin
(1990) present another view. They write that this genre of research
"relies on criteria other than validity, reliability, and generalizability" (p. 7) and that these criteria are "under development in the
research community" (p. 7). They note that "each inquirer must
search for, and defend, the criteria that best apply to his or her
work;" (p. 7) they go on to propose "apparency, verisimilitude, and
transferability as possible criteria" (p. 7).

Wolcott (1994) takes yet another direction, arguing "the absurdity of validity" (p. 364). Instead of validity, what he seeks "is something else, a quality that points more to identifying critical elements and wringing plausible interpretations from them, something one can pursue without becoming obsessed with finding the right or ultimate answer, the correct version, the Truth" (pp. 366–367). For Wolcott the "something else" is understanding.

Most educators conducting qualitative investigations do not want to wait for the research community to develop a consensus as to the appropriate criteria for assessing validity and reliability, if indeed that is even possible. While the theoretical debate goes on, there are immediate needs to be met in the field. As Stake (1994) notes, knowledge gained in an investigation "faces hazardous passage from writer to reader. The writer needs ways of safeguarding the trip" (p. 241). Further, qualitative researchers need to respond to the concerns of outsiders, many of whom may be unfamiliar with or blatantly challenging of the credibility of qualitative research. Exhibit 10.1 is list of questions commonly asked of my students during defenses of qualitative research; each question asks something about the validity or reliability of qualitative research.

Fortunately, several strategies can be used to enhance the validity and reliability of qualitative studies. The following sections address the specific concerns in qualitative research with respect to internal validity, reliability, and external validity and suggest appropriate strategies for dealing with each of these issues.

Internal Validity

Internal validity deals with the question of how research findings match reality. How congruent are the findings with reality? Do the findings capture what is really there? Are investigators observing or measuring what they think they are measuring? Internal validity in all research thus hinges on the meaning of reality. Becker (1993) humorously points out that "reality is what we choose not to question at the moment," and "the leading cause of stress amongst those in touch with it" (p. 220). On a more serious note, Ratcliffe (1983) offers an interesting perspective on assessing validity in every kind of research. It should be remembered, he suggests, that (1) "data do not speak for themselves; there is always an

**Exhibit 10.1. Challenging the
Trustworthiness of Qualitative Research.**

---

1. What can you possibly tell from an *n* of 1 (3, 15, 29, etc.)?
2. What is it worth just to get one person's interpretation of someone else's interpretation of what is going on?
3. How can you generalize from a small, nonrandom sample?
4. If the researcher is the primary instrument for data collection and analysis, how can we be sure the researcher is a valid and reliable instrument?
5. How do you know the researcher isn't biased and just finding out what he or she expects to find?
6. Doesn't the researcher's presence so alter the participant's behavior as to contaminate the data?
7. Don't people often lie to field researchers?
8. If somebody else did this study, would they get the same results?

---

interpreter, or a translator" (p. 149); (2) that "one cannot observe or measure a phenomenon/event without changing it, even in physics where reality is no longer considered to be single-faceted"; and (3) that numbers, equations, and words "are all abstract, symbolic representations of reality, but not reality itself" (p. 150). Validity, then, must be assessed in terms of something other than reality itself (which can never be grasped).

One of the assumptions underlying qualitative research is that reality is holistic, multidimensional, and ever-changing; it is not a single, fixed, objective phenomenon waiting to be discovered, observed, and measured as in quantitative research. Assessing the isomorphism between data collected and the "reality" from which they were derived is thus an inappropriate determinant of validity. In writing about his scientific journey to the Sea of Cortez more than fifty years ago, Steinbeck (1941) eloquently contrasted the two views of reality. For example, he wrote:

> The Mexican sierra has 'XVII–15–1X' spines in the dorsal fin. These can easily be counted. But if the sierra strikes hard on the line so that our hands are burned, if the fish sounds and nearly

escapes and finally comes in over the rail, his colors pulsing and his tail beating the air, a whole new relational externality has come into being—an entity which is more than the sum of the fish plus the fisherman. The only way to count the spines of the sierra unaffected by this second relational reality is to sit in a laboratory, open an evil smelling jar, remove a stiff colorless fish from formalin solution, count the spines, and write the truth 'D. XVII–15–1X.' There you have recorded a reality which cannot be assailed—probably the least important reality concerning either the fish or yourself. . . . The man with his pickled fish has set down one truth and has recorded in his experience many lies. The fish is not that color, that texture, that dead, nor does he smell that way [p. 2].

Then what *is* being observed in qualitative research, and how does a researcher assess the validity of those observations? What is being observed are people's constructions of reality—how they understand the world.

Reality, according to Lincoln and Guba (1985), is "a multiple set of mental constructions . . . made by humans; their constructions are on their minds, and they are, in the main, accessible to the humans who make them" (p. 295). And because human beings are the primary instrument of data collection and analysis in qualitative research, interpretations of reality are accessed directly through their observations and interviews. We are thus "closer" to reality than if a data collection instrument had been interjected between us and the participants. Most agree that when reality is viewed in this manner, internal validity is a definite strength of qualitative research. In this type of research it is important to understand the perspectives of those involved in the phenomenon of interest, to uncover the complexity of human behavior in a contextual framework, and to present a holistic interpretation of what is happening.

LeCompte and Preissle (1993) list four factors that lend support to the claim of high internal validity of ethnographic research:

First, the ethnographer's common practice of living among participants and collecting data for long periods provides opportunities for continual data analysis and comparison to refine constructs; it ensures a match between researcher categories and participant realities. Second, informant interviews, a major ethnographic data source, are phrased in the empirical categories of participants; they are less abstract than many instruments used in other research designs. Third, participant observation, the ethnographer's second key source of data—is conducted in natural settings reflecting the life experiences of participants more accurately than do more contrived or laboratory settings. Finally, ethnographic analysis incorporates researcher reflection, introspection, and self-monitoring that Erickson (1973) calls disciplined subjectivity, and these expose all phases of the research to continual questioning and reevaluation [p. 342].

According to my research experience as well as the literature on qualitative research, an investigator can use six basic strategies to enhance internal validity:

1. *Triangulation*—using multiple investigators, multiple sources of data, or multiple methods to confirm the emerging findings. (See Denzin, 1970, for a discussion of triangulation.) This procedure for establishing validity in case studies was cited in an article by Foreman (1948) more than forty years ago. He recommended using independent investigators "to establish validity through pooled judgment" (p. 413) and using outside sources to validate case study materials. In a more recent article, Mathison (1988) points out that triangulation may produce data that are inconsistent or contradictory. She suggests shifting the notion of triangulation away from "a technological solution for ensuring validity" and instead relying on a "holistic understanding" of the situation to construct "plausible explanations about the phenomena being studied" (p. 17).

2. *Member checks*—taking data and tentative interpretations back to the people from whom they were derived and asking them if the results are plausible. A number of writers suggest doing this continuously throughout the study.

3. *Long-term observation* at the research site or repeated observations of the same phenomenon—gathering data over a period of time in order to increase the validity of the findings. (See the discussion of field observations in Chapter Six.)

4. *Peer examination*—asking colleagues to comment on the findings as they emerge.

5. *Participatory or collaborative modes of research*—involving participants in all phases of research from conceptualizing the study to writing up the findings. (See Merriam and Simpson, 1995, for a discussion of participatory research.)

6. *Researcher's biases*—clarifying the researcher's assumptions, worldview, and theoretical orientation at the outset of the study.

Reliability

Reliability refers to the extent to which research findings can be replicated. In other words, if the study is repeated will it yield the same results? Reliability is problematic in the social sciences simply because human behavior is never static. Even those in the hard sciences are asking similar questions about the constancy of phenomena. Reliability in a research design is based on the assumption that there is a single reality and that studying it repeatedly will yield the same results. This is a central concept of traditional experimental research, which focuses on discovering causal relationships among variables and uncovering laws to explain phenomena.

Qualitative research, however, is not conducted so that the laws of human behavior can be isolated. Rather, researchers seek to describe and explain the world as those in the world experience it. Since there are many interpretations of what is happening, there is no benchmark by which to take repeated measures and establish reliability in the traditional sense. "If the researcher's self is the prime instrument of inquiry, and the self-in-the-world is the best source of knowledge about the social world, and social reality is held to be an emergent property of interacting selves, and the meanings people live by are malleable as a basic feature of social life, then concern over reliability—in the postpositivist sense—is fanciful" (Bednarz, 1985, p. 303).

The connection between reliability and internal validity from a traditional perspective rests for some on the assumption that a study is more valid if repeated observations in the same study or replications of the entire study have produced the same results. This logic relies on repetition for the establishment of truth; but, as everyone knows, measurements, observation, and people can be repeatedly wrong. A thermometer may repeatedly record boiling water at 85 degrees Fahrenheit; it is very reliable since the measurement is consistent, but not at all valid. And in the social sciences, simply because a number of people have experienced the same phenomenon does not make the observations more reliable. All reports of personal experience are not necessarily unreliable, any more than all reports of events witnessed by a large number of people are reliable. An audience's account of a magician, for example, is not as reliable as that of the stagehand who watched the show from behind the curtain.

The notion of reliability with regard to instrumentation can be applied to qualitative case studies in a sense similar to its meaning in traditional research (Lincoln and Guba, 1985). Just as a researcher refines instruments and uses statistical techniques to ensure reliability, so too the human instrument can become more reliable through training and practice. Furthermore, the reliability of documents and personal accounts can be assessed through various techniques of analysis and triangulation.

Because what is being studied in education is assumed to be in flux, multifaceted, and highly contextual, because information gathered is a function of who gives it and how skilled the researcher is at getting it, and because the emergent design of a qualitative case study precludes a priori controls, achieving reliability in the traditional sense is not only fanciful but impossible. Furthermore, for the reasons discussed, replication of a qualitative study will not yield the same results. That fact, however, does not discredit the results of the original study. Several interpretations of the same data can be made, and all stand until directly contradicted by new evidence.

Since the term *reliability* in the traditional sense seems to be something of a misfit when applied to qualitative research, Lincoln and Guba (1985, p. 288) suggest thinking about the "dependability" or "consistency" of the results obtained from the data. That is, rather than demanding that outsiders get the same results, a researcher wishes outsiders to concur that, given the data collected, the results make sense—they are consistent and dependable. The question then is not whether findings will be found again but *whether the results are consistent with the data collected.* Investigators can use several techniques to ensure that results are dependable:

The investigator's position. The investigator should explain the assumptions and theory behind the study, his or her position vis-à-vis the group being studied, the basis for selecting informants and a description of them, and the social context from which data were collected (LeCompte and Preissle, 1993).

Triangulation. Especially in terms of using multiple methods of data collection and analysis, triangulation strengthens reliability as well as internal validity.

Audit Trail. Just as an auditor authenticates the accounts of a business, independent judges can authenticate the findings of a study by following the trail of the researcher (Guba and Lincoln, 1981). "If we cannot expect others to replicate our account, the best we can do is explain how we arrived at our results" (Dey, 1993, p. 251). In order for an audit to take place, the investigator must describe in detail how data were collected, how categories were derived, and how decisions were made throughout the inquiry.

External Validity

External validity is concerned with the extent to which the findings of one study can be applied to other situations. That is, how generalizable are the results of a research study? Guba and Lincoln (1981) point out that even to discuss the issue, the study must be internally valid, for "there is no point in asking whether meaningless information has any general applicability" (p. 115). On the other hand, an investigator can go too far in controlling for factors that might influence outcomes, with the result that findings can be generalized only to other highly controlled, largely artificial situations.

The question of generalizability has plagued qualitative investigators for some time. Part of the difficulty lies in thinking of generalizability in the same way as do investigators using experimental or correlational designs. In these situations, ability to generalize to other settings or people is ensured through a priori conditions such as assumptions of equivalency between the sample and population from which it was drawn, control of sample size, random sampling, and so on. Of course even in these circumstances, generalizations are made within specified levels of confidence.

It has also been argued that applying generalizations from the aggregated data of enormous, random samples to individuals is hardly useful. A study might reveal, for example, that absenteeism is highly correlated with poor academic performance—that 80 percent of students with failing grades are found to be absent more than half the time. If student Alice has been absent more than half the time, does it also mean that she is failing? There is no way to know without looking at her record. Actually, an individual case study of Alice would allow for a much better prediction of her academic performance, for then the particulars that are important to her situation could be discovered. The best that research from large random samples can do vis-à-vis an individual is to "make teachers and other clinicians more informed gamblers" (Donmoyer, 1990, p. 181). In qualitative research, a single case or small nonrandom sample is selected precisely *because* the researcher wishes to understand the particular in depth, not to find out what is generally true of the many.

Overall, the issue of generalizability centers on whether it is possible to generalize from a single case, or from qualitative inquiry in general, and if so in what way? Those who view external validity in terms of traditional research design take one of two positions. Either they assume that one cannot generalize and thus regard generalizability as a limitation of the method, or they attempt to strengthen external validity by using standard sampling procedures. Within a single case, for example, a researcher can randomly sample from a subunit—say, teachers in a school—and then treat the data quantitatively. Another strategy is to use many cases to study the same phenomenon. In multicase or cross-case analysis, the use of predetermined questions and specific procedures for coding and analysis enhances the generalizability of findings in the traditional sense (Burlingame and Geske, 1979; Firestone and Herriott, 1984; James, 1981; Miles and Huberman, 1994; Schofield, 1990; Yin, 1994).

When multisite studies are impractical or the phenomenon of interest is unique, the question of external validity remains. Is generalization from a small, nonrandom sample possible? Only, most writers contend, if "generalization" is reframed to reflect the assumptions underlying qualitative inquiry. Reconceptualizations of generalizability to be discussed here include working hypotheses (Cronbach, 1975; Donmoyer, 1990), concrete universals (Erickson, 1986), naturalistic generalization (Stake, 1978), and user or reader generalizability (Wilson, 1979; Walker, 1980).

Cronbach (1975) proposes *working hypotheses* to replace the notion of generalizations in social science research. He makes the point that since generalizations decay in time, even in the hard sciences, they should not be the aim of social science research:

> Instead of making generalization the ruling consideration in our research, I suggest that we reverse our priorities. An observer collecting data in one particular situation is in a position to appraise a practice or proposition in that setting, observing effects in context. In trying to describe and account for what happened, he will give attention to whatever variables were controlled but he will give equally careful attention to uncontrolled conditions, to personal characteristics, and to events that occurred during treatment and measurement. As he goes from situation to situation, his first task is to describe and interpret the effect anew in each locale, perhaps taking into account factors unique to that locale or series of events. . . . Generalization comes late. . . .
>
> When we give proper weight to local conditions, any generalization is a working hypothesis, not a conclusion [pp. 124–125].

Working hypotheses not only take account of local conditions, they offer the educator some guidance in making choices—the results of which can be monitored and evaluated in order to make better future decisions. This practical view of generalization is shared by Patton (1990), who argues that qualitative research should "provide perspective rather than truth, empirical assessment of local decision makers' theories of action rather than generation and verification of universal theories, and context-bound extrapolations rather than generalizations" (p. 491).

Donmoyer (1990), however, points to some problems with applying working hypotheses derived from a single case study to other situations. First, much of the understanding gained in a case study is tacit and cannot be "translated into propositional form, the sort of form implied by the term *working hypotheses*" (p. 187, emphasis in original). Working hypotheses also fail to capture the interactive aspects of creating common meanings between researcher and participants, fail to convey the affective, visceral dimension of the knowledge, and fail to communicate the sense or meaning the researcher has made of the phenomenon.

For Erickson (1986) the production of generalizable knowledge is an inappropriate goal for interpretive research. In attending to the particular, concrete universals will be discovered. "The search is not for *abstract universals* arrived at by statistical generalizations from a sample to a population," he writes, "but for *concrete universals* arrived at by studying a specific case in great detail and then comparing it with other cases studied in equally great detail" (p. 130). The general lies in the particular; that is, what we learn in a particular situation we can transfer or generalize to similar situations subsequently encountered. This is, in fact, how most people cope with everyday life. I get one speeding ticket from a trooper pulling out from behind a concrete buttress; subsequently, I slow down whenever I come upon concrete buttresses on any road. I have taken a particular incident and formed a concrete universal. Erickson makes this same point with regard to teaching.

> When we see a particular instance of a teacher teaching, some aspects of what occurs are absolutely generic, that is, they apply cross-culturally and across human history to all teaching situations. This would be true despite tremendous variation in those situations—teaching that occurs outside school, teaching in other societies, teaching in which the teacher is much younger than the learners, teaching in Urdu, in Finnish, or in a mathematical language, teaching narrowly construed cognitive skills, or broadly construed social attitudes and beliefs. . . .
>
> Each instance of a classroom is seen as its own unique system, which nonetheless displays universal properties of teaching. These properties are manifested in the concrete, however, not in the abstract [p. 130].

The idea that the general resides in the particular, that we can extract a universal from a particular, is also what renders great literature and other art forms enduring. While we may never live at the South Pole, we can understand loneliness by reading Byrd's account; we can come up with concrete generalizations about power and corruption by listening to the Watergate tapes, although we are not likely to be president. (See Greene, 1988, and Eisner, 1991, 1993, for more on artistic expression and qualitative research).

Similar to concrete universals is what Stake (1978, 1994, 1995) calls *naturalistic generalization*. Drawing on tacit knowledge, intuition, and personal experience, people look for patterns that explain their own experience as well as events in the world around them. "Full and thorough knowledge of the particular" allows one to see similarities "in new and foreign contexts" (1978, p. 6). This process of naturalistic generalization is arrived at "by recognizing similarities of objects and issues in and out of context and by sensing the natural covariations of happenings" (1978, p. 6). These generalizations develop from experience and, like Cronbach's "working hypotheses," can guide but not predict a person's actions.

A fourth way of viewing external validity is to think in terms of the reader or user of the study. *Reader or user generalizability* involves leaving the extent to which a study's findings apply to other situations up to the people in those situations. Called *case-to-case* transfer by Firestone (1993), "It is the reader who has to ask, what is there in this study that I can apply to my own situation, and what clearly does not apply?" (Walker, 1980, p. 34). This is a common practice in law and medicine, where the applicability of one case to another is determined by the practitioner. Kennedy (1979) and Lincoln and Guba (1985) contend that the researcher is less concerned with generalizing than the reader or user. Nevertheless, the researcher has an obligation to provide enough detailed description of the study's context to enable readers to compare the "fit" with their situations.

To enhance the possibility of the results of a qualitative study generalizing in any of these senses (working hypotheses, concrete universals, naturalistic generalization, user generalization), the following strategies can be used:

Rich, thick description—providing enough description so that readers will be able to determine how closely their situations match the research situation, and hence, whether findings can be transferred.

Typicality or modal category—describing how typical the program, event, or individual is compared with others in the same class, so that users can make comparisons with their own situations (LeCompte and Preissle, 1993). In Wolcott's (1973) case study of a school principal, for example, he tells how he sought a male elementary school principal who was responsible for one school, and who regarded himself as a career principal, rather than using the principalship to move to a higher position.

Multisite designs—using several sites, cases, situations, especially those that maximize diversity in the phenomenon of interest; this will allow the results to be applied by readers to a greater range of other situations. This variation can be achieved through purposeful or random sampling.

By way of summarizing this discussion of validity and reliability, we can look back at the questions in Exhibit 10.1. Nearly all are framed from assumptions underlying positivist or quantitative research. If, however, we begin from the worldview of qualitative inquiry in which there are multiple constructions of reality, where the researcher is the primary instrument of data collection and analysis, and where understanding and meaning are of paramount importance, these same issues take on a new slant. And, as outlined in this chapter, there are adequate "safeguards" for the "hazardous passage from writer to reader" (Stake, 1994, p. 241).

Ethics

Concerns about validity and reliability are common to all forms of research, as is the concern that the investigation be conducted in an ethical manner. Early researchers in both the physical and the social sciences paid little attention to ethical issues inherent in both the production and application of research knowledge. Not until the horror of Nazi concentration camp experiments was revealed, until questions were raised about the uses of nuclear energy, and until physical and psychological abuses of subjects came to light, was the autonomy of researchers called into question. The first set of principles ever established to guide researchers in conducting experiments with human subjects dates to the Nuremberg Code established as a result of the Nuremberg military tribunals of 1945. Since then, many professions have developed codes of ethics pertaining to their field's research activities. Such codes function as guidelines "that alert researchers to the ethical dimensions of their work" (Punch, 1986, p. 37). The ethical code for anthropologists addresses relations with those studied, responsibility to the discipline, to students, to sponsors, and to the researcher's own government and the host government. In psychology and sociology, the codes deal with weighing the costs and benefits of an investigation, with safeguards to protect the rights of participants, and with ethical considerations in the presentation of research findings (Diener and Crandall, 1978). These are in fact the concerns of all social scientists (Sieber, 1992).

Moreover the federal government has established regulations to protect human subjects in biomedical, behavioral, and social research. Professional codes and federal regulations deal with issues common to all social science research—the protection of subjects from harm, the right to privacy, the notion of informed consent, and the issue of deception. Federal regulations in particular are somewhat problematic when applied to qualitative research because they are based on a model of research that assumes random sampling, experimental intervention, and so on.

The investigator-participant relationship and the risks differ considerably between experimental and qualitative research. Cassell (1982) proposes a continuum for analyzing risk and benefit in different types of research. At one end is biomedical experimentation; the investigator has considerable power. Other categories, placed in descending order of control, are psychological experimentation, face-to-face surveys, mailed surveys, field or participant observation studies, nonreactive observation, and secondary analysis of data. Obviously, wherever the investigator holds great power and control, there is a danger of abuse and thus a great need for guidelines and regulations (Cassell, 1982).

In qualitative studies, ethical dilemmas are likely to emerge with regard to the collection of data and in the dissemination of findings. Overlaying both the collection of data and the dissemination of findings is the researcher-participant relationship. For example, this relationship and the research purpose determine how much the researcher reveals about the actual purpose of the study—how informed the consent can actually be—and how much privacy and protection from harm is afforded the participants. Punch (1994) points to the current tension between more traditional forms of ethnography in which "total immersion" and "going native" are to be avoided and feminist, ethnic, and action research agendas in which a totally interactive, collaborative, and political stance is assumed. "This debate," he writes, "has illuminated certain research dilemmas in an acute and fresh way" (p. 86). (For more discussion on this debate, see Grossberg, Nelson, and Treichler (1992); Reinharz (1992); Welch (1991); Wolf (1992).)

Ethics in Data Collection

The standard data collection techniques of interviewing and of observation in qualitative research present their own ethical dilemmas. As Stake (1994) observes, "Qualitative researchers are guests in the private spaces of the world. Their manners should be good and their code of ethics strict" (p. 244). Interviewing—whether it is highly structured with predetermined questions or semistructured and open-ended—carries with it both risks and benefits to the informants. Respondents may feel their privacy has been invaded, they may be embarrassed by certain questions, and they may tell things they had never intended to reveal.

In-depth interviewing may have unanticipated long-term effects. What are the residual effects of an interview with a teacher who articulates, for the first time perhaps, anger and frustration with his position? Or the administrator who becomes aware of her own lack of career options through participation in a study of those options? Or the adult student who is asked to give reasons for failing to read? Painful, debilitating memories may surface in an interview, even if the topic appears routine or benign.

However, an interview may improve the condition of respondents when, for example, they are asked to review their successes or are stimulated to act positively in their own behalf. Most people who agree to be interviewed enjoy sharing their knowledge, opinions, or experiences. Some gain valuable self-knowledge; for others the interview may be therapeutic—which brings up the issue of the researcher's stance. Patton (1990) points out that the interviewer's task "is first and foremost to gather data, not change people" (p. 354). The interviewer is neither a judge nor a therapist nor "a cold slab of granite—unresponsive to the human issues, including great suffering and pain, that may unfold during an interview" (p. 354). Patton and others recommend being able to make referrals to resources for assistance in dealing with problems that may surface during an interview.

Observation, a second means of collecting data in a qualitative study, has its own ethical pitfalls, depending on the researcher's involvement in the activity. Observations conducted without the awareness of those being observed raise ethical issues of privacy and informed consent. Webb and others (1981), in their book on nonreactive measures, suggest that there is a continuum of ethical issues based on how "public" the observed behavior is. At one end, and least susceptible to ethical violations, is the public behavior of public figures. At midposition are public situations that "may be regarded as momentarily private," such as lovers in a park (p. 147). At the other end are situations involving "'spying' on private behavior" where distinct ethical issues can be raised (p. 148).

Participant observation raises questions for both the researcher and for those being studied. On the one hand, the act of observation itself may bring about changes in the activity, rendering it somewhat atypical. On the other, participants may become so accustomed to the researcher's presence that they may engage in activity they will later be embarrassed about, or reveal information they had not intended to disclose. Further, an observer may witness behavior that creates its own ethical dilemmas, especially behavior involving abuse or criminal activity (Hopper and Moore, 1990). What if inappropriate physical contact between instructor and participant is witnessed while observing a volunteer CPR training session? Or a helpless teen is attacked by the group under study? Or a researcher witnesses utterly ineffective, perhaps potentially damaging teacher behavior? Knowing when and how to intervene is perhaps the most perplexing ethical dilemma facing qualitative investigators. "Blanket injunctions such as 'never intervene' offer no practical aid. In the reciprocal relationship that arises between fieldworker and hosts, it seems immoral—and perhaps it is—to stand back and let those who have helped you be menaced by danger, exploitation, and death" (Cassell, 1982, p. 156). Taylor and Bogdan (1984) conclude that while "the literature on research ethics generally supports a noninterventionist position in fieldwork," failure to act is itself "an ethical and political choice" (p. 71) that researchers must come to terms with.

Somewhat less problematic are the documents a researcher might use in a case study. At least public records are open to anyone's scrutiny, and data are often in aggregated (and hence anonymous) form. But what of documents related to a continuing education program, for example, that reveal a misappropriation of funds? Or documents showing that course-load assignments are based on certain favors being extended? And personal records pose potential problems unless they are willingly surrendered for research purposes. As for data collected by other researchers and used in secondary analysis, the issue here is whether or not the respondent's "tacit consent to the subsequent analysis can be taken for granted" (Kelman, 1982, p. 81). Kelman believes that it can be taken for granted and that "serious ethical problems arise only when respondents agree to provide information for one purpose and the data are then used for a clearly different purpose" (p. 81).

Analysis and Dissemination

Analyzing data may present other ethical problems. Since the researcher is the primary instrument for data collection, data have been filtered through his or her particular theoretical position and biases. Deciding what is important—what should or should not be attended to when collecting and analyzing data—is almost always up to the investigator. Opportunities thus exist for excluding data contradictory to the investigator's views. Sometimes these biases are not readily apparent to the researcher. Nor are there practical guidelines for all the situations a researcher might face. Diener and Crandall (1978) offer sound advice. "There is simply no ethical alternative to being as nonbiased, accurate, honest as is humanly possible in all phases of research. In planning, conducting, analyzing, and reporting his work the scientist should strive for accuracy, and whenever possible, methodological controls should be built in to help. . . . Biases that cannot be controlled should be discussed in the written report. Where the data only partly support the predictions, the report should contain enough data to let readers draw their own conclusions" (p. 162).

Disseminating findings can raise further ethical problems. If the research has been sponsored, the report is made to the sponsoring agency, and the investigator loses control over the data and its subsequent use. Cassell (1978) points out that qualitative research on deviant or disadvantaged groups "can be used to control those who one studied, or to explain differences between them and the majority" (p. 141), thus providing a rationale for withholding assistance.

The question of anonymity is not particularly problematic in survey or experimental studies, when data are in aggregated form. At the other end of the continuum is a qualitative case study that, by definition, is an intensive investigation of a specific phenomenon of interest. The case may even have been selected because it was unique, unusual, or deviant in some way. At the local level, it is nearly impossible to protect the identity of either the case or the people involved. In addition, "The cloak of anonymity for characters may not work with insiders who can easily locate the individuals concerned or, what is even worse, *claim* that they can recognize them when they are, in fact, wrong" (Punch, 1994, p. 92).

Consider two recent popular works, *Primary Colors* (Anonymous, 1996) and *Midnight in the Garden of Good and Evil* (Berendt, 1994). The first is a thinly disguised fictional work describing Bill Clinton's 1992 presidential election campaign, and the other is a true story of a murder trial in Savannah, Georgia. After over a year of speculation, accusations, and denials, the author of *Primary Colors* was revealed. In Berendt's book, some real people were named, other characters were given pseudonyms, and others were composites—all of whom were soon known to the residents of Savannah and beyond. These two examples illustrate how difficult, if not impossible, it is to protect the identity of the situation and the participants in case studies.

Exposure of a case through publication or other means of dissemination poses several risks: the danger of presenting the case in a manner offensive to the participants, "the violation of anonymity, subjecting an individual or group to unwelcome publicity," or "exposing people to legal, institutional, or governmental sanctions because of behavior revealed by the fieldworker" (Cassell, 1978, p. 141). Questions about the researcher's ethical responsibility abound. "Should material be 'cleared' with the group under study, and if so, with which members or factions within the group? How does one weigh the public's 'right to know' against an individual's or group's 'right to privacy'" (Cassell, 1978, p. 141)? Kimmel (1988) recommends (1) considering possible consequences of the research before undertaking it, (2) presenting results with as little distortion as possible, while maximizing the potential benefits of the research, and (3) taking special care in disseminating the results.

While policies, guidelines, and recommendations for dealing with the ethical dimensions of qualitative research are available to researchers, actual ethical practice comes down to the individual researcher's own values and ethics. All possibilities cannot be anticipated, nor can a researcher's own responses. As Punch (1994) points out, "Acute moral and ethical dilemmas . . . often have to be resolved *situationally,* and even spontaneously" (p. 84). While an investigator can be informed by guidelines and others' experiences, ultimately, the researcher's own conscience informs the decision. Deyhle, Hess, and LeCompte (1992) underscore this point. "One is not suddenly faced with ethical decisions when one goes into the field. He or she is faced with behaving in an ethical manner at every moment; doing qualitative research in the field simply creates specialized situations with more extensive ramifications that must be examined" (p. 639).

Summary

As in any research, validity, reliability, and ethics are major concerns. Every researcher wants to contribute results that are believable and trustworthy. Since a qualitative approach to research is based upon different assumptions and a different worldview than traditional research, most writers argue for employing different criteria in assessing qualitative research.

The question of internal validity—the extent to which research findings are congruent with reality—is addressed by using triangulation, checking interpretations with individuals interviewed or observed, staying on-site over a period of time, asking peers to comment on emerging findings, involving participants in all phases of the research, and clarifying researcher biases and assumptions. Reliability—the extent to which there is consistency in the findings—is enhanced by the investigator explaining the assumptions and theory underlying the study, by triangulating data, and by leaving an audit trail, that is, by describing in detail how the study was conducted and how the findings were derived from the data. Finally, the extent to which the findings of a qualitative study can be generalized to other situations—external validity—continues to be the object of much debate. Working hypotheses, concrete universals, naturalistic generalization, and user or reader generalizability are discussed as alternatives to the statistical notion of external validity.

Although researchers can turn to guidelines and regulations for help in dealing with some of the ethical concerns likely to emerge in qualitative research, the burden of producing a study that has been conducted and disseminated in an ethical manner lies with the individual investigator. No regulation can tell a researcher when the questioning of a respondent becomes coercive, when to intervene in abusive or illegal situations, or how to ensure that the study's findings will not be used to the detriment of those involved. The best a researcher can do is to be conscious of the ethical issues that pervade the research process and to examine his or her own philosophical orientation vis-à-vis these issues.

Chapter Eleven

Writing Reports and Case Studies

For most educators, doing research means designing a study that addresses some problem arising from practice, collecting and analyzing data relevant to the problem, and finally, interpreting the results. Often neglected, especially by graduate students and practitioners who do much of the research in education, is the important step of reporting and disseminating results. The research is of little consequence if no one knows about it; other educators have no way to benefit from what the researcher learned in doing the study. For qualitative research in particular, one of the serious problems arises at "the point where rich data, careful analysis, and lofty ideas meet the iron discipline of writing" (Woods, 1985, p. 104).

Several factors contribute to this stage of the research process being particularly daunting. First, because data collection and analysis is continuous and simultaneous in qualitative research, there is no clean cutoff—no time when everything else stops and writing begins. Second, a great amount of qualitative data needs to be sorted through, selected, and woven into a coherent narrative. Finally, there is no standard format for reporting such data (Wolcott, 1990). Nearly twenty-five years ago Lofland (1974) commented on the lack of consensus. "Qualitative field research seems distinct in the degree to which its practitioners lack a public, shared, and codified conception of how what they do is done, and how what they report should be formulated" (p. 101). Lofland's observation is even more true today, where "in the wake of feminist and postmodernist critiques of traditional qualitative writing practices, qualitative work has been appearing in new forms; genres are blurred, jumbled" (Richardson, 1994, p. 520).

In this chapter I will first offer suggestions as to how you can prepare for the writing of the report. In the second and major portion, I will examine the options available to researchers with regard to the content and dissemination of the final report. A final section addresses writing up case study reports. While qualitative research reports can take an oral, pictorial, or even dramatic form, the focus of this chapter is on the more common written form.

Preparing to Write

There is nothing more frustrating than sitting down to a blank piece of paper or blank computer screen and not being able to write. Unfortunately, there is no formula to make this an easy task. You can read tips on how to write, talk to those who write a lot, read exemplary accounts—but, like learning to swim, there is no substitute for plunging in and doing it. This is not to say that it is a totally serendipitous or haphazard process. Writing up the results of your study can be greatly facilitated by attending to the following tasks prior to writing: determining the audience, selecting a focus, and outlining the report.

Determining the Audience

The first and one of the most important considerations in preparing to write your final report is deciding whom the report is for. Schatzman and Strauss (1973) call this process *audience conjuring*. "Since one can hardly write or say anything without there being some real or imagined audience to receive it, any description necessarily will vary according to the audience to which it is directed. Audiences 'tell' what substances to include, what to emphasize, and the level and complexity of abstractions needed to convey essential facts and ideas" (p. 118). Once it is clear who will be reading the report, you can ask what that audience would want to know about the study. The answer to that question can help structure the content of the report and determine the style of presentation.

The primary audience interested in your results might be the general public, policy makers, the funding source, practitioners, the scientific community at large, or members of the site or project studied. Each audience would have a different interest in the research and would require a somewhat different approach. Take, for example, a qualitative study of nursing home residents learning to use computers for study and entertainment. The general public, reading about the study in a popular magazine, would respond to a human interest report that highlighted one resident's experience. Policy makers, though, are concerned with policy options. "Here the central interest is . . . in how the study can inform the current decision situation of the policymaker" (Erickson, 1986, p. 153). Policy makers involved in legislation for the aged or nursing home administration, for example, might want to know how the program has affected the management of staff and residents, whether funding should be channeled into the project, and so on.

The funding source for the study—a computer company, for example—would have its own questions, such as how the residents fared with their computers or whether this population represents a market.

Practitioners would be most interested in whether the research setting sufficiently resembles their own situation to warrant adopting the same practice. "Practitioners may say they want tips," writes Erickson (1986), "but experienced practitioners understand that the usefulness and appropriateness of any prescriptions for practice must be judged in relation to the specific circumstances of practice in their own setting. Thus the interest in learning by positive and negative example from a case study presupposes that the case is in some ways comparable to one's own situation" (p. 153). With regard to the example, practitioners in recreation and leisure studies, adult education, and gerontology might be particularly interested in the computer's role in enhancing the residents' ability to learn. Thus the implicit comparison would be between the residents and setting of the study and the residents and setting of the practitioner.

The general scientific community—that is, other researchers interested in the problem—would need to know such technical aspects of the study as how the data were collected and analyzed and what was done to ensure reliability and validity. With this information they could judge the study's value and its contribution to knowledge.

Finally, the study's results might be presented to those who participated. The main concern of participants, Erickson (1986) points out, relates to "their personal and institutional reputations" (p. 154). If the findings about residents' use of computers are to be helpful to the residents and staff, "the reports must be sensitive to the variety of personal and institutional interests that are at stake in the kinds of information that are presented about people's actions and thoughts, and in the ways these thoughts and actions are characterized in the reports" (p. 154).

Determining the audience should help a researcher define the relative emphasis of different components of the research report. It may be even more helpful to address the report to a particular person in that audience. Spradley (1980) quotes advice from an editor regarding a target reader. "Pick out some real person *whom you know*, then set down your materials so this person will understand what you are saying. When you have a 'target reader,' you effect a single level of presentation" (pp. 168–169). Yin (1994) suggests not only examining the selected audience closely but reading other reports "that have successfully communicated with it. Such prior reports may offer helpful clues for composing a new report" (p. 132).

Selecting a Focus

The next step is to select a focus for the report. The focus depends on the audience for which it is being written, the original purpose of the study, and the level of abstraction obtained during analysis of the data (see Chapter Nine).

To illustrate how audience, purpose, and level of data analysis can be taken into consideration in determining the focus of a report, take the example of teaching nursing home residents to use computers. A report for a practitioner-oriented journal or magazine could have as its focus the benefits of introducing computers into this environment; or the focus might be on tips for instructing nursing home residents in computer usage. In either case, a full description of the nursing home setting would be important; the research study itself would be briefly summarized in jargon-free language; the benefits or tips would be highlighted.

If the write-up of this same study were for a dissertation committee or scholarly research journal, the focus would reflect the purpose of the study—cognitive strategies employed by nursing home residents in learning to use computers, for example. If the study had developed a substantive theory, that would be the focus of the write-up. The report or article would emphasize the methodology of the study and the analysis and interpretation of the findings.

Bogdan and Biklen (1992) suggest another type of focus—the thesis. A *thesis* is a proposition put forth to be argued and defended that often arises out of the discrepancy between what some theory or previous research says should happen in a situation and what actually does happen. Because of its argumentative nature, the thesis is a good attention-getting device and particularly suited to popular accounts of research. In preparing a report of the previously mentioned research for a policy group or funding agency, for example, this more propositional focus might ask whether buying computers for nursing home residents is a waste of money.

The important thing is that some focus be chosen for the study. As Spradley (1980) says, "In order to communicate with your audience you need to have something to say. . . . A thesis is the central message, the point you want to make" (p. 169). Thus the focus depends on the audience being addressed and the message the researcher wants to convey.

Outlining the Report

Before writing the report, all relevant data must be gone through, culled for extraneous material, and organized in some manner. Ideally you have been doing this all along. At the very minimum you should have devised some system for keeping track of the voluminous data typical of qualitative investigations, your analysis of that data, and your own reflections on the process (see Chapter Eight). With these resources at hand, *and* with your audience and focus determined, making an outline is the next step.

Some writers say they just sit down and write with no outline; perhaps they only have a vague notion of what they want to say. Except for these extraordinary and usually highly creative writers, most everyone else can be immeasurably aided in their writing by even a sketchy outline. The mere act of jotting down some of the major points you want to be sure to cover reveals whether you have anything to say or not. Trying to write something—anything—is a good clue as to whether you have done enough background reading, analyzed your data enough, or thought about it enough. As Dey (1993) points out, "What you cannot explain to others, you do not understand yourself. Producing an account of our analysis is not just something we do for an audience. It is also something we do for ourselves" (p. 237).

An easy way to outline is to write down all the topics that might be covered in the report. Next, arrange the topics in some order that will be understood by the intended audience. All research reports need an introduction defining the problem that was studied and, depending on the audience, information about the methodology. The main body of the report contains the findings in the form of topics that have been listed and organized in some way. A conclusion summarizes the study and its findings and offers some commentary on the findings.

Beginning to Write

From the outline, you can begin to write the first draft of the report. The outline breaks the writing task into manageable units, making the task less overwhelming. As I stated earlier, there is no substitute for actually *writing*—all the preparation in the world does not save you from having to put words on paper or characters on a screen. The act of writing itself causes something to happen. "It seems, in fact, that one does not truly begin to think until one concretely attempts to render thought and analysis into successive sentences" (Lofland, 1971, p. 127). The combination of thinking while writing leads to seeing new ideas or revising the outline when certain sections do not make sense. "One is never truly inside a topic—or on top of it—until he faces the hard task of explaining it to someone else. It is in the process of externalizing (writing) one's outline descriptions, analyses, or arguments that they first become visible to oneself as 'things' 'out there' that are available for scrutiny. When they become available as external objects—as text—one can literally see the weaknesses—points overlooked, possibilities unattended, assertions unsupported or unillustrated" (Lofland, 1971, p. 127). This is why Dey (1993) considers writing "another tool in our analytic tool-kit." It is partially "through the challenge of explaining ourselves to others [that] we can help to clarify and integrate the concepts and relationships we have identified in our analysis" (p. 237).

All writers occasionally experience writer's block. Lofland (1971) suggests that it is probably more accurate to call it a "thinking block" (p. 127). Wolcott (1990) agrees. "Writing is a great way to discover what we are thinking, as well as to discover gaps in our thinking. Unfortunately, that means we must be prepared to catch ourselves red-handed when we seem not to be thinking at all. The fact should not escape us that when the writing is not going well, we probably have nothing (yet) to say; most certainly we are not yet able to say it" (p. 21). And while organization and outlines are important and helpful, "one can also become a prisoner of his organization" (Lofland, 1971, p. 128).

If writer's block occurs, several tactics may be tried. First, writing *anything* is better than not writing. The material may or may not be used later, but forcing yourself to write something may trigger more thinking and writing. A second strategy is to set deadlines for completing a certain number of pages, and meet these deadlines no matter what is written. Werner and Schoepfle (1987, p. 297) suggest shifting to a different medium of communication—writing a letter about the research to a friend, for example, or giving a talk, formal or informal, on the topic. A tape recording of the lecture or conversation can later be used as a stimulus for writing.

The first draft of the report is just that—a first draft. No matter how rough or disjointed some sections may be, it is infinitely easier to work from something than from nothing. The first draft can be given to colleagues, friends, or participants for comments. Incorporating their suggestions with your own editing will result in a more refined draft that may be close to the final version. In any case, writing the initial draft is the most laborious and time-consuming phase. Successive revisions are much less tedious; gradually the report takes shape, and you can feel a sense of accomplishment as the research process comes to a close.

In summary, the writing up of a research study can be made easier by breaking the task into smaller steps. According to Werner and Schoepfle (1987), "Planning is the most important part of writing" (p. 302). With a well-thought-out strategy for tackling the report, it becomes a manageable undertaking. One such strategy has been described here. First, assemble all the materials related to the study in an organized fashion. Second, determine the intended audience, since different audiences will be interested in different questions and components of the study. Third, select a focus that meets the interest of the intended audience and addresses the original purpose of the study. Fourth, outline the report once the central message has been determined. Finally, begin writing. The outline may be refined, adjusted, or revised entirely to coincide with the thoughts and ideas you have while writing. It is also wise to have others read the first draft before undertaking revisions that lead to the final form of the report.

Content of a Qualitative Study Report

In the first part of this chapter I presented a strategy for engaging in the writing process. This section addresses some of the questions qualitative investigators face regarding the content of the report. What are the common components of a report? Where should the methodology, references to other research, data displays, and other such elements be placed? How should description be integrated with analysis? And, How can some balance be maintained between the two? Also discussed are outlets for disseminating the final report.

Components of a Qualitative Research Report

There is no standard format for reporting qualitative research. Diversity in style of reporting qualitative research was "rampant" over twenty years ago (Lofland, 1974, p. 110), and is even more "experimental" today (Richardson, 1994, p. 520). The contents of a case study report depend on the audience's interest as well as the investigator's purpose in doing the research in the first place. Practitioners or the general public, for example, will not be much interested in methodological information, whereas colleagues and other researchers will find such information crucial for assessing the study's contribution to the field. The best that I can offer here is a presentation of the basic components of most qualitative reports and the options available for handling different parts of the report.

The relative emphasis given each section, as well as the overall form of the report, can vary widely. Nevertheless, all reports discuss the nature of the problem investigated, the way the investigation was conducted, and the findings that resulted. In standard research reports, the problem that gave rise to the study is laid out early in the report. This section usually includes references to the literature, the theoretical framework of the study, a problem statement and the purpose of the study, and research questions that guided the study (see Chapter Three). At the very least, the reader must have some clue as to what this study is all about, even in the more postmodern, experimental write-ups. Tierney's (1993) ethnographic fiction of a university's nondiscrimination policy, for example, opens by quoting the policy. This is followed by descriptive portraits of six personalities involved in the policy change. In quoting the twenty-seven–word policy statement at the opening of his report, we at least know that the study takes place at a university and involves discrimination in some way.

Early in some reports, especially qualitative case studies, is a description of the context of the study, or where the inquiry took place. In forms of qualitative research where interviewing is the major or only source of data, a general description of the sample as a whole is given in the methodology section. Some interview-based studies also include short portraits of each participant.

The methodology section includes, at the minimum, how the sample was selected, how data were collected and analyzed, and what measures were taken to ensure validity and reliability. Becoming quite common in reports of qualitative research is an additional section on the investigator—his or her training, experience, philosophical orientation, and biases. In a qualitative case study of his Russian immigrant grandfather, for example, Abramson (1992) includes a discussion of the biases inherent in translating his grandfather's Hebrew diaries, as well as his own personal biases, which included a tendency to "pathologize" the man. Of this tendency he writes:

> Though I never knew him, I knew his offspring (my father) well. I did not like my father. He was frequently volatile, impulsive, and out-of-control. He also had a raging temper and was plagued with obsessional fears. . . . He seemed stuck in the role of 'master

sergeant,' his rank in the army. . . . On the positive side, my father was very bright, was a gifted musician, and could occasionally be charming. . . . Since my father did not 'spring from the cosmos,' I have assumed—whether fair or not—that there was a causal relationship between his behavior and that of my grandfather. Thus, as a consequence, I am predisposed to malign Samuel Abramson [pp. 12–13].

In addition to some attention to the problem of the study and information as to how it was carried out, every report offers the findings derived from the analysis of the data. Basically, findings are the outcome of the inquiry, what you, the investigator learned or came to understand about the phenomenon. For this section of the report there are few guidelines. Richardson (1994) reviews a range of creative possibilities for presentation of a study's findings:

> Margery Wolf, in *A Thrice-Told Tale* (1992), takes the same event and tells it as fictional story, field notes, and a social scientific paper. John Steward, in *Drinkers, Drummers and Decent Folk* (1989), writes poetry, fiction, ethnographic accounts, and field notes about Village Trinidad. Valerie Walkerdin's *Schoolgirl Fictions* (1990) develops/displays the theme that "masculinity and femininity are fictions which take on the status of fact" (p. xiii) by incorporating into the book journal entries, poems, essays, photographs of herself, drawings, cartoons, and annotated transcripts. Ruth Linden's *Making Stories, Making Selves: Feminist Reflections on the Holocaust* (1992) intertwines autobiography, academic writing, and survivors' stories [p. 522].

While the examples given are alternatives, the most common way findings are presented in a qualitative report is to organize them according to the categories, themes, or theory derived from the data analysis (see Chapter Nine). Typically, a "findings" section begins with a brief overview of the findings, followed by presentation of *each* separate finding supported by quotes from interviews or field notes or references to documentary evidence. Exhibit 11.1 is an abbreviated example taken from a study of the negative outcomes of learning from life experience (Merriam, Mott, and Lee, 1996). Note the overview of the findings at the beginning. This overview functions like a map so the reader can

Exhibit 11.1. Sample "Findings" Section of a Research Report.

Findings

As stated earlier, the purpose of this study was to understand the process involved when the negative interpretation of a life experience results in growth-inhibiting outcomes. We uncovered a process consisting of three major components. First, a defining aspect of the self is challenged by a life experience. The experience is then interpreted to protect the self—this is the learning that results in growth-inhibiting outcomes. If and when the threat is reduced, meaning-making can lead to possible future growth.

A defining aspect of the self is challenged

Some life experiences become learning experiences and others do not. Those that get our attention are ones that link with our personal history. As Boud, Cohen and Walker (1993: 9) suggest, 'our personal history affects the way in which we experience and what we acknowledge as experience'. Thus, the experience not only links with our personal history, it challenges some defining, central aspect of the self. Greg, for example, saw himself as a caretaker, as one who supports and is responsible for others. Greg explained that he had always had

> very clear external definitions of what it means to be a parent, father, spouse, husband, friend, whatever . . . I was the caretaker for the family . . . I would just be walking along and think, 'Holy Cow! I'm divorced! Little Greg doesn't get divorced!'

In a very different experience, Roger recounted how his tour of duty in Vietnam nearly 20 years ago was 'a rite of passage to manhood in my family', that he 'felt proud . . . very proud. I was raised to be patriotic . . . to believe in country'. However, his image of himself as a proud patriot was challenged both by the reality of being there and his return home:

> You find out you're not fighting for God, country, mom, and apple pie. You're fighting for yourself and your friends and to get the hell out and get it over with . . . If you do survive, when you do come home, you lost the war. It's your fault, you're the drug-crazed baby killer . . . We came back losers.

In perhaps the most extreme example of the self being challenged by an experience, Ruth finds out at 28 years old that she had been sold to her adoptive parents as an infant. Her entire identity is shaken by this knowledge. While she remembered herself as being 'a very trusting, loving person', upon finding out about the adoption, she described herself as having

> a fragmentary sense of self . . . I don't know how to find my identity. Where did I come from? Where is my origin? . . . I ask, 'what is my real identity, where is the foundation, where is the basis of integrity of myself?'

Source: Merriam, Mott, and Lee (1996, pp. 12–13). Reprinted with permission.

follow the presentation. The first finding—"A defining aspect of the self is challenged"—is introduced, followed by interview data in support of the finding.

Knowing how much data to include in support of a category or theme is a judgment call. You need enough to be convincing, but not so much that the reader becomes buried. The findings are also discussed, either along with their presentation or in a separate section often titled "Discussion." It is in the discussion that you tell the reader what you make of the findings. Were there any surprises? How do they compare with what is already known? What conclusions do you draw overall? What unique contribution does your study make to the knowledge base in this area?

Placement of Component Parts

Where should the methodology section, the references to previous research and literature, and the visual displays be placed? Again the answer depends on the sophistication and interest of the target audience. For many audiences, the methodology section would be placed in an appendix to the report. Referring to an ethnographic study, Werner and Schoepfle (1987) write, "The average reader is not interested in how the ethnography was obtained as long as he or she retains a feeling for the quality, validity, and reliability of the monograph. On the other hand, for fellow ethnographers a methodological section may be of great importance. Under no circumstances should it be left out, but its placement should be dictated by the anticipated readership" (p. 282).

Qualitative studies in professional journals present a discussion of methodology early in the article—often as part of the introduction of the problem or immediately following it. Boggs's (1986) article reports the results of a case study of the role of educational activities in an environmental campaign of a local citizens group called HART (Huron Agricultural Resources Tomorrow). The methodology section consists of a one-page explanation of how the case study was chosen and how data were gathered. Here is an excerpt from the methodology:

> A case study . . . is a detailed examination of one setting, one single subject, one single depository of documents, or some particular event. Several theoretical perspectives and several disciplines can provide the basis for such a detailed examination. . . . The focus of this examination . . . was on the self and community education undertaken by HART to achieve its objectives.
>
> Four sources of data were relevant in this case study. First, HART leaders and members were interviewed over a period of eight months. These persons were asked to describe the HART experience—its origins, purposes, activities, successes, and failures. They were asked to elaborate on the measures taken to educate themselves and the Harbor Beach community on the power plant initiative. The chairperson of the education committee was interviewed twice. Second, a scrapbook of newspaper clippings chronicled the public story. The scrapbook presented the perspectives of HART, Detroit Edison, elected officials, government agency personnel, the newspaper editor, and the general public in letters-to-the-editor. . . . A third data source was the newsletter published every two months for distribution to the HART membership. . . . A fourth source of data was the educational materials prepared by HART. . . . The period of time in which data were collected and analyzed was roughly Autumn 1979 to Spring 1982 [Boggs, 1986, p. 5].

Where should the references to literature relevant to the problem being studied be placed? In experimental or survey research, a review of previous research and writing is part of the introduction and development of the problem. Glaser (1978) argues for a much later handling of relevant literature in grounded theory studies so the researcher will not be unduly influenced by others' ideas regarding the problem under study. In this way the researcher can remain open to discovering new insights. Lincoln and Guba (1985) raise an interesting question. "If the literature is to be critiqued via the case, should not the case writer know in what sense, so as to be sure to include materials that would make such a critique possible" (p. 369)? Thus if a qualitative case study is being undertaken as a critique of some theory, principle, or accepted piece of folk wisdom, the investigator should establish that fact with appropriate reference to the literature early in the report. However, if someone else's categorical scheme is being used to interpret the data collected (rather than evolving one from the data), such references should be made just prior to use of the material. Finally, discussion of the study's findings might very well incorporate references to other reports in pointing out where the study's findings deviate from previous work or support it.

Thus references to relevant literature can be placed early in the report when describing the problem, in a section reviewing previous work, or in the section devoted to presentation and interpretation of the study's results. Keep in mind the intended audience and the desired length of the report when making this decision.

What about charts, tables, and figures? Their placement must also be considered in writing the final report. Miles and Huberman (1994) note that the typical mode of displaying qualitative research has been through words in a narrative text. Used by itself, narrative text is a "weak and cumbersome form of display" that is hard on both analysts and readers. For policy makers in particular, "long case studies are almost useless" due to lack of the "time required to comprehend a long account and draw conclusions for their work" (p. 91).

As I pointed out in Chapter Nine, displaying qualitative data in the form of a chart, matrix, table, or figure can be an aid in analyzing that data. Such displays show the relationships, common threads, and even problems with the analysis to date. Displaying data in a final report permits the consumer of the report to see the same sorts of things; at the same time readers can quickly grasp complexities in the analysis that would take an enormous amount of narrative writing to convey. Displays provide something of a shorthand version of the findings. They should be used judiciously, however. Their use is recommended "only if it snaps important ideas or significant relationships into sharp focus for the reader more quickly than other means of presentation" (Van Dalen, 1966, p. 431).

In using visual displays in a study report, the researcher should

- Keep the display simple, including only the information that is necessary to understanding the presentation.
- Keep the number of displays to a minimum. Using just a few figures to represent important ideas will draw attention to those ideas.
- Mention the display in the text, keeping the display as close to its discussion as possible.

Displays should be an integrated part of the study narrative. That is, displays accompanied by a sentence or two leave too much interpretation up to the reader. The researcher must at least explain how the data displayed in the table or figure or chart illustrate some aspect of the case, whether it is descriptive or interpretive information.

Description and Analysis

One of the most difficult dilemmas to resolve in writing up qualitative research is deciding how much concrete description to include as opposed to analysis and interpretation and how to integrate one with the other so that the narrative remains interesting and informative. Lofland's (1974) review of styles of reporting qualitative field research found that some writers' presentations of supporting data amounted to overkill. "Inflicted unedited upon readers, four or five page extracts are used to illustrate single points" (p. 104). At the other extreme were writers so enamored with the conceptual frame of their study that "the actual report emerge[s] more or less divorced from the adequate empirical materials—direct quotes and direct descriptions—remaining in the field worker's files" (p. 108). Reviewers of qualitative sociology reports, Lofland writes, have a rule of thumb that "sixty to seventy percent of the report is events, anecdotes, episodes, and the like, and some thirty to forty percent is conceptual framework" (p. 107). Strauss (1987) makes the point that a study that builds a grounded theory will understandably rely more heavily on analytic commentary than on raw data.

Whether this 60–40 or 70–30 split is a good guideline for writing up qualitative research in education remains to be tested by checking what gets published in the field. The discussion does, however, point to a real problem in writing up the results of a qualitative study. Some balance needs be achieved between description and interpretation.

Erickson's (1986) differentiation among particular description, general description, and interpretive commentary may be helpful in determining this balance. These three components are units in the process of data analysis, and they also can become "basic elements of the written report of the study" (p. 149). That is, the raw data are reported as particular description, patterns discovered in the data are reported as general description, and ever higher levels of abstraction become interpretive commentary. "Such commentary is interpolated between particular and general description to help the reader make connections between the details that are being reported and the more abstract argument being . . . reported" (p. 149).

Particular description consists of quotes from people interviewed, quotes from field notes, and narrative vignettes of everyday life "in which the sights and sounds of what was being said and done are described in the natural sequence of their occurrence in real time" (Erickson, 1986, pp. 150–151). *General description* is needed to tell the reader whether the vignettes and quotes are typical of the data as a whole. "Failing to demonstrate these patterns of distribution—to show generalization *within the corpus*—is perhaps the most serious flaw in much reporting of fieldwork research" (Erickson, 1986, p. 151). *Interpretive commentary,* the third element in a case study report, provides a framework for understanding the particular and general descriptions just discussed. According to Erickson (1986):

> The interpretive commentary that precedes and follows an instance of particular description is necessary to guide the reader to see the analytic type of which the instance is a concrete token. . . . Interpretive commentary thus points the reader to those details that are salient for the author, and to the meaning-interpretations of the author. Commentary that follows the particular vignette or quote stimulates the retrospective interpretation of the reader. Both the anticipatory and the subsequent commentary are necessary if the reader is not to be lost in a thicket of uninterpretable detail [p. 152].

Erickson recognizes the difficulty of alternating between "the extreme particularity of detail found in the vignette (or in an exact citation from field notes or in a direct quote from an interview) and the more general voice of the accompanying interpretive commentary" (p. 152). Report writers tend to err in presenting too much description or "adopting a voice of medium general description—neither concrete enough nor abstract enough" (p. 152). Since there are no set guidelines on how to achieve the right balance between the particular and the general, between description and analysis, the qualitative investigator usually learns how to balance the two through trial and error. Reading published reports or consulting experienced colleagues might also be helpful in learning how to balance description and analysis.

Disseminating the Study Report

Depending on the study's sponsor, its purpose, and the intended audience, the format used in reporting the results can vary. For certain groups, executive summaries or specialized condensations are effective. Or the narrative could be replaced with a set of open-ended questions and answers drawn from the data (Yin, 1994). This format is particularly useful for reporting multiple-case studies. "A reader need only examine the answers to the same question or questions within each case study to begin making cross-case comparisons. Because each reader may be interested in different questions, the entire format facilitates the development of a cross-case analysis tailored to the specific interests of its readers" (Yin, 1994, p. 135). Still another possibility is to prepare analytic summaries with supporting data in appendixes (Rist, 1982).

Patton (1990) even questions the need for a final report in some studies, especially those with a focus on evaluation. He has found that final reports "have less impact than the direct, face-to-face interactions" with those interested in using the results of the evaluation. In his opinion, "the burden of proof lies with the evaluation users to justify production of a full report" (p. 428). Certainly oral delivery in the form of conference presentations, debriefings, press conferences, and the like serves the purpose of communicating and disseminating the results of some research. In fact, a study's findings could be presented in the form of film, videodisc, or pictorial display.

Most researchers are interested in disseminating the results of their studies beyond a sponsor and participants. Such dissemination is done primarily through conferences or journals in the field. Conferences are organized by professional associations, institutions, and agencies and are usually open to anyone interested in the topic. Any conference is an avenue for disseminating the results of research—depending, of course, on the conference's goals and whether or not you can frame the report in terms of those goals. A qualitative study on teachers' influence on social studies curriculum, for example, could be presented at a conference on research, curriculum issues, teaching, or social studies.

Publishing the study in a professional journal means familiarizing yourself with the journal's format, style, procedures for submission, and focus. There is no point in sending a qualitative study to a journal that publishes only experimental research, even if the topic matches the journal's content. Since there is wide diversity in qualitative reporting, it is a good idea to find examples of qualitative studies in the journal to serve as prototypes. Most fields of education—curriculum and supervision, science education, adult education, and so on—have at least one journal that will consider qualitative research for publication. Journals in related fields such as anthropology, sociology, and psychology might also publish studies dealing with educational issues, and there is at least one journal devoted to this type of work, titled *International Journal of Qualitative Studies in Education*.

Other modes of dissemination might be through the in-house publications of professional associations, foundations, social service agencies, and community organizations. And, of course, qualitative studies sometimes get published in book form. Often such books are produced by presses associated with the university or organization where the study was done. Occasionally, a commercial press will publish research results that have wide appeal. Preston's (1995) account in *The Hot Zone* of an outbreak of a strain of Ebola virus among monkeys in Reston, Virginia, is an example.

Case Study Reports

Nearly everything presented in this chapter about writing the final report is also applicable to qualitative case studies. Some particulars with regard to writing up a case study should be attended to, however. Perhaps the major point about case studies to keep in mind is that they are richly descriptive in order to afford the reader the vicarious experience of having been there. "The case study," Patton (1990) writes, "should take the reader into the case situation, a person's life, a group's life, or a program's life" (p. 387). Detailed description of particulars is needed so that the reader can vicariously experience the setting of the study; detailed description is also necessary for the reader to assess the evidence upon which the researcher's analysis is based.

Donmoyer (1990) offers three compelling rationales for conveying the vicarious experience of a case study to the reader. First is the advantage of *accessibility*. "Case studies can take us to places where most of us would not have an opportunity to go" (p. 193). This does not have to refer to exotic places. Case studies allow us to experience situations and individuals in our own settings that we would not normally have access to. A second advantage to case studies is *seeing through the researcher's eyes*. By this Donmoyer means that case studies may allow us to see something familiar but in new and interesting ways. The third advantage he identifies is *decreased defensiveness*. "Vicarious experience is less likely to produce defensiveness and resistance to learning" (p. 196). People can learn from a case study, perhaps more willingly than from actual experience. "Resistance to accommodating novelty" in a case study, for example, "will not be as great as when a threat is experienced in real life" (p. 197).

Of course, in order for a reader to vicariously experience a phenomenon, the writer must transport the reader to the setting. This is done through writing a vividly descriptive narrative of the setting and the situation. These descriptions can be any length, depending on whether they are describing the context generally, or illustrating a specific point. Exhibit 11.2 is a description of one of Billy Graham's crusade meetings and one of a set of case descriptions in a study by Houle (1984) of different patterns of learning. This case explores oratory as a basic teaching method. Note how the rich, thick description transports the reader to the event.

Exhibit 11.2. Example of a Descriptive Case Study.

If you entered the great hall of McCormick Place in Chicago on a June evening in 1971, you were immediately confronted by a long row of tables at which books and phonograph records were for sale, with, for example, a $4.95 authorized biography of Graham going at the special rate of $2.50. Beyond those tables were 38,000 seats, but your choice among them was limited. Some were held for those with "blue and white tickets," whatever that might mean. Some were set aside for groups. Some were reserved for counselors, ushers, and the press. Most of the seats near the door were kept for latecomers. Men with bull-horns were needed to direct the general flow of traffic, but for the most part in-comers were gently urged in one direction by ushers and prevented from going in other directions by barriers. Eventually you came to the place where you could exercise a choice but it was not a wide one. Every seat must be taken, and people were held shoulder to shoulder by linked chairs. When one section was full, another was opened. There must be close, direct, human contact of a physical sort. . . .

The ushers are indispensable to the entire process. They range from perhaps twenty-five to seventy-five years of age; they are neatly dressed with carefully folded handkerchiefs in their breast pockets; they have fresh haircuts; and they have been either born to their calling or conditioned by years of service on Sunday mornings. Each has four to six rows of seats under his care and sees himself as the kindly shepherd of the people sitting in them. Authority rises above these first-line men in an orderly hierarchy; there are aisle captains and section captains and presumably a floor captain. These men are constantly busy; once the need to seat their flock has been met, they confer with one another endlessly, answer questions from the audience, volunteer information about the evening's program, and, if need be, care for distress or disturbance.

The setting itself is in no sense dramatic, only big. No bold design catches the eye, no banners wave, no striking symbols are to be seen. Later on, there will be no sudden darkenings of the room or the stadium, no beams of light picking out an isolated figure in the darkness, no use of projected images, no hidden electric fans causing banners to wave. No orchestra will play; the only music will be provided by piano or organ. None of the devices of modern industrial design or of the packaging of performance are visible.

The evocation is of something far different and far more familiar. The meeting place feels comfortable to its audiences because it has been made to look as much as possible like customary places of lower- and middle-class pomp and ceremony; the Protestant church, the high school

Exhibit 11.2. (continued)

auditorium, or the converted gymnasium or movie theater that is being used for graduation exercises. The people present know where they are because they have been there so often. Only the scale has changed. In Chicago, a banner stretching across the background of the rostrum said: "Jesus said, 'I am the way, the truth, and the life.' John 14:6"; it was fifty feet long. The chorus was made up not of twenty or a hundred voices but of two thousand. The platform was very large. The piano and organ were electrically amplified, so that 38,000 people could hear every note. The runway that projected forward from the platform was edged with the familiar shapes of ferns and ornamental trees. At the base of the lectern was an arrangement of flowers like those at christenings, weddings, and funerals—but incomparably larger. The hall itself was brilliantly lighted throughout, but, in addition, three massed rows of spotlights focused on the platform. . . .

A strong sense of community pervades the hall. It is felt most deeply by the members of a local church congregation who know one another, come from the same community, have planned and undertaken the trip, sit together, and will go home in the same bus. As the service proceeds, the feeling of togetherness spreads to the entire assemblage. We have so much in common. We heard the choir rehearsing before the service. We focused our cameras on the young man who stood silently at the lectern for a half hour before the service; when Billy comes out we are sure to get good photographs. Isn't it wonderful how many people are pouring in? We applaud during the program whenever the success of the Crusade is mentioned. We sing familiar songs. We rise and sit down as directed. We look up passages in the Bibles we have brought. We laugh comfortably at the witticisms. We catch our breaths with astonishment when a celebrity is introduced. We make our financial contributions willingly, eager to help the great Crusade go on. We speak to one another approvingly of the number of young people present this evening. When a speaker makes a telling point, we say "amen." We talk about past Crusades and hope for future ones. We exchange gossip about Billy and the members of his team. We nudge our children and remind them that this is a night they will remember all their lives. We make plans to see all future telecasts, especially the one of tonight's program. We say over and over again how nice it is that Billy has had a chance to come back to Chicago-land, which means so much to him; other people may claim him but he is really one of ours, having gone to one of our colleges and having had his first pastorate here. . . .

The pace quickens. With no introduction, Graham bounds to the lectern at the front end of the long runway. He welcomes the group, gives thanks to various people, tells the audience how close Chicago "and the tri-state area" are to his own heart, makes a little witticism, and describes in detail what will be happening each subsequent evening during the Crusade. He is succeeded by several events: Barrows recommending a magazine, a hymn by the choir, another solo by another artist, Barrows recommending a book, a hymn by the choir and audience, and then an introduction of the second most important event of the evening. It is a talk by someone who has found God, often by listening to Graham. The speaker may be a big league baseball player, a handicapped person in a wheelchair, a former member of a youth gang or of the White House staff, or a leader of the advertising profession. This speech is brief, well-rehearsed, and movingly spoken. Then another song by soloist and choir. Then comes the main event of the evening.

The man who is the focal point of this elaborate setting and process is taller than his co-workers, erect, and with a springing step. His face is exactly like the one shown in his newspaper photographs except, of course, that it is not black and white but ruddy. His hair sweeps back to a moderate length, its smooth perfection sometimes set off by a little duck tail. His face is lean and his build athletic.

His countenance is mobile, although he never smiles. He uses his hands with extraordinary effectiveness and swiftness and has a large repertoire of gestures, each distinct but flowing into one another with smooth perfection. The right-handed index finger is pointed toward the audience or toward heaven. He clenches one or both fists, or his hands rapidly revolve around one another. A characteristic gesture is made with either hand. It is a swift vertical movement, followed by a swift horizontal one. "He sent his son" (vertical movement) "to die for you" (horizontal movement). The symbolism of the cross must be evident to many and subliminal to others. A frequent mannerism is to thrust his head forward from his body with the chin stretched out as far as possible and the lips tightly pressed. It is a defiant look that says, "I have said something you must hear; if you don't, it is at your cost." His most celebrated posture comes at the end, while he is waiting for people to come forward. Then he stands erect except for a bowed head, his eyes closed, his upper lip resting on his clasped hands.

His voice is vibrant and alive. He knows, as does any orator, that it lies at the heart of his success. While sitting on the platform, he sprays his throat surreptitiously with a hand atomizer, and he takes a sudden last sip of water before he goes forward to preach. His voice has been thoroughly trained, and he uses it to the full limit of its not extraordinary range. His accent is American of the middle-South variety, particularly noticeable in his final "r's" and "o's"; he says "fathuh" and "heah" and

Exhibit 11.2. (continued)

"tomorruh." He thunders and he speaks softly and sometimes does one immediately following the other. He can be the great spellbinder, his blue eyes flashing fire. He can speak confidentially. He can be mildly humorous, although only rarely. And yet, although anybody who has ever taken a course in public speaking would realize that Graham is using his voice with great art, he never seems conscious of doing so. The days of the acquisition of mastery are far behind him.

Source: Houle (1984, pp. 79–86). Reprinted with permission.

In another example, Lightfoot (1983) illustrates with a short vignette how one school attendance officer "rearranges the traditional patterns of power and exchange" (p. 6) between the school and poor minority parents. The vignette also illustrates the officer's "honor of parents, his integration of empathy and toughness, his belief in the capacities of each individual student" (p. 96):

At Epstein's desk a quiet, shy Black boy is trying to get permission to reenter school after several weeks of absence. His mother has been in a serious car accident and since her hospitalization, he has not come to school. The boy, who is frail and awkward, looks strikingly vulnerable and Epstein's tone seems to noticeably soften. A call is made to the boy's aunt who is at work. "I'm going to dial the number," says Epstein, "but you say hello to your aunt, so she won't get scared. Tell her it's Mr. Epstein from the attendance office. Then I'll talk to her." The boy repeats Epstein's words verbatim and hands the phone across the desk to him. Epstein is gentle and respectful. "Hello, how are you? We wanted to call to confirm Robert's absences. He has been absent a lot and we've received no notes from home. . . . He'll fail his subjects unless we hear from you confirming his absences." There is a long pause in which the aunt must be offering an explanation. Epstein follows with a few questions and then closes by saying, "Okay, we'll try to help him. He seems like a nice boy. Take care now and thanks for your time." Robert has been on the edge of his chair, his body erect and tense, during the telephone conversation. His eyes search Epstein's face. Epstein returns his full gaze and says with a stronger voice, "Let me tell you something important. What happened to your mom is very serious. No doubt about it. It was very scary, extremely frightening . . . but rather than be absent through all of the hard times, you must come to school. Come here and we'll talk about it. . . . Just think if Mom comes out of the hospital and you've failed your subjects, she's going to be very sad and disappointed. . . . There are lots of people around here who you can get to know, who could care about you. But you have to be in school." . . . Robert seems to hang on each word and looks comforted, not chastised [Lightfoot, 1983, p. 99].

There are a number of ways to organize a case study report such that the sense of immediacy, of being there, is maintained. Van Maanen (1988) identifies seven styles: realistic, impressionistic, confessional, critical, formal, literary, and jointly told, and there are other, more experimental forms (Richardson, 1994). Currently, there are two common patterns. Some writers present a descriptive narrative first, followed by analysis and interpretation. This is what Houle (1984) did in his book, wherein the final chapter offers generalizations about learning drawn from across the individual cases. Another common organization is to integrate descriptions and vignettes with commentary. This is how Abramson (1992) wrote the case study of his Russian immigrant grandfather.

Stake (1995) points out that the case report usually falls somewhere between storytelling and the traditional research report. According to Stake, the development of most case study reports follows one of several paths: "a chronological or biographical development of the case; a researcher's view of coming to know the case"; or "description one by one of several major components of the case" (p. 127). He also offers an outline tailored to case studies but encompassing all the elements of a qualitative research report discussed earlier in this chapter. This outline with his commentary is presented in Exhibit 11.3.

In summary, writing a case study report is not a lot different from writing up any report of qualitative research. In both situations, it is crucial to consider the audience, which in turn, helps determine the style and voice of the report, as well as how much attention should be devoted to each of the necessary component parts. Case studies, which have as their goal to convey understanding, must contain enough description to provide a vicarious experience for the reader.

Exhibit 11.3. Outline of a Case Study Report.

Entry vignette	I want my readers immediately to start developing a vicarious experience, to get the feel of the place, time.
Issue identification, purpose and method of study	Although most of my readers care little about my methods, I want to tell them something about how the study came to be, who I am, and what issues I think will help us to understand the case.
Extensive narrative description to further define case and contexts	I want to present a body of relatively uncontestable data, not completely without interpretation, but a description not unlike they would make themselves had they been there. If I have controversial data to present, I am likely to present them, if I can, as views of a contender or witness.
Development of issues	Somewhere, perhaps in the middle, I want to carefully develop a few key issues, not for the purpose of generalizing beyond the case but for understanding the complexity of the case. It is often here that I will draw on other research or on my understanding of other cases.
Descriptive detail, documents, quotations, triangulating data	Some of the issues need further probing. This should be the place for the most confirming experiential data. I will indicate not only what I have done to confirm the observations (my triangulations) but what I have done to try to disconfirm them.
Assertions	It is my intent to provide information that allows the readers to reconsider their knowledge of the case or even to modify existing generalizations about such cases. Nevertheless, having presented a body of relatively uninterpreted observations, I will summarize what I feel I understand about the case and how my generalizations about the case have changed conceptually or in level of confidence.
Closing vignette	I like to close on an experiential note, reminding the reader that the report is just one person's encounter with a complex case.

Source: Stake (1995, p. 123). Reprinted with permission.

Summary

This chapter has focused on the writing of a qualitative study report. Without the important step of reporting and disseminating results, the research process would not be complete. Research in education is important for extending the knowledge base of the field as well as for understanding and improving practice. Research can contribute to both theory and practice, but only if it is communicated beyond the research situation. Suggestions for writing the report were as follows. First, the writer should compile all the relevant data and then determine the intended audience. The next step is to settle on the main message—that is, the focus or theme of the study. An outline reflecting the study's focus is essential for dealing with a large amount of material. The researcher is then ready to write the first draft.

The major portion of the chapter focused on the content of a qualitative research report. The essential elements of the study problem, methodology, and findings were reviewed, along with the issues of placing component parts, balancing description with analysis, and disseminating the research findings. The chapter closed with a discussion of special considerations in writing a qualitative case study report.

Writing the final report is much like the entire process of conducting a qualitative research study: it is as much an art as a science. While we have examples, guidelines, and other peoples' experiences to draw upon, the process as well as the end product will reflect the uniqueness, peculiarities, and idiosyncracies of each research situation. In this book I have provided some guidelines, shared my experiences, and provided numerous examples of how to handle the various components of qualitative research and their application to case studies. There is, however, no substitute for actually engaging in the process of shaping a research problem, collecting and analyzing data, and writing up findings. I hope that this book will make your journey easier.

References

Abramson, P. R. *A Case for Case Studies.* Thousand Oaks, Calif.: Sage, 1992.

Adelman, C., Jenkins, D., and Kemmis, S. "Rethinking Case Study: Notes from the Second Cambridge Conference." In *Case Study: An Overview.* Case Study Methods 1 (Series). Victoria, Australia: Deakin University Press, 1983.

Adler, P. A., and Adler, P. "Observational Techniques." In N. K. Denzin and Y. S. Lincoln (eds.), *Handbook of Qualitative Research.* Thousand Oaks, Calif.: Sage, 1994.

Agar, M. "The Right Brain Strikes Back." In N. G. Fielding and R. M. Lee (eds.), *Using Computers in Qualitative Research.* London: Sage, 1991.

Akeroyd, A. V. "Personal Information and Qualitative Research Data: Some Practical and Ethical Problems Arising from Data Protection Legislation." In N. G. Fielding and R. M. Lee (eds.), *Using Computers in Qualitative Research.* London: Sage, 1991.

Alcoff, L. "The Problem of Speaking for Others." *Cultural Critique,* 1991, *20,* 5–32.

Allatt, P., and Benson, L. D. "Computing and Qualitative Analysis: Issues in Research Methods Teaching." In N. G. Fielding and R. M. Lee (eds.), *Using Computers in Qualitative Research.* London: Sage, 1991.

Altheide, D. L. "Ethnographic Content Analysis." *Qualitative Sociology,* 1987, *10*(1), 65–77.

Anonymous, *Primary Colors: A Novel of Politics.* New York: Random House, 1996.

Armstrong, D. "Finding a 'Role' for the Ethnograph in the Analysis of Qualitative Data." In R. G. Burgess (ed.), *Computing and Qualitative Research.* Vol. 5. Greenwich, Conn.: JAI Press, 1995.

Araujo, L. "Designing and Refining Hierarchical Coding Frames." In U. Kelle (ed.), *Computer-Aided Qualitative Data Analysis: Theory, Methods, and Practice.* London: Sage, 1995.

Auster, C. J. "Manuals for Socialization: Examples from Girl Scout Handbooks 1913–1984." *Qualitative Sociology,* 1985, *8*(4), 359–367.

Aviram, O. "Appearance and Reality in a Stressful Educational Setting:

Practices Inhibiting School Effectiveness in an Israeli Boarding School." *Qualitative Studies in Education,* 1993, *6*(1), 33–48.

Bateson, M. C. *Composing a Life.* New York: Penguin Books, 1990.

Becker, H. S. "Social Observation and Social Case Studies." In *International Encyclopedia of the Social Sciences.* Vol. 11. New York: Crowell, 1968.

Becker, H. S. *Doing Things Together.* Evanston, IL: Northwestern University Press, 1986a.

Becker, H. S. *Writing for Social Scientists.* Chicago: University of Chicago Press, 1986b.

Becker, H. S. "Theory: The Necessary Evil." In D. J. Flinders and G. E. Mills (eds.), *Theory and Concepts in Qualitative Research.* New York: Teachers College Press, 1993.

Bednarz, D. "Quantity and Quality in Evaluation Research: A Divergent View." *Evaluation and Program Planning,* 1985, *8,* 289–306.

Berendt, J. *Midnight in the Garden of Good and Evil.* New York: Random House, 1994.

Bierema, L. L. "How Executive Women Learn Corporate Culture." *Human Resource Development Quarterly,* 1996, *7*(2), 145–164.

Blankenship, J. C. "Attrition Among Male Nursing Students." Unpublished doctoral dissertation, Department of Adult Education, University of Georgia, Athens, 1991.

Bogdan, R. C. *Participant Observation in Organizational Settings.* Syracuse, N.Y.: Syracuse University Press, 1972.

Bogdan, R. C., and Biklen, S. K. *Qualitative Research for Education: An Introduction to Theory and Methods.* (2nd ed.) Needham Heights, Mass.: Allyn & Bacon, 1992.

Boggs, D. L. "A Case Study of Citizen Education and Action." *Adult Education Quarterly,* 1986, *37*(1), 1–13.

Bohannan, L. "Shakespeare in the Bush." Reprinted in J. M. Morse (ed.), *Qualitative Health Research.* Thousand Oaks, Calif.: Sage, 1992.

Borg, W. R., and Gall, M. D. *Educational Research.* (5th ed.) White Plains, N.Y.: Longman, 1989.

Boshier, R. "Popular Discourse Concerning AIDS: Its Implications for Adult Education." *Adult Education Quarterly,* 1992, *42,* 125–135.

Bowering, D. J. (ed.). *Secondary Analysis of Available Data Bases.* New Directions for Program Evaluation, no. 22. San Francisco: Jossey-Bass, 1984.

Brandt, R. "Observations of B's Lesson on Overhead Transparencies." Unpublished report, University of Georgia, Athens, April 1987.

Bromley, D. B. *The Case-Study Method in Psychology and Related Disciplines.* New York: Wiley, 1986.

Burgess, R. G. (ed.). *Field Research: A Source Book and Field Manual.* London: Allen & Unwin, 1982.

Burlingame, M., and Geske, T. G. "State Politics and Education: An Examination of Selected Multiple-State Case Studies." *Educational Administration Quarterly,* 1979, *15*(2), 50–75.

Burnett, J. *Useful Toil.* Harmondsworth, England: Penguin, 1977.

Carr, W., and Kemmis, S. *Becoming Critical: Education, Knowledge and Action Research.* London: Falmer Press, 1986.

Cassell, J. "Risk and Benefit to Subjects of Fieldwork." *American Sociologist,* 1978, *13*(3), 134–143.

Cassell, J. "Does Risk-Benefit Analysis Apply to Moral Evaluation of Social Research?" In T. L. Beauchamp, R. R. Faden, R. J. Wallace, Jr., and L. Walters (eds.), *Ethical Issues in Social Science Research.* Baltimore: Johns Hopkins University Press, 1982.

Chein, I. "Appendix: An Introduction to Sampling." In L. H. Kidder (ed.), *Selltiz, Wrightsman & Cook's Research Methods in Social Relations.* (4th ed.) Austin, Tex.: Holt, Rinehart and Winston, 1981.

Clandinin, D. J., and Connelly, F. M. "Personal Experience Methods." In N. K. Denzin and Y. S. Lincoln (eds.), *Handbook of Qualitative Research.* Thousand Oaks, Calif.: Sage, 1994.

Clark, G. K. *The Critical Historian.* Portsmouth, N.H.: Heinemann Educational Books, 1967.

Coffey, A., and Atkinson, P. *Making Sense of Qualitative Data.* Thousand Oaks, Calif.: Sage, 1996.

Collins, T. S., and Noblit, G. W. *Stratification and Resegregation: The Case of Crossover High School, Memphis, Tennessee.* Memphis: Memphis State University, 1978. (ED 157 954)

Connelly, F. M., and Clandinin, D. J. "Stories of Experience and Narrative Inquiry." *Educational Researcher,* 1990, *9*(5), 2–14.

Conrad, P., and Reinharz, S. "Computers and Qualitative Data: Editors' Introductory Essay." *Qualitative Sociology,* 1984, 7(1 and 2), 3–15.

Constas, M. A. "Qualitative Analysis as a Public Event: The Documentation of Category Development Procedures." *American Educational Research Journal,* 1992, *29*(2), 253–266.

Cooper, H. M. *The Integrative Research Review: A Systematic Approach.* Thousand Oaks, Calif.: Sage, 1984.

Cordeiro, P. A., and Carspecken, P. F. "How a Minority of the Minority Succeed: A Case Study of Twenty Hispanic Achievers." *Qualitative Studies in Education,* 1993, *6*(4), 277–290.

Cordingley, E. B. "The Upside and Downside of Hypertext Tools: The KANT Example." In N. G. Fielding and R. M. Lee (eds.), *Using Computers in Qualitative Research.* London: Sage, 1991.

Cortazzi, M. *Narrative Analysis.* London: Falmer Press, 1993.

Cotterill, P., and Letherby, G. "The 'Person' in the Researcher." In R. G. Burgess (ed.), *Issues in Qualitative Research.* Studies in Qualitative Methodology. Vol. 4. Greenwich, Conn.: JAI Press, 1994.

Courtenay, B. C., Merriam, S. B., and Reeves, T. "The Centrality of Meaning-Making in Transformational Learning: How HIV-positive Adults Make Sense of their Lives." *Adult Education Quarterly,* forthcoming.

Cronbach, L. J. "Beyond the Two Disciplines of Scientific Psychology." *American Psychologist,* 1975, *30,* 116–127.

D'Andrade, R. G. "Afterword." In R. G. D'Andrade and C. Strauss (eds.), *Human Motives and Cultural Models.* Cambridge, England: Cambridge University Press, 1992.

Denzin, N. K. *The Research Act: A Theoretical Introduction to Sociological Methods.* Chicago: Aldine, 1970.

Denzin, N. K. *The Research Act: A Theoretical Introduction to Sociological Methods.* (2nd ed.) New York: McGraw-Hill, 1978.

Denzin, N. K., and Lincoln, Y. S. (eds.). *Handbook of Qualitative Research.* Thousand Oaks, Calif.: Sage, 1994

Dewey, J. *How We Think.* Lexington, Mass.: Heath, 1933.

Dexter, L. A. *Elite and Specialized Interviewing.* Evanston, Ill.: Northwestern University Press, 1970.

Dey, I. *Qualitative Data Analysis.* London: Routledge, 1993.

Dey, I. "Reducing Fragmentation in Qualitative Research." In U. Kelle (ed.), *Computer-Aided Qualitative Data Analysis: Theory, Methods, and Practice.* London: Sage, 1995.

Deyhle, D. L., Hess, G. A., Jr., and LeCompte, M. D. "Approaching Ethical Issues for Qualitative Researchers in Education." In M. D. LeCompte, W. L. Millroy, and J. Preissle (eds.), *The Handbook of Qualitative Research in Education.* Orlando, Fla.: Academic Press, 1992.

Diener, E., and Crandall, R. *Ethics in Social and Behavioral Research.* Chicago: University of Chicago Press, 1978.

Dominick, J., and Cervero, R. "A Case Study of a Problem-Solving Workshop for Northeast Georgia Health Districts." Unpublished paper, Department of Adult Education, University of Georgia, Athens, 1987.

Donmoyer, R. "Generalizability and the Single-Case Study." In E. W. Eisner and A. Peshkin (eds.), *Qualitative Inquiry in Education: The Continuing Debate.* New York: Teachers College, 1990.

Donmoyer, R. "Educational Research in an Era of Paradigm Proliferation: What's a Journal Editor to Do?" *Educational Researcher,* 1996, *25*(2), 19–25.

Dukes, W. F. (N=1). *Psychological Bulletin,* 1965, 64, 75–79.

Eisner, E. W. "On the Differences Between Scientific and Artistic Approaches to Qualitative Research." *Educational Researcher,* 1981, *10*(4), 5–9.

Eisner, E. W. The Enlightened Eye: Qualitative Inquiry and the Enhancement of Educational Practice. Old Tappan, N.J.: Macmillan, 1991.

Eisner, E. W. "Forms of Understanding and the Future of Educational Research." *Educational Researcher,* 1993, *22*(7), 5–11.

Erickson, F. "What Makes School Ethnography 'Ethnographic'?" *Anthropology and Education Quarterly,* 1973, *4*(2), 10–19.

Erickson, F. "Qualitative Methods in Research on Teaching." In M. C. Whittrock (ed.), *Handbook of Research on Teaching.* (3rd ed.) Old Tappan, N.J.: Macmillan, 1986.

Etheridge, C. P., Hall, M. L., and Etheridge, G. W. "From Volunteer to Advocate: The Empowerment of an Urban Parent." *Qualitative Studies in Education,* 1995, *8*(2), 109–119.

Fielding, N. G., and Lee, R. M. "Confronting CAQDAS: Choice and Contingency." In R. G. Burgess (ed.), *Computing and Qualitative Research.* Vol. 5. Greenwich, Conn.: JAI Press, 1995.

Firestone, W. A. "Meaning in Method: The Rhetoric of Quantitative and Qualitative Research." *Educational Researcher,* 1987, *16*(7), 16–21.

Firestone, W. A. "Alternative Arguments for Generalizing from Data as Applied to Qualitative Research." *Educational Researcher,* 1993, *22*(4), 16–23.

Firestone, W. A., and Herriott, R. E. "Multisite Qualitative Policy Research: Some Design and Implementation Issues." In D. M. Fetterman (ed.), *Ethnography in Educational Evaluation.* Thousand Oaks, Calif.: Sage, 1984.

Fisher, J. C. "A Framework for Describing Developmental Change Among Older Adults." *Adult Education Quarterly,* 1993, *43*(2), 76–89.

Fontana, A., and Frey, J. H. "Interviewing: The Art of Science." In N. K. Denzin and Y. S. Lincoln (eds.), *Handbook of Qualitative Research.* Thousand Oaks, Calif: Sage, 1994.

Foreman, P. B. "The Theory of Case Studies." *Social Forces,* 1948, *26*(4), 408–419.

Foster, J. "The Dynamics of Gender in Ethnographic Research: A Personal View." In R. G. Burgess (ed.), *Issues in Qualitative Research.* Studies in Qualitative Methodology. Vol. 4. Greenwich, Conn: JAI Press, 1994.

Frankenberg, R. "Participant Observers." In R. G. Burgess (ed.), *Field Research: A Sourcebook and Field Manual.* London: Allen & Unwin, 1982.

Freidheim, E. A. "Field Research and Word Processor Files: A Technical Note." *Qualitative Sociology,* 1984, *7*(1, 2), 90–97.

Gage, N. L. "The Paradigm Wars and Their Aftermath." *Educational Researcher,* 1989, *18*(7), 4–10.

Gans, H. J. "The Participant Observer as a Human Being: Observations on the Personal Aspects of Fieldwork." In R. G. Burgess (ed.), *Field Research: A Sourcebook and Field Manual.* London: Allen & Unwin, 1982.

Gassaway, B. M., Elder, W. L., and Campbell, J. "Word Processors for Qualitative Sociologists: A Review Essay." *Qualitative Sociology,* 1984, 7(1, 2), 157–168.

Geller, T. "Deus ex Machina: Searching for God on the Net." *The Net, 1,* 1996.

Gibson, M. A. *Accommodation Without Assimilation: Sikh Immigrants in an American High School.* Ithaca, N.Y.: Cornell University Press, 1988.

Glaser, B. G. *Theoretical Sensitivity.* Mill Valley, Calif.: Sociology Press, 1978.

Glaser, B. G. *Examples of Grounded Theory: A Reader.* Mill Valley, Calif.: Sociology Press, 1993.

Glaser, B. G., and Strauss, A. L. *The Discovery of Grounded Theory.* Chicago: Aldine, 1967.

Glesne, C., and Peshkin, A. *Becoming Qualitative Researchers: An Introduction.* White Plains, N.Y.: Longman, 1992.

Goetz, J. P., and LeCompte, M. D. *Ethnography and Qualitative Design in Educational Research.* Orlando, Fla.: Academic Press, 1984.

Gold, R. "Roles in Sociological Field Observations." *Social Forces,* 1958, *36,* 217–223.

Good, C., and Scates, D. *Methods of Research.* Englewood Cliffs, N.J.: Appleton-Century-Crofts, 1954.

Greene, J. C. "Qualitative Program Evaluation: Practice and Promise." In N. K. Denzin and Y. S. Lincoln (eds.), *Handbook of Qualitative Research,* Thousand Oaks, Calif.: Sage, 1994.

Greene, M. "Qualitative Research and the Uses of Literature." In R. W. Sherman and R. B. Webb (eds.), *Qualitative Research in Education: Focus and Methods.* London: Falmer Press, 1988.

Grossberg, L., Nelson, C. and Treichler, P. A. (eds.), *Cultural Studies.* New York: Routledge, 1992.

Guba, E. G. *Toward a Methodology of Naturalistic Inquiry in Educational Evaluation.* Monograph Series no. 8. Los Angeles: Center for the Study of Evaluation, University of California, 1978.

Guba, E. G. "What Have We Learned About Naturalistic Evaluation?" *Evaluation Practice,* 1987, *8*(1), 23–43.

Guba, E. G., and Lincoln, Y. S. *Effective Evaluation.* San Francisco: Jossey-Bass, 1981.

Guba, E. G., and Lincoln, Y. S. "Competing Paradigms in Qualitative Research." In N. K. Denzin and Y. S. Lincoln (eds.), *Handbook of Qualitative Research.* Thousand Oaks, Calif.: Sage, 1994.

Hamel, J. *Case Study Methods*. Qualitative Research Methods. Vol. 32. Thousand Oaks: Sage, 1993.

Hammersley, M., Scarth, J., and Webb, S. "Developing and Testing Theory: The Case of Research on Pupil Learning and Examinations." In R. G. Burgess (ed.), *Issues in Educational Research: Qualitative Methods*. London: Falmer Press, 1985.

Harper, D. "On the Authority of the Image: Visual Methods at the Crossroads." In N. K. Denzin and Y. S. Lincoln (eds.), *Handbook of Qualitative Research*. Thousand Oaks, Calif.: Sage, 1994.

Harris, J.F.Z. "A Comparative Case Study of the Program Planning Process in Learning in Retirement Institutes." Unpublished doctoral dissertation, Department of Adult Education, University of Georgia, Athens, 1995.

Hatch, J. A., and Wisniewski, R. (eds.). *Life History and Narrative*. London: Falmer Press, 1995.

Hawkins, R. P. "Developing a Behavior Code." In D. P. Hartmann (ed.), *Using Observers to Study Behavior*. New Directions for Methodology of Social and Behavioral Science, no. 14. San Francisco: Jossey-Bass, 1982.

Herzog, M.J.R. "School Censorship Experiences of Teachers in Southern Appalachia." *Qualitative Studies in Education*, 1995, *8*(2), 137–148.

Hesse-Biber, S. "Unleashing Frankenstein's Monster? The Use of Computers in Qualitative Research." In R. G. Burgess (ed.), *Computing and Qualitative Research*. Vol. 5. Greenwich, Conn.: JAI Press, 1995.

Hesse-Biber, S., and Dupuis, P. "Hypothesis Testing in Computer-Aided Qualitative Research." In U. Kelle (ed.), *Computer-Aided Qualitative Data Analysis: Theory, Methods, and Practice*. London: Sage, 1995.

Hoaglin, D. C., and others. *Data for Decisions*. Cambridge, Mass.: Abt Books, 1982.

Hodder, I. "The Interpretation of Documents and Material Culture." In N. K. Denzin and Y. S. Lincoln (eds.), *Handbook of Qualitative Research*. Thousand Oaks, Calif.: Sage, 1994.

Holsti, O. R. *Content Analysis for the Social Sciences and Humanities*. Reading, Mass.: Addison-Wesley, 1969.

Honigmann, J. J. "Sampling in Ethnographic Fieldwork." In R. G. Burgess (ed.), *Field Research: A Sourcebook and Field Manual*. London: Allen & Unwin, 1982.

Hopper, C. B., and Moore, J. "Women in Outlaw Motorcycle Gangs." *Journal of Contemporary Ethnography*, 1990, *18*(4), 363–387.

Houle, C. O. *Patterns of Learning: New Perspectives on Life-Span Education*. San Francisco: Jossey-Bass, 1984.

Howard, D.C.P. "Human-Computer Interactions: A Phenomenological Examination of the Adult First-Time Computer Experience." *Qualitative Studies in Education*, 1994, 7(1) 33–49.

Huber, G. L. "Qualitative Hypothesis Examination and Theory Building." In U. Kelle (ed.), *Computer-Aided Qualitative Data Analysis: Theory, Methods, and Practice.* London: Sage, 1995.

Huber, G. P., and Van de Ven, A. H. (eds.). *Longitudinal Field Research Methods.* Thousand Oaks, Calif.: Sage, 1995.

Jacob, E. "Qualitative Research Traditions: A Review." *Review of Educational Research,* 1987, *57*(1), 1–50.

Jacob, E. "Clarifying Qualitative Research: A Focus on Tradition." *Educational Researcher,* 1988, *17*, 16–19, 22–24.

James, P. "The Study of Educational Policy Making: A Critique of the Case Study Method." *Educational Administration,* 1981, *9*(3), 80–89.

Janesick, V. J. "The Dance of Qualitative Research Design: Metaphor, Methodolatry, and Meaning." In N. K. Denzin and Y. S. Lincoln (eds.), *Handbook of Qualitative Research.* Thousand Oaks, Calif.: Sage, 1994.

Jarvie, I. C. "The Problem of Ethical Integrity in Participant Observation." In R. G. Burgess (ed.), *Field Research: A Sourcebook and Field Manual.* London: Allen & Unwin, 1982.

Johnson-Bailey, J., and Cervero, R. M. "An Analysis of the Educational Narratives of Reentry Black Women." *Adult Education Quarterly,* 1996, *46*(3), 142–157.

Josselson, R., and Lieblich, A. (eds.). *The Narrative Study of Lives.* Vol. 3: *Interpreting Experience.* Thousand Oaks, Calif.: Sage, 1995.

Kaplan, A. *The Conduct of Inquiry: Methodology for Behavioral Science.* San Francisco: Chandler, 1964.

Katz, J. "A Theory of Qualitative Methodology: The Social Science System of Analytic Fieldwork." In R. M. Emerson (ed.), *Contemporary Field Research.* New York: Little, Brown, 1983.

Katz, L. "The Experience of Personal Change." Ph.D. dissertation, Union Graduate School, Union Institute, Cincinnati, Ohio, 1987.

Kelle, U. "An Overview of Computer-Aided Methods in Qualitative Research." In U. Kelle (ed.), *Computer-Aided Qualitative Data Analysis: Theory, Methods, and Practice.* London: Sage, 1995.

Kelle, U., and Laurie, H. "Computer Use in Qualitative Research and Issues of Validity." In U. Kelle (ed.), *Computer-Aided Qualitative Data Analysis: Theory, Methods, and Practice.* London: Sage, 1995.

Kelle, U., and others. "Hypothesis Examination in Qualitative Research." In U. Kelle (ed.), *Computer-Aided Qualitative Data Analysis: Theory, Methods, and Practice.* London: Sage, 1995.

Kellogg, W. A., and Richards, T. J. "The Human Factors of Information on the Internet." In J. Nielson (ed.), *Advances in Human-Computer Interaction.* Vol. 5. Norwood, N.J.: Ablex, 1995.

Kelman, H. C. "Ethical Issues in Different Social Science Methods." In T. L. Beauchamp, R. R. Faden, R. J. Wallace, Jr., and L. Walters (eds.), *Ethical Issues in Social Science Research.* Baltimore: Johns Hopkins University Press, 1982.

Kemmis, S. "The Imagination of the Case and the Invention of the Study." In *Case Study: An Overview.* Case Study Methods 1 (Series). Victoria, Australia: Deakin University Press, 1983.

Kennedy, M. M. "Generalizing from Single Case Studies." *Evaluation Quarterly,* 1979, *3,* 661–679.

Kenny, W. R., and Grotelueschen, A. D. *Making the Case for Case Study.* Occasional Paper, Office for the Study of Continuing Professional Education. Urbana-Champaign: College of Education, University of Illinois, 1980.

Kidder, L. H. "Qualitative Research and Quasi-Experimental Frameworks." In M. B. Brewer and B. E. Collins (eds.), *Scientific Inquiry and the Social Sciences.* San Francisco: Jossey-Bass, 1981a.

Kidder, L. H. *Selltiz, Wrightsman & Cook's Research Methods in Social Relations.* (4th ed.) Austin, Tex.: Holt, Rinehart and Winston, 1981b.

Kidder, L. H., and Fine, M. "Qualitative and Quantitative Methods: When Stories Converge." In M. M. Mark and R. L. Shotland (eds.), *Multiple Methods in Program Evaluation.* New Directions for Program Evaluation, no. 35. San Francisco: Jossey-Bass, 1987.

Kimmel, A. J. *Ethics and Values in Applied Social Research.* Applied Social Research Methods Series. Vol. 12. Thousand Oaks, Calif.: Sage, 1988.

Kline, B. "A Case Study of a Return-to-Industry Program: An Inservice Approach for Vocational Instructors at a Two-Year Post-Secondary Institution." Unpublished doctoral dissertation, Department of Vocational Education, Virginia Polytechnic Institute and State University, 1981.

Kuckartz, U. "Case-Oriented Quantification." In U. Kelle (ed.), *Computer-Aided Qualitative Data Analysis: Theory, Methods, and Practice.* London: Sage, 1995.

Lancy, D. F. *Qualitative Research in Education: An Introduction to the Major Traditions.* White Plains, N.Y.: Longman, 1993.

Lawrenson, D. "Oral History: Neither Fish Nor Fowl." In R. B. Burgess (ed.), *Issues in Qualitative Research.* Studies in Qualitative Methodology. Vol. 4. Greenwich, Conn.: JAI Press, 1994.

LeCompte, M. D., and Preissle, J. "Toward an Ethnology of Student Life in Schools and Classrooms: Synthesizing the Qualitative Research Tradition." In M. D. LeCompte, W. L. Millroy, and J. Preissle (eds.), *The Handbook of Qualitative Research in Education.* Orlando, Fla.: Academic Press, 1992.

LeCompte, M. D., and Preissle, J., with Tesch, R. *Ethnography and Qualitative Design in Educational Research.* (2nd ed.) Orlando, Fla.: Academic Press, 1993.

Lee, R. M., and Fielding, N. G. "Computing for Qualitative Research: Options, Problems, and Potential." In N. G. Fielding and R. M. Lee (eds.), *Using Computers in Qualitative Research.* London: Sage, 1991.

Lee, R. M., and Fielding, N. G. "Users' Experiences of Qualitative Data Analysis Software." In U. Kelle (ed.), *Computer-Aided Qualitative Data Analysis: Theory, Methods, and Practice.* London: Sage, 1995.

Lenzo, K. "Validity and Self-Reflexivity Meet Poststructuralism: Scientific Ethos and the Transgressive Self." *Educational Researcher,* 1995, *24*(14), 17–23.

Levinson, D. J., and others. *The Seasons of a Man's Life.* New York: Knopf, 1978.

Levinson, D. J., and Levinson, J. D. *The Seasons of a Woman's Life.* New York: Ballantine, 1996.

Lightfoot, S. L. *The Good High School.* New York: Basic Books, 1983.

Lijphart, A. "Comparative Politics and the Comparative Method." *American Political Science Review,* 1971, *65,* 682–694.

Lincoln, Y. S. "Emerging Criteria for Quality in Qualitative and Interpretive Research." *Qualitative Inquiry,* 1995, *1*(1), 275–289.

Lincoln, Y. S., and Guba, E. G. *Naturalistic Inquiry.* Thousand Oaks, Calif.: Sage, 1985.

Lofland, J. *Analyzing Social Settings: A Guide to Qualitative Observation and Analysis.* Belmont, Calif.: Wadsworth, 1971.

Lofland, J. "Styles of Reporting Qualitative Field Research." *American Sociologist,* 1974, *9,* 101–111.

Lofland, J., and Lofland, L. H. Analyzing Social Settings: A Guide to Qualitative Observation and Analysis. (3rd ed.) Belmont, Calif.: Wadsworth, 1995.

Lonkila, M. "Grounded Theory as an Emerging Paradigm for Computer-Assisted Qualitative Data Analysis." In U. Kelle (ed.), *Computer-Aided Qualitative Data Analysis: Theory, Methods, and Practice.* London: Sage, 1995.

Lyman, P. "Reading, Writing, and Word Processing: Toward a Phenomenology of the Computer Age." *Qualitative Sociology,* 1984, *7*(1 and 2), 75–89.

MacDonald, B., and Walker, R. "Case Study and the Social Philosophy of Educational Research." In D. Hamilton and others (eds.), *Beyond the Numbers Game.* London: Macmillan Education, 1977.

McCorduck, P. "Sex, Lies, and Avatars: A Profile of Sherry Turkle." *Wired,* April 1996.

McMillan, J. H., and Schumacher, S. *Research in Education*. New York: Little, Brown, 1984.

McTaggart, R. "Principles for Participatory Research." *Adult Education Quarterly*, 1991, *41*(3), 168–187.

Malcolm, C., and Welch, W. "Case Study Evaluations: A Case in Point." In W. W. Welsh (ed.), *Case Study Methodology in Educational Evaluation*. Proceedings of the 1981 Minnesota Evaluation Conference. Minneapolis: Minnesota Research and Evaluation Center, 1981.

Mangabeira, W. "Qualitative Analysis and Microcomputer Software: Some Reflections on a New Trend in Sociological Research." In R. G. Burgess (ed.), *Computing and Qualitative Research*. Vol. 5. Greenwich, Conn.: JAI Press, 1995.

Manning, P. K., and Cullum-Swan, B. "Narrative, Content, and Semiotic Analysis." In N. K. Denzin and Y. S. Lincoln (eds.), *Handbook of Qualitative Research*. Thousand Oaks, Calif.: Sage, 1994.

Mathison, S. "Why Triangulation?" *Educational Researcher*, 1988, *17*, 13–17.

Medina, M. P. "Adult Literacy in a Rural Setting: A Family Case Study of Literacy Use and Meaning." Unpublished doctoral dissertation, Department of Educational Leadership, Florida State University, 1987.

Merriam, S. B. *Coping with Male Mid-Life: A Systematic Analysis Using Literature as a Data Source*. Washington, D.C.: University Press, 1980.

Merriam, S. B. *Case Study Research in Education: A Qualitative Approach*. San Francisco: Jossey-Bass, 1988.

Merriam, S. B. "The Structure of Simple Reminiscence." *The Gerontologist*, 1989, *29*(6), 761–767.

Merriam, S. B. (ed.). *An Update on Adult Learning Theory*. New Directions for Adult and Continuing Education, no. 57. San Francisco: Jossey-Bass, 1993.

Merriam, S. B., and Simpson, E. L. *A Guide to Research for Educators and Trainers of Adults*. (2nd ed.) Malabar, Fla.: Robert E. Krieger, 1995.

Merriam, S. B., Mott, V. W., and Lee, M. "Learning That Comes from the Negative Interpretation of Life Experience." *Studies in Continuing Education*, 1996, *18*(1), 1–23.

Miles, M. B., and Huberman, A. M. *Qualitative Data Analysis: An Expanded Sourcebook*. (2nd ed.) Thousand Oaks, Calif.: Sage, 1994.

Mishoe, S. C. "The Effects of Institutional Context on Critical Thinking in the Workplace." Proceedings of the 36th Annual Adult Education Research Conference, University of Alberta, Edmonton, Alberta, Canada, May 1995.

Moore, D. T. "Learning at Work: Case Studies in Non-School Education." *Anthropology and Education Quarterly*, 1986, *17*(3), 166–184.

Moore, G. A. *Crossing the Chasm: Marketing and Selling Technology to Mainstream Customers.* New York: HarperCollins, 1991.

Mott, V. W. "The Role of Intuition in the Reflective Practice of Adult Education." Proceedings of the 35th Annual Adult Education Research Conference, University of Tennessee, Knoxville, May 1994.

Moustakas, C. *Heuristic Research: Design, Methodology, and Applications.* Thousand Oaks, Calif.: Sage, 1990.

Moustakas, C. *Phenomenological Research Methods.* Thousand Oaks, Calif.: Sage, 1994.

Munro, P. "Continuing Dilemmas of Life History Research." In D. J. Flinders and G. E. Mills (eds.), *Theory and Concepts in Qualitative Research.* New York: Teachers College Press, 1993.

Murdock, G. P. *Outline of World Cultures.* (5th rev. ed.) New Haven, Conn.: Human Relations Area Files, 1983.

Murdock, G. P., and others. *Outline of Cultural Materials.* (5th ed.) New Haven, Conn.: Human Relations Area Files, 1982.

Namuth, T., and others. "Adultery: A New Furor Over an Old Sin." *Newsweek,* September 30, 1996.

Norman, D. A. *Things That Make Us Smart: Defending Human Attributes in the Age of the Machine.* Reading, Mass: Addison-Wesley, 1993.

Offerman, M. "A Case Study of Failed Consortia of Higher Education." Unpublished doctoral dissertation, Department of Leadership and Educational Policy Studies, Northern Illinois University, 1985.

Olesen, V. "Feminisms and Models of Qualitative Research." In N. K. Denzin and Y. S. Lincoln (eds.), *Handbook of Qualitative Research.* Thousand Oaks, Calif.: Sage, 1994.

Patton, M. Q. "Quality in Qualitative Research: Methodological Principles and Recent Developments." Invited address to Division J of the American Educational Research Association, Chicago, April 1985.

Patton, M. Q. *Creative Evaluation.* (2nd ed.) Thousand Oaks, Calif.: Sage, 1987.

Patton, M. Q. *Qualitative Evaluation Methods.* (2nd ed.) Thousand Oaks, Calif.: Sage, 1990.

Patton, M. Q. *Utilization-Focused Evaluation.* (3rd ed.) Thousand Oaks, Calif.: Sage, 1996.

Perka, P. L., Matherly, C. A., Fishman, D. E., and Ridge, R. H. "Using Photographs to Examine Environmental Perceptions of African-American and White Greek Members: A Qualitative Study." *College Student Affairs Journal,* 1992, *12*(1), 7–16.

Peshkin, A. *God's Choice: The Total World of a Fundamentalist Christian School.* Chicago: University of Chicago Press, 1986.

Peshkin, A. "In Search of Subjectivity—One's Own." *Educational Researcher,* 1988, *17*(7), 17–22.

Pfaffenberger, B. *Microcomputer Applications in Qualitative Research.* Vol. 14. London: Sage, 1988.

Phillips, G. M., and Barnes, S. B. "Is Your Epal an Ax-Murderer?" *Interpersonal Computing and Technology,* 1995, *3*(4), 12–41.

Posner, J. "Urban Anthropology: Fieldwork in Semifamilial Settings." In W. B. Shaffier, R. A. Stebbins, and A. Turowetz (eds.), *Fieldwork Experience.* New York: St. Martin's Press, 1980.

Prein, G. Kelle, U., and Bird, K. "An Overview of Software." In U. Kelle (ed.), *Computer-Aided Qualitative Data Analysis: Theory, Methods, and Practice.* London: Sage, 1995.

Prein, G., Kelle, U., Richards, L., and Richards, T. "Using Linkages and Networks for Theory Building." In U. Kelle (ed.), *Computer-Aided Qualitative Data Analysis: Theory, Methods, and Practice.* London: Sage, 1995.

Prein, G., and others. "Between Quality and Quantity." In U. Kelle (ed.), *Computer-Aided Qualitative Data Analysis: Theory, Methods, and Practice.* London: Sage, 1995.

Preskill, H. "The Use of Photography in Evaluating School Culture." *Qualitative Studies in Education,* 1995, *8*(2), 183–193.

Preston, R. *The Hot Zone.* New York: Random House, 1995.

Punch, M. *The Politics and Ethics of Fieldwork.* Qualitative Research Methods Series. Vol. 3. Thousand Oaks, Calif.: Sage, 1986.

Punch, M. "Politics and Ethics in Qualitative Research." In N. K. Denzin and Y. S. Lincoln (eds.), *Handbook of Qualitative Research.* Thousand Oaks, Calif.: Sage, 1994, 83–97.

Ragin, C. "Using Qualitative Comparative Analysis to Study Configurations." In U. Kelle (ed.), *Computer-Aided Qualitative Data Analysis: Theory, Methods, and Practice.* London: Sage, 1995.

Ratcliffe, J. W. "Notions of Validity in Qualitative Research Methodology." *Knowledge: Creation, Diffusion, Utilization,* 1983, *5*(2), 147–167.

Rathje, W. L. "Trace Measures." In L. Sechrest (ed.), *Unobtrusive Measurement Today.* New Directions for Methodology of Social and Behavioral Science, no. 1. San Francisco: Jossey-Bass, 1979.

Reichardt, C. S., and Cook, T. D. "Beyond Qualitative Versus Quantitative Methods." In T. D. Cook and C. S. Reichardt (eds.), *Qualitative and Quantitative Methods in Evaluation Research.* Thousand Oaks, Calif.: Sage, 1979.

Reichardt, C. S., and Rallis, S. F. (eds.). *The Qualitative-Quantitative Debate: New Perspectives.* New Directions for Program Evaluation, no. 61. San Francisco: Jossey-Bass, 1994.

Reid, A. O., Jr. "Computer Management Strategies for Text Data." In B. F. Crabtree and W. L. Miller (eds.), *Doing Qualitative Research*. Vol. 3. London: Sage, 1992.

Reinharz, S. *On Becoming a Social Scientist: From Survey Research and Participant Observation to Experiential Analysis*. San Francisco: Jossey-Bass, 1979.

Reinharz, S. *Feminist Methods in Social Research*. New York: Oxford University Press, 1992.

Reybold, L. E. "The Epistemological Development of Malaysian Women: At the Intersection of Culture and Cognition." Unpublished doctoral dissertation, Department of Adult Education, University of Georgia, Athens, 1996.

Richards, L. "Transition Work! Reflections on a Three-Year Nud-Ist Project." In R. G. Burgess (ed.), *Computing and Qualitative Research*. Vol. 5. Greenwich, Conn.: JAI Press, 1995.

Richards, L., and Richards, T. "The Transformation of Qualitative Method: Computational Paradigms and Research Processes." In N. G. Fielding and R. M. Lee (eds.), *Using Computers in Qualitative Research*. London: Sage, 1991.

Richards, T., and Richards, L. "Using Computers in Qualitative Research." In N. K. Denzin and Y. S. Lincoln (eds.), *Handbook of Qualitative Research*. London: Sage, 1994.

Richards, T., and Richards, L. "Using Hierarchical Categories in Qualitative Data Analysis." In U. Kelle (ed.), *Computer-Aided Qualitative Data Analysis: Theory, Methods, and Practice*. London: Sage, 1995.

Richardson, L. "Writing: A Method of Inquiry." In N. K. Denzin and Y. S. Lincoln (eds.), *Handbook of Qualitative Research*, Thousand Oaks, Calif.: Sage, 1994.

Richman, J. "Male Sociologist in a Woman's World: Aspects of a Medical Partnership." In R. G. Burgess (ed.), *Issues in Qualitative Research*. Studies in Qualitative Methodology. Vol. 4. Greenwich, Conn.: JAI Press, 1994.

Riley, M. W. *Sociological Research*. Vol. 1: *A Case Approach*. Orlando, Fla.: Harcourt Brace, 1963.

Rist, R. C. "On the Application of Ethnographic Inquiry to Education: Procedures and Possibilities." *Journal of Research in Science Teaching*, 1982, *19*, 439–450.

Robinson, W. S. "The Logical Structure of Analytic Induction," *American Sociological Review*, 1951, *16*, 812–818.

Rogers, E. *Diffusion of Innovations*. (4th ed.) New York: Free Press, 1995.

Roller, E., Mathes, R., and Eckert, T. "Hermeneutic-Classificatory Content Analysis." In U. Kelle (ed.), *Computer-Aided Qualitative Data Analysis: Theory, Methods, and Practice*. London: Sage, 1995.

Rosenfeldt, A. B. "Faculty Commitment to the Improvement of Teaching Via Workshop Participation." Unpublished doctoral dissertation, Department of Vocational Education, Virginia Polytechnic Institute and State University, 1981.

Rowden, R. W. "The Role of Human Resource Development in Successful, Small to Mid-Sized Manufacturing Businesses: A Comparative Case Study." Unpublished doctoral dissertation, Department of Educational Policy Studies, Georgia State University, Atlanta, 1994.

Rowden, R. W. "The Role of Human Resource Development in Successful Small to Mid-Sized Manufacturing Businesses: A Comparative Case Study." *Human Resource Development Quarterly*, 1995, *6*(4), 355–373.

Rowden, R. W. "How Human Resource Development Helps Small Businesses to Maintain a Competitive Edge: A Comparative Case Study." In E. F. Holton III (ed.), *1996 Conference Proceedings of the Academy of Human Resource Development*. Minneapolis, Feb. 29–March 3, 1996, pp. 27–32.

Rubin, L. B. *Just Friends: The Role of Friendship in Our Lives*. New York: HarperCollins, 1985.

Sanders, J. R. "Case Study Methodology: A Critique." In W. W. Welsh (ed.), *Case Study Methodology in Educational Evaluation*. Proceedings of the 1981 Minnesota Evaluation Conference. Minneapolis: Minnesota Research and Evaluation Center, 1981.

Schatzman, L., and Strauss, A. L. *Field Research*. Englewood Cliffs, N.J.: Prentice Hall, 1973.

Schofield, J. W. "Increasing the Generalizability of Qualitative Research." In E. W. Eisner and A. Peshkin (eds.), *Qualitative Inquiry in Education*. New York: Teachers College Press, 1990.

Schrum, L. "Framing the Debate: Ethical Research in the Information Age." *Qualitative Inquiry*, 1995, *1*(3), 311–326.

Schrum, L., and Harris, J. "Ethical Electronic Research: Creating a Dialogue." Unpublished report presented at the Qualitative Research in Education Annual Conference, Athens, Ga., 1996.

Schultz, J. G. "Developing Theoretical Models/Conceptual Frameworks in Vocational Education Research." *Journal of Vocational Education Research*, 1988, *13*(3), 29–43.

Schwandt, T. A. "Theory for the Moral Sciences: Crisis of Identity and Purpose." In D. J. Flinders and G. E. Mills (eds.), *Theory and Concepts in Qualitative Research*. New York: Teachers College Press, 1993.

Seidel, J. "Method and Madness in the Application of Computer Technology to Qualitative Data Analysis." In N. G. Fielding and R. M. Lee (eds.), *Using Computers in Qualitative Research*. London: Sage, 1991.

Seidel, J. V., and Clark, J. A. "The Ethnograph: A Computer Program for the Analysis of Qualitative Data." *Qualitative Sociology*, 1984, 7(1, 2), 110–125.

Seidel, J., and Kelle, U. "Different Functions of Coding in the Analysis of Textual Data." In U. Kelle (ed.), *Computer-Aided Qualitative Data Analysis: Theory, Methods, and Practice.* London: Sage, 1995.

Seidman, I. E. *Interviewing as Qualitative Research.* New York: Teachers College Press, 1991.

Selltiz, C., Jahoda, M., Deutsch, M., and Cook, S. W. *Research Methods in Social Relations.* Austin, Tex.: Holt, Rinehart and Winston, 1959.

Shaw, K. E. "Understanding the Curriculum: The Approach Through Case Studies." *Journal of Curriculum Studies*, 1978, 10(1), 1–17.

Sherman, R. R., and Webb, R. B. "Qualitative Research in Education: A Focus." In R. R. Sherman and R. B. Webb (eds.), *Qualitative Research in Education: Focus and Methods.* Bristol, Pa.: Falmer Press, 1988.

Sibert, E., and Shelly, A. "Using Logic Programming for Hypothesis Generation." In U. Kelle (ed.), *Computer-Aided Qualitative Data Analysis: Theory, Methods, and Practice.* London: Sage, 1995.

Sieber, J. E. *Planning Ethically Responsible Research.* Thousand Oaks, Calif.: Sage, 1992.

Smith, A. G., and Louis, K. S. (eds.). "Multimethod Policy Research: Issues and Applications." *American Behavioral Scientist*, 1982, 26(1), 1–144.

Smith, J. K., and Heshusius, L. "Closing Down the Conversation: The End of the Quantitative-Qualitative Debate." *Educational Researcher*, 1986, 15(1), 4–13.

Smith, L. M. "An Evolving Logic of Participant Observation, Educational Ethnography and Other Case Studies." In L. Shulman (ed.), *Review of Research in Education.* Itasca, Ill.: Peacock, 1978.

Spiegelberg, H. A. *The Phenomenological Movement.* Vol. 2. The Hague, Netherlands: Marinus Nijhoff, 1965.

Spradley, J. P. *The Ethnographic Interview.* Austin, Tex.: Holt, Rinehart and Winston, 1979.

Spradley, J. P. *Participant Observation.* Austin, Tex.: Holt, Rinehart and Winston, 1980.

Sprokkereef, A., Lakin, E., Pole, C. J., and Burgess, R. G. "The Data, the Team, and the Ethnograph." In R. G. Burgess (ed.), *Computing and Qualitative Research.* Vol. 5. Greenwich, Conn.: JAI Press, 1995.

Stacey, M. "From Being a Native to Becoming a Researcher: Meg Stacey and the General Medical Council." In R. B. Burgess (ed.), *Issues in Qualitative Research.* Studies in Qualitative Methodology. Vol. 4. Greenwich, Conn.: JAI Press, 1994.

Stake, R. E. "The Case Study Method in Social Inquiry." *Educational Researcher*, 1978, 7, 5–8.

Stake, R. E. "Case Study Methodology: An Epistemological Advocacy." In
W. W. Welsh (ed.), *Case Study Methodology in Educational Evaluation.*
Proceedings of the 1981 Minnesota Evaluation Conference. Min-
neapolis: Minnesota Research and Evaluation Center, 1981.

Stake, R. E. "Case Studies." In N. K. Denzin and Y. S. Lincoln (eds.),
Handbook of Qualitative Research. Thousand Oaks, Calif.: Sage, 1994.

Stake, R. E. *The Art of Case Study Research.* Thousand Oaks, Calif.: Sage,
1995.

Stanfield II, J. H. "Ethnic Modeling in Qualitative Research." In N. K.
Denzin and Y. S. Lincoln (eds.). *Handbook of Qualitative Research.*
Thousand Oaks, Calif.: Sage, 1994.

Stanley, L., and Temple, B. "Doing the Business? Evaluating Software
Packages to Aid the Analysis of Qualitative Data Sets." In R. G.
Burgess (ed.), *Computing and Qualitative Research.* Vol. 5. Greenwich,
Conn.: JAI Press, 1995.

Steinbeck, J. *Sea of Cortez.* New York: Viking Penguin, 1941.

Stenhouse, L. "Case Study and Case Records: Towards a Contemporary
History of Education." *British Educational Research Journal,* 1978, *4*(2),
21–39.

Stenhouse, L. "Case Study Methods." In J. P. Keeves (ed.), *Educational
Research, Methodology, and Measurement: An International Handbook.*
Sydney: Pergamon Press, 1988.

Strauss, A. L. *Qualitative Analysis for Social Sciences.* Cambridge, England:
Cambridge University Press, 1987.

Strauss, A. L., and Corbin, J. *Basics of Qualitative Research: Grounded Theory
Procedures and Techniques.* Thousand Oaks, Calif.: Sage, 1990.

Strauss, A. L., and Corbin, J. "Grounded Theory Methodology: An
Overview." In N. K. Denzin and Y. S. Lincoln (eds.), *Handbook of
Qualitative Research.* Thousand Oaks, Calif.: Sage, 1994.

Strauss, A., Schatzman, L., Bucher, R., and Sabshin, M. *Psychiatric Ideologies
and Institutions.* (2nd ed.) New Brunswick, N.J.: Transaction, 1981.

Swisher, K. "Authentic Research: An Interview on the Way to the Pon-
derosa." *Anthropology & Education Quarterly,* 1986, *17,* 185–188.

Taylor, S. J., and Bogdan, R. *Introduction to Qualitative Research Methods.*
(2nd ed.) New York: Wiley, 1984.

Tesch, R. *Qualitative Research: Analysis Types and Software Tools.* London:
Falmer Press, 1990.

Tesch, R. "Software for Qualitative Researchers: Analysis Needs and Program Capabilities." In N. G. Fielding and R. M. Lee (eds.), *Using
Computers in Qualitative Research.* London: Sage, 1991.

Thomas, W. I., and Znaniecki, F. *The Polish Peasant in Europe and America.*
New York: Knopf, 1927.

Thornton, S. J. "The Quest for Emergent Meaning: A Personal Account." In D. J. Flinders and G. E. Mills (eds.), *Theory and Concepts in Qualitative Research.* New York: Teachers College Press, 1993.

Tierney, W. G. "The Cedar Closet." *Qualitative Studies in Education,* 1993, *6*(4), 303–314.

Tisdell, E. J. "Power Relations in Higher Education Classes of Nontraditional-Age Adults: A Comparative Case Study." Unpublished doctoral dissertation, Department of Adult Education, University of Georgia, Athens, 1992.

Tisdell, E. J. "Interlocking Systems of Power, Privilege, and Oppression in Adult Higher Education Classes." *Adult Education Quarterly,* 1993, *43*(4), 203–226.

Vaillant, G. E. *Adaptation to Life.* New York: Little, Brown, 1977.

Van Dalen, D. B. *Understanding Educational Research.* New York: McGraw-Hill, 1966.

Van Maanen, J. *Tales of the Field: On Writing Ethnography.* Chicago: University of Chicago Press, 1988.

Walker, R. "The Conduct of Educational Case Studies: Ethics, Theory and Procedures." In W. B. Dockerell and D. Hamilton (eds.), *Rethinking Educational Research.* London: Hodder & Stoughton, 1980.

Weaver, A., and Atkinson, P. "From Coding to Hypertext Strategies for Microcomputing and Qualitative Data Analysis." In R. G. Burgess (ed.), *Computing and Qualitative Research.* Vol. 5. Greenwich, Conn.: JAI Press, 1995.

Webb, E. T., and others. *Unobtrusive Measures.* Skokie, Ill.: Rand McNally, 1966.

Webb, E. T., and others. *Nonreactive Measures in the Social Sciences.* (2nd ed. of *Unobtrusive Measures*) Boston: Houghton Mifflin, 1981.

Weber, R. P. "Computer-Aided Content Analysis: A Short Primer." *Qualitative Sociology,* 1984, *7*(1, 2), 126–147.

Weeks, S. "Interview." Unpublished transcript, University of Athens, Ga., n.d.

Weitzman, E. A., and Miles, M. B. *Computer Programs for Qualitative Data Analysis: A Software Sourcebook.* Thousand Oaks, Calif.: Sage, 1995.

Welch, S. "An Ethic of Solidarity." In H. Giroux (ed.), *Postmodernism, Feminism, and Cultural Politics.* Albany: State University of New York Press, 1991.

Werner, O., and Schoepfle, G. M. *Systematic Fieldwork: Ethnographic Analysis and Data Management.* Vol. 2. Thousand Oaks, Calif.: Sage, 1987.

West, J., and Oldfather, P. "Pooled Case Comparison: An Innovation for Cross-Case Study." *Qualitative Inquiry,* 1995, *1*(4), 452–464.

Whyte, W. F. "Interviewing in Field Research." In R. G. Burgess (ed.), *Field Research: A Source Book and Field Manual.* London: Allen & Unwin, 1982.

Wilson, S. "Explorations of the Usefulness of Case Study Evaluations." *Evaluation Quarterly,* 1979, *3,* 446–459.

Wolcott, H. F. *The Man in the Principal's Office: An Ethnography.* Austin, Tex.: Holt, Rinehart and Winston, 1973.

Wolcott, H. F. "How to Look Like an Anthropologist Without Really Being One." *Practicing Anthropology,* 1980, *3*(2), 6–7, 56–59.

Wolcott, H. F. *Writing Up Qualitative Research.* Thousand Oaks: Sage, 1990.

Wolcott, H. F. "Posturing in Qualitative Inquiry." In M. D. LeCompte, W. L. Millroy, and J. Preissle (eds.), *The Handbook of Qualitative Research in Education.* Orlando, Fla.: Academic Press, 1992.

Wolcott, H. F. *Transforming Qualitative Data: Description, Analysis, and Interpretation.* Thousand Oaks, Calif.: Sage, 1994.

Wolf, M. *A Thrice-Told Tale.* Stanford, Calif.: Stanford University Press, 1992.

Woods, P. "New Songs Played Skillfully: Creativity and Technique in Writing Up Qualitative Research." In R. G. Burgess (ed.), *Issues in Educational Research: Qualitative Methods.* London: Falmer Press, 1985.

Yin, R. K. *Case Study Research: Design and Methods.* (2nd ed.) Thousand Oaks, Calif.: Sage, 1994.

Zeph, C. "Career Development for Community Adult Educators: Interrelating Personal and Professional Development." *Adult Education Quarterly,* 1991, *41,* 217–232.

Name Index

A

Anonymous, 217
Abramson, P. R., 33, 116, 228–229, 243
Adelman, C., 28
Adler, P., 101
Adler, P. A., 101
Agar, M., 172, 175
Akeroyd, A. V., 172, 174–175
Alcoff, L., 200
Allatt, P., 172, 175
Altheide, D. L., 123, 160
Araujo, L., 168, 172, 175
Armstrong, D., 171
Atkinson, P., 156, 158, 171
Auster, C. J., 113
Aviram, O., 12, 20

B

Barnes, S. B., 130
Bateson, M. C., 72
Becker, H. S., 29, 45, 50, 119, 201
Bednarz, D., 205
Benson, L. D., 173, 175
Berendt, J., 217
Bierema, L. L., 59, 60, 62
Biklen, S. K., 35, 97, 99, 115, 119, 162, 183, 224
Bird, K., 171
Blankenship, J. C., 11, 13
Bogdan, R. C., 35, 84, 97, 99–100, 105, 115, 119, 121, 152, 162, 179, 183, 215, 224
Boggs, D. L., 232
Bohannan, L., 7
Borg, W. R., 40, 97, 161
Boshier, R., 57

Brandt, R., 110
Bromley, D. B., 32
Bucher, R., 76
Burgess, R. G., 60, 116, 121, 171, 174
Burlingame, M., 208

C

Carr, W., 4
Carspecken, P. F., 12, 14
Cassell, J., 213, 215–217
Cervero, R. M., 47, 120, 157, 188–189
Chein, I., 61
Clandinin, D. J., 157–158, 200
Coffey, A, 156, 158
Collins, T. S., 33, 41
Connelly, F. M., 157–158, 200
Conrad, P., 166
Constas, M. A., 179
Cook, S. W., 113, 116, 121, 125
Cook, T. D., 33
Cooper, H. M., 50, 53
Corbin, J., 17–18, 49, 57, 156, 164
Cordeiro, P. A., 12, 14
Cordingley, E. B., 173, 175
Cortazzi, M., 158
Cotterill, P., 86
Courtenay, B. C., 12, 76, 165
Crandall, R., 213, 216
Cronbach, L. J., 29, 199, 208–209, 211
Cullum-Swan, B., 160

D

D'Andrade, R. G., 13
Denzin, N. K., 10, 74, 84, 160, 204
Deutsch, M., 113, 116, 121, 125
Dewey, J., 56
Dexter, L. A., 71–72, 83, 85, 125

Dey, I., 70, 156, 165, 168, 172, 175, 180, 192, 207, 225
Deyhle, D. L., 218
Diener, E., 213, 216
Dominick, J., 120
Donmoyer, R., 200, 208–209, 238
Dukes, W. F., 36
Dupuis, P., 168, 172, 175

E

Eckert, T., 168, 172, 175
Eisner, E. W., 210
Erickson, F., 208, 210, 222–223, 235–236
Etheridge, C. P., 19
Etheridge, G. W., 19

F

Fielding, N. G., 171, 173, 175
Fine, M., 8
Firestone, W. A., 8, 152, 199, 208, 211
Fisher, J. C., 12, 18
Fishman, D. E., 119
Fontana, A., 71, 86
Foreman, P. B., 204
Foster, J., 86
Frankenberg, R., 104
Freidheim, E. A., 173
Freud, S., 36
Frey, J. H., 71, 86

G

Gage, N. L., 8
Gall, M. D., 40, 97, 161
Gans, H. J., 101–102
Geller, T., 128
Geske, T. G., 208
Gibson, M. A., 19
Glaser, B. G., 17–18, 22, 49, 52–53, 62–64, 120, 124, 126, 159, 181, 183, 190–192, 232
Glesne, C., 80
Goetz, J. P., 7, 62, 97–98, 190
Gold R., 100
Good, C., 32
Greene, J. C., 39
Greene, M., 210

Grossberg, L., 214
Grotelueschen, A. D., 39
Guba, E. G., 7, 21, 23–24, 29, 39, 42, 64, 113, 121, 124, 126, 179–180, 185, 196, 199–200, 203, 206–207, 211, 232–232

H

Hall, M. L., 19
Hamel, J., 37, 43
Hammersley, M., 48
Harper, D., 113
Harris, J., 132
Harris, J.F.Z., 135–141, 148
Hatch, J. A., 158
Hawkins, R. P., 97
Herriott, R. E., 208
Herzog, M.J.R., 11, 13
Heshusius, L., 8
Hess, G. A., 218
Hesse-Biber, S., 168, 172–173, 175
Hoaglin, D. C., 30
Hodder, I., 117
Holsti, O. R., 112
Honigmann, J. J., 61
Hopper, C. B., 215
Howard, D.C.P., 16–17
Houle, C. O., 238, 242–243
Huber, G. L., 168, 172, 175
Huber, G. P., 30
Huberman, A. M., 27, 40, 62–63, 156, 184, 187, 195, 208, 233

J

Jacob, E., 10
Jahoda, M., 113, 116, 121, 125
James, P., 208
Janesick, V. J., 57
Jarvie, I. C., 102
Jenkins, D., 28
Johnson-Bailey, J., 47, 157, 188–189
Josselson, R, 158

K

Katz, L., 158, 160
Kelle, U., 168, 171–173, 175
Kellogg, W. A., 131

Kelman, H. C., 216
Kemmis, S., 4, 28, 200
Kennedy, M. M., 211
Kenny, W. R., 39
Kidder, L. H., 8, 94–95, 115, 160
Kimmel, A. J., 217
Kline, B., 33, 83, 120
Kuckartz, U., 168, 172, 175

L

Lakin, E., 171, 174
Lancy, D. F., 5–6, 10, 24
Laurie, H., 172–173, 175
Lawrenson, D., 40
LeCompte, M. D., 7, 14–15, 22, 37, 39, 61–62, 97–98, 112, 115, 121, 171–173, 179, 181, 188, 190, 203–204, 207, 211, 218
Lee, R. M., 171, 173, 175
Lee, M., 229, 231
Lenzo, K., 200
Letherby, G., 86
Levinson, D. J., 11, 13, 57
Levinson, J. D., 11,13
Lieblich, A., 158
Lightfoot, S. L., 40, 194, 242
Lijphart, A., 38
Lincoln, Y. S., 7, 10, 21, 23–24, 29, 39, 42, 64, 113, 121, 124, 126, 179–180, 185, 196, 199–200, 203, 206–207, 211, 232–233
Lofland, L. H., 156–157
Lofland, J., 105, 152, 156–157, 220, 225–227, 234
Lonkila, M., 173, 175
Lyman, P., 174

M

MacDonald, B., 29, 42
McCorduck, P., 128
McMillan, J. H., 53, 56–57
McTaggart, R., 101
Malcolm, C., 110–111
Mangabeira, W., 168, 171, 173
Manning, P. K., 160
Matherly, C. A., 119
Mathes, R., 168, 172, 175

Mathison, S., 204
Medina, M. P., 39
Merriam, S. B., 4, 12, 16, 27, 46, 53–55, 76, 101, 128, 165, 184, 190, 205, 229, 231
Miles, M. B., 27, 40, 62–63, 156, 168, 170–175, 184, 187, 195, 208, 233
Mishoe, S. C., 96
Moore, D. T., 38
Moore, G. A., 176
Moore, J., 215
Mott, V. W., 12, 16, 229, 231
Moustakas, C., 17, 158–159
Munro, P., 86, 101
Murdock, G. P., 115, 156

N

Namuth, T., 128
Nelson, C., 214
Noblit, G. W., 33, 41
Norman, D. A., 131

O

Offerman, M., 90
Oldfather, P., 115, 196
Olesen, V., 86, 101

P

Patton, M. Q., 6, 10, 15, 23, 39, 61–64, 69, 71–72, 76, 84, 95, 97–98, 102, 114, 137, 183, 188, 194, 209, 214, 236, 238
Perka, P. L., 119
Peshkin, A., 14, 23, 80
Pfaffenberger, B., 173
Phillips, G. M., 130
Piaget, J., 36–37
Pole, C. J., 171, 174
Posner, J., 102
Prein, G., 168, 171–172, 175
Preissle, J., 14–15, 22, 37, 39, 61, 97, 113, 115, 121, 171–173, 179, 181, 188, 203–204, 207, 211
Preskill, H., 119
Preston, R., 237
Punch, M., 212–213, 217–218

R

Ragin, C., 168, 172, 175
Rallis, S. F., 8
Ratcliffe, J. W., 201
Rathje, W. L., 117–118
Reeves, T., 12, 76, 165
Reichardt, C. S., 8, 33
Reid, A. O., 167, 169–170, 172
Reinharz, S., 101, 104, 166, 214
Reybold, L. E., 190
Richards, L., 167–168, 170–175
Richards, T. J., 131, 167–168, 170–173, 175
Richardson, L., 221, 227, 229, 243
Richman, J., 86
Ridge, R. H., 119
Riley, M. W., 121, 124–125
Rist, R. C., 236
Robinson, W. S., 160
Rogers, E., 176
Roller, E., 168, 172, 175
Rosenfeldt, A. B., 191
Rowden, R. W., 135–139, 143–145, 149, 183
Rubin, L. B., 72

S

Sabshin, M., 76
Sanders, J. R., 33
Scarth, J., 48
Scates, D., 32
Schatzman, L., 76, 221
Schoepfle, G. M., 157, 186, 226, 231
Schofield, J. W., 208
Schrum, L. 129, 132
Schultz, J. G., 46
Schumacher, S., 53, 56–57
Schwandt, T. A., 48–49
Seidel, J., 173, 175
Seidman, I. E., 86–87
Selltiz, C., 113, 116, 121, 125
Shaw, K. E., 29, 39
Shelly, A., 168, 172, 175
Sherman, R. R., 6
Sibert, E., 168, 172, 175
Sieber, J. E., 213

Simpson, E. L., 4, 16, 53–55, 101, 128, 205
Smith, J. K., 8, 19, 27
Spiegelberg, H. A., 16
Spradley, J. P., 110, 223–224
Sprokkereef, A., 171, 174,
Stacey, M., 86
Stake, R. E., 27–28, 30–32, 39, 65, 193, 201, 208, 211–212, 214, 243–244
Stanfield II, J. H., 86
Stanley, L., 167, 169–171, 173
Steinbeck, J., 202–203
Stenhouse, L., 40, 195
Strauss, A. L., 17–18, 49, 57, 62–63, 76, 120, 124, 126, 156, 159, 164, 181, 183, 190–192, 221, 234
Swisher, K., 102

T

Taylor, S. J., 84, 97, 99–100, 105, 121, 152, 179, 215
Temple, B., 167, 169–171, 173
Tesch, R., 5, 10, 157, 167, 170–174, 176, 181,
Thomas, W. I., 117
Thorton, S. J., 48
Tierney, W. G., 228
Tisdell, E. J., 12, 59, 136–139, 145–149
Treichler, P. A., 214

V

Vaillant, G. E., 37
Van Dalen, D. B., 233
Van de Ven, A. H., 30
Van Maanen, J., 243

W

Walker, R., 29, 42, 208, 211
Weaver, A., 171
Webb, E. T., 113, 115, 117–118, 125–126, 215
Webb, R. B., 6
Webb, S., 48
Weeks, S., 80
Weitzman, E. A., 167–168, 170–175
Welch, S., 214

Welch, W., 110–111, 214
Werner, O., 157, 186, 226, 231
West, J., 115, 196
Whyte, W. F., 91
Wilson, S., 29–30, 208
Wisniewski, R., 158
Wolf, M., 214
Wolcott, H. F., 10, 14, 26–27, 69, 95,
   148, 201, 211, 220, 226
Woods, P., 220

Y

Yin, R. K., 27, 29, 32, 35, 40, 44,
   194–195, 208, 223, 236

Z

Znaniecki, F., 117

Subject Index

A

Action research, 10
Analytic induction, 160–161

B

Basic qualitative study, 11; examples of, 11–13
Biases: personal, 21–23, 42–43, 216

C

Case history, 32
Case method, 32
Case study, 18–19; as a bounded system, 27–28; characteristics of, 29–33; data collection in, 137–148; definition of, 27, 29, 32; descriptive, 38; educational uses of, 34–37; ethnographic, 34–35; evaluative, 39–40; heuristic, 30–31; historical, 35–36 interpretive, 38–39; limitations of, 42–43; multiple, 40; particularistic, 29; psychological, 36–37; sample in, 64–66; strengths of, 40–42; theoretical framework in, 135–137; when to use, 32–34, 39
Case study report: advantages of, 238; as distinguished from other written reports, 238; organizing, 343. *See also* Written report
Case survey, 195
Casework, 32
Categories: analytical, 178; borrowing of, 183; construction of, 179–187; guidelines for developing, 185–187; judging efficacy of, 183–184; naming, 182–183

Coding: definition of, 164; levels of, 164–166
Computers: and ethical considerations, 174–175; limitations of, 167–168; 172–175; possibilities for, 168, 175–177; qualitative software for, 170–172; sorting data by, 186–187; word processing functions of, 169–170
Constant comparative method, 18, 159, 179, 191–192
Content analysis, 159–160
Critical research, 4–5
Critical theory, 4–5
Cross-case analysis, 195

D

Data: coding of, 164–166; definition of, 69; managing, 164–166; sorting of, 185–187; unit of, 179
Data analysis: analytic induction method of, 160–161; and category construction, 179–187; constant comparative method of, 159, 191–192; content analysis method of, 159–160; data collection during, 161–164; definition of, 178; and descriptive account resulting from, 178–179; ethnographic method of, 156–157; in case studies, 193–196; limitations of computer-assisted, 167–168, 172–175; narrative method of, 157–158; overview of computer-assisted, 166–168; phenomenological method of, 158–159; possibilities for computer-assisted, 168, 175–177; and theory

building, 187–193; using qualitative software, 170–172; using standard office software, 169–170. *See also* Categories; Computers; Theory

Documents: analyzing, 123; collecting data from, 120–123; definition of, 112–113; determining authenticity of, 121–123; limitations of, 124–125 personal, 115–117; physical material as, 112–113, 117–118; public, 113–115; researcher-generated, 118–120; strengths of, 125–127. *See also* On-line documents

E

Educational Resources Information Center (ERIC), 196

Emic perspective, 6–7

Ethics: in case studies, 42–43, 215–216; and computers, 174, 131–132; in disseminating findings, 216–218; in document use, 215–216; and federal regulations, 213; and individual researcher, 218; in interviews, 214; in observation, 215; professional codes of, 213; in traditional research, 212–213

Ethnographic analysis, 156–157

Ethnographic case study, 34–35

Ethnographic study, 13–15; techniques of collecting data for, 14

Etic perspective, 6–7

External validity: definition of, 207; issues of, 207–208; strategies for enhancing, 211–212; ways of viewing, 208–212. *See also* Generalizability

F

Feminist theory, 4

Field notes: definition of, 104; observer comments on, 105–106, 110–111; sample of, 107–110; techniques for recording, 105

Fieldwork, 7

Fieldwork journal, 110

G

Generalizability, 207–208; as concrete universals, 210; naturalistic, 211; strategies to enhance, 211–212; user or reader, 211; as working hypotheses, 209. *See also* External validity

Grounded theory study, 17–18, 190–191

H

Historical case study, 35–36

Hypotheses: generating, 190–191; working, 209

I

Internal validity: assessing, 203; assumptions underlying, 202–203; connected to reliability, 205–206; definition of, 201; in ethnographic research, 203–204; strategies to enhance, 204–205

Interpretive research, 4–5

Interview: assessing data collected during, 91; definition of, 71–72; interviewer and respondent interaction during, 85–87; methods of recording data from, 87–88, 91; organization of, 83–85; sample, 89–90; semistructured, 74; structured, 74; unstructured, 74–75; when to conduct, 72

Interview questions: examples of good, 75–78; examples of poor, 78–79; use of probes in, 80–81

Interview guide, 81–83

Interview log, 88, 91

L

Literature review: definition of, 55; placement of, 51–52; purpose of, 49–51; steps in conducting, 53–55; when to conduct, 52–53

N

Narrative method of data analysis, 157–158

O

Observation: as a research tool, 94–96; as distinguished from interviews, 94; participant, 103–104; recording of, 104–106, 110–111; three stages of, 98–100; what to observe in, 96–100; when to use, 95–96

Observer: as collaborative partner, 101; as complete observer, 101; as complete participant, 100; as observer (participant), 101; as participant (observer), 101; changing roles of, 102–103; effects of, 103–104

On-line documents: collecting data using, 127–131; ethical issues with, 131–132

P

Phenomenological analysis, 158–159
Phenomenological study, 15–17
Physical trace material, 112–113
Positivist research, 4–5
Problem statement, 46–47, 57–60; definition of, 58
Psychological case study, 36–37

Q

Qualitative researcher characteristics, 20–24
Qualitative research: characteristics of, 5–9; philosophical orientation of, 1; types of, 10–20

R

Reliability: assumptions underlying, 205; connected to internal validity, 205–206; definition of, 205; general nature of, 201–205; strategies to enhance, 206–207
Research questions, 60–61
Research problem: 47; identification of, 55–59
Researcher: as communicator, 23–24; as primary instrument, 7, 20, 22; sensitivity, 21–22; tolerance for ambiguity, 20–21
Rich description, 8, 211

S

Sampling: definition of, 60; in case studies, 64–66; nonprobability, 61; number of units in, 64; probability, 61; purposive (or purposeful), 61–62; types of purposive, 62–64
Substantive theory, 17–18

T

Theoretical framework: definition of, 45; how to identify, 46–47; in case studies, 135–137; pervasiveness of, 47–49
Theorizing, 188–190
Theory: defined, 187–188; generating, 187–193; grounded, 190–191; role of speculation in developing, 190; use of constant comparative method in generating, 191–193
Thick description, 29–30, 211
Triangulation, 204, 207
Trustworthiness, 198–201

V

Validity: general nature of, 198–201. See also Internal validity and External validity

W

Written report: balancing description and analysis in, 234–236; components of, 227–231; determining audience for, 221–223; determining focus for, 223–224; displaying data in, 233–234; disseminating, 236–237; drafting, 225–227; general description in, 235; interpretive commentary in, 235; outlining, 224–225; overcoming writer's block in producing, 226; particular description in, 235; placement of component parts of, 231–234; problems in starting, 220–221; publishing, 237. See also Case study report